HEART-SICK

BIOPOLITICS: MEDICINE, TECHNOSCIENCE,
AND HEALTH IN THE 21ST CENTURY

GENERAL EDITORS: MONICA J. CASPER AND LISA JEAN MOORE

Missing Bodies: The Politics of Visibility
Monica J. Casper and Lisa Jean Moore

*Against Health: How Health
Became the New Morality*
Edited by Jonathan M. Metzl
and Anna Kirkland

*Is Breast Best? Taking on the
Breastfeeding Experts and the New
High Stakes of Motherhood*
Joan B. Wolf

Biopolitics: An Advanced Introduction
Thomas Lemke

*The Material Gene: Gender, Race, and
Heredity after the Human Genome Project*
Kelly E. Happe

*Cloning Wild Life: Zoos, Captivity, and
the Future of Endangered Animals*
Carrie Friese

*Eating Drugs: Psychopharmaceutical
Pluralism in India*
Stefan Ecks

*Phantom Limb: Amputation, Embodiment,
and Prosthetic Technology*
Cassandra S. Crawford

*Heart-Sick: The Politics of Risk,
Inequality, and Heart Disease*
Janet K. Shim

Heart-Sick

The Politics of Risk, Inequality, and Heart Disease

Janet K. Shim

NEW YORK UNIVERSITY PRESS

New York and London

NEW YORK UNIVERSITY PRESS
New York and London
www.nyupress.org

Portions of chapters 3 and 6 have appeared in Shim, Janet K. 2005. "Constructing 'race' across the science–lay divide: Racial formation in the epidemiology and experience of cardiovascular disease." *Social Studies of Science* 35(3): 405–36. Portions of chapter 3 have also appeared in a book chapter: Shim, Janet K. 2010. "The stratified biomedicalization of heart disease: Expert and lay perspectives on racial and class inequality." Pp. 218–41 in *Biomedicalization: Technoscience, Health and Illness in the U.S.*, edited by Adele E. Clarke, Laura Mamo, Jennifer R. Fosket, Jennifer R. Fishman, and Janet K. Shim. Durham, N.C.: Duke University Press.

References to Internet websites (URLs) were accurate at the time of writing.
Neither the author nor New York University Press is responsible
for URLs that may have expired or changed since the manuscript was prepared.

LIBRARY OF CONGRESS CATALOGING-IN-PUBLICATION DATA
Shim, Janet K., 1969–
Heart-sick : the politics of risk, inequality, and heart disease / Janet K. Shim.
pages cm
Includes bibliographical references and index.
ISBN 978-0-8147-8683-3 (cl : alk. paper) — ISBN 978-0-8147-8685-7 (pb : alk. paper)
1. Heart—Diseases—Political apects. 2. Discrimination in medical care. 3. Minorities—Medical care. 4. Health services accessibility. I. Title.
RC682.S48 2014
362.1961'2—dc23
2013048345

New York University Press books are printed on acid-free paper,
and their binding materials are chosen for strength and durability.
We strive to use environmentally responsible suppliers and materials t
o the greatest extent possible in publishing our books.

Manufactured in the United States of America

10 9 8 7 6 5 4 3 2 1

Also available as an ebook

In loving memory of my mother,
Young Ja Shim,
who gave me so much,
and taught me about
courage, compassion, and love.

CONTENTS

Acknowledgments   ix

Introduction   1

1. The Politics of Disease Causation   29

2. Disciplining Difference: A Selective Contemporary
   History of Cardiovascular Epidemiology   48

3. The Contested Meanings and Intersections of Race   77

4. An Apparent Consensus on Class   112

5. The Dichotomy of Gender   139

6. Individualizing "Difference" and the Production
   of Scientific Credibility   162

Conclusion   191

Appendix: Methodology   215

Notes   225

References   245

Index   271

About the Author   277

ACKNOWLEDGMENTS

The acknowledgments are what I always open to first in any book I'm reading. I like that they show the social and biographical history of the work and the author as part of a networked web of scholarship and support. But in all the times I've read others' acknowledgments, I've never imagined how difficult it would be to write something that could do justice to all that I owe to others. My debts are great and my gratitude is deep.

My thanks go first and foremost to the participants of my study. They warmly welcomed me into their homes and offices, bore with good grace my many probing questions, and freely shared with me their feelings, frustrations, biographies, and life experiences. They did so with no expectation of reciprocity, though I did try in small ways to make my interactions with them more of an exchange than one-way data collection. That people are so willing to give of themselves and their time for little more than a belief in another's project is something that will never cease to surprise and delight me. All of the participants in this study treated the interview experience with great care, respect, and thoughtfulness. For making this book possible, I am deeply indebted to them. I hope they recognize themselves in these pages.

In large part, it was the experience of conducting the research described in this book—of producing knowledge and sharing it with colleagues and students—which brought me to the realization that I wanted to pursue a career in the academy. However, it was the unerring, constant support of multiple mentors that made me feel this was even possible. I consider myself immeasurably rich in mentors and welcome this opportunity to thank them publicly: Howard Pinderhughes, for his unwavering belief that scholarship and activism can coexist, and for knowing when to step in and when to step back; Adele Clarke, for her incredible intellectual and interpersonal generosity, and for all her cheerleading, which never failed to revive me when I felt deflated; and Sharon Kaufman, for her stalwart faith that I could do more and better than I thought I could, and for showing me through example how to get there. The research I describe in this book also benefited from another group of mentors—Steven Epstein, Michael Omi, and Gay Becker—who could always be counted on to provide another reading of a chapter, insightful comments all along the way, and sincere and frank validation that the research I was doing was meaningful. Their generous reviews and reactions to the arguments contained here served as wonderful guides as I wrote this book.

I have the extraordinary luck of having landed in a department that embodies and enacts all of what it means to be collegial. I cannot imagine having weathered the past five years without the encouragement, collaboration, and support of my colleagues: Susan Chapman, Adele Clarke, Shari Dworkin, Ruth Malone, Howard Pinderhughes, and Zachary Zimmer. Quite simply, we take care of one another, and we have each others' backs. I hear enough to know that this is rare indeed, and I am enormously grateful to have been the beneficiary of such care. And while I often find myself explaining why our sociology program is located in a School of Nursing, I also relish pointing out how this makes for a program that is surrounded by committed, caring scholars who know many a thing or two about health, illness, and healing. They have welcomed me into their fold, and I appreciate their warm support and our cross-disciplinary dialogue. And finally, I have had more than my share of phenomenal students; our engagement and ongoing conversations sustain and excite me, and I look forward to many more years of continued discovery together.

Colleagues near and far have also had a hand in this book, and I have gained immeasurably from their scholarship, which inspires my own, and from their friendship as well. These include: Adele Clarke, Troy Duster, Shari Dworkin, Steven Epstein, Jennifer Fishman, Jennifer Fosket, Joan Fujimura, Kelly Joyce, Sharon Kaufman, Laura Mamo, Virginia Olesen, Michael Omi, John S.W. Park, Howard Pinderhughes, Ann Russ, Teresa Scherzer, Sara Shostak, and Stefan Timmermans. I also appreciated the opportunity to present this research to multiple audiences and am thankful for their engagement with and comments on my work. This book is thus the collective product of conversations at meetings of the American Sociological Association, the American Anthropological Association, and the Society for Social Studies of Science, and talks given at Harvard University, London School of Economics, Massachusetts Institute of Technology, Pitzer College, Pomona College, Portland State University, University of New Mexico, and the University of California campuses at Berkeley, Davis, Riverside, and San Francisco.

I also gratefully acknowledge the generous support of the following sources of funding, without which this research could not have been completed: an Agency for Healthcare Research and Quality Dissertation Research Grant (R03 HS10582), a Doctoral Dissertation Improvement Grant from the National Science Foundation (SES-0114986), a National Institute on Aging grant (Sharon Kaufman, Principal Investigator, R01 AG20962), the Graduate Division of UCSF, and intramural support from the UCSF School of Nursing.

New York University Press has been a wonderful publishing home for me. Monica Casper and Lisa Jean Moore, the general editors of the Biopolitics series, and Ilene Kalish at NYU Press have been supportive guides and enthusiastic champions all along the way. My thanks additionally go to Caelyn Cobb and Dorothea Halliday, also at NYU Press, for helping to bring my work to press. Adi Hovav also provided stellar editorial suggestions and advice that improved the entire manuscript.

My love goes to Elsa Chen, David Chiu, Ramie Dare, Phong Le, Debby Lu, and John Park, longtime companions in my life. By some kismet, we have all managed to land in California, and I'm so grateful to them for reminding me of life beyond my computer, for making me laugh, and for providing kinship, love, and support.

And finally, I come to my family. To my *ohana* in Hawai'i—Sau Thi Le, Tai Thanh Ly, Nhung Ly, and Ngoc, Max, Sam, and Eden Murata—I give my deep thanks for welcoming me into their midst. My father, Poong Sup Shim, has always been a stalwart supporter (I will forever be amused by—and appreciate—the huge sigh of relief he let out when I told him I had received tenure). I am thankful for these last few years during which our relationship has become closer and deeper. My sister, Jae Young Shim, has been the gentlest of sisters, constant in her presence and support, and I will be always grateful for how she took such loving care of me and our family. My smart and engaging nephew, Brendan Tsuda, was born just as the research I describe in this book began, and he provided me with all manner of fun and joyful distractions. My mother, Young Ja Shim, was one of the bravest and strongest people I know. Having come of age in a time and place where her trajectory and options were limited, she made sure to tell me throughout my life that I should make my own choices and find my own way. She communicated in large ways and small her constant support for my taking the road less traveled. And I continue to be blessed by all that she taught me. This book is inspired by and dedicated to her.

Last, to the main men in my life: my husband, Dat Ly, and my son, Kanoa Shim-Ly. Words cannot describe the constancy of love and support with which Dat has enveloped me throughout our many years together. Without his faith in me, my work, our love, and our future, I do not know what or where I would be. Kanoa has been the brightest light in my life, and watching him grow and learn, sharing in his fun and laughter, experiencing the world through his eyes, and caring for and being cared for by him has been an incredible joy. The two of them fill my heart and remind me of the beauty and wonder of life. They are my compass, my anchor, my home.

Introduction

Juanita Miller lives in a first-floor apartment on a quiet residential street in a predominantly African American community in the San Francisco Bay Area. Her neighborhood, lined with older two-story homes now split into smaller apartment units, is just blocks away from an industrial strip located in the shadows of an elevated highway. I came to visit Ms. Miller on an overcast afternoon in late summer. She took a long time to come to the door. A tall black woman in her fifties, she moved slowly and gingerly, wincing in pain from the arthritis that the recent wet weather had aggravated and breathing laboriously because of her congestive heart failure. The living room in which we sat was crowded with sofas and loveseats, a china cabinet, a huge stuffed animal, and Ms. Miller's wheelchair. She preferred to sit in the wheelchair because it had leg rests that she used to alternately elevate and then lower her legs during my visit. She had sustained a fall recently and was also recovering from an infection on her leg—a complication of diabetes that had almost required amputation.

My interview with Ms. Miller turned out to be the longest one I conducted. Her medical history of arthritis, diabetes, hypertension, multiple heart attacks, and congestive heart failure was lengthy and complicated. Telling the story of their incidence, development, diagnosis, and treatment inevitably involved extended forays into her personal history. Her subjection to racial and gender discrimination at school, on the job, and at home; her drive to surpass the devaluing expectations of family, teachers, and employers; her experiences of domestic violence and single motherhood; and her lifelong engagement in social and labor activism all became part of the medical story. Ms. Miller did not mince her words as she attributed her bad health to a lifetime of the strains and stresses of this social biography. In her view, "Who has the most checkers, that's who has the better chance of surviving." She made it clear that she had not been given many checkers in life and had had to fight for those few that she did have. At the end of our interview, as she walked me to the door, I commented on how informed she seemed to be about her medical conditions, and how much I'd learned from her. She replied, "I've been the landlady of this body for over fifty years. I *know* what makes me sick."

Mulling over Ms. Miller's words on my way home, I could not help but be reminded of my encounter with an epidemiologist at a scientific conference some five months earlier. She was exhibiting a poster of her research on the disparities in cardiovascular risk factors between black and white women. According to her findings, black women in her study had more risk factors for heart disease than their white counterparts. When I asked the scientist what she made of this finding, she responded that "socioeconomic status, including occupational category, combined family income, educational level, and insurance status, might have a lot to do with it." She also hypothesized that diet, sedentary lifestyle, culture, education, and perhaps access to health care may play a role.

The researcher then added that she was involved in another study in which investigators were exploring what prompted people experiencing cardiovascular symptoms to see a medical provider for evaluation. She noted this to me, she said, because black women, in addition to being disproportionately at risk for heart disease, have also been shown to have high rates of delaying care, which to her had sounded a bit like "blaming the victim." She suspected that not seeking care had more to do with structural barriers such as lack of time, child care, transportation, access to care, and so on. She related that she had shared these thoughts with the rest of her research team, only to be contradicted by the study's nursing coordinators—who she noted were black—who told her that "'black women could come in but don't.'" They argued that there were also poor white women who had as many barriers yet still sought treatment for symptoms. The principal investigator subsequently speculated to me that maybe "there is a black culture—welfare moms, or whatever—with low education who maybe missed out on the public health messages of the past ten years." This researcher ultimately attributed the disproportionately high cardiovascular risk of black women to a presumed propensity to delay care and a lack of skill in symptom recognition. These traits, she suggested, were rooted in a pathological culture combined with insufficient education. In advancing these arguments, she bypassed the very kinds of forces that Ms. Miller had so emphatically implicated: the powerful influence of race, gender, and class in stratifying education, economic opportunities, and material conditions, and their subsequent effects on her well-being.

Juxtaposing this epidemiologist's account with Ms. Miller's narrative raises a host of questions: Why such divergent views? How do Ms. Miller and this epidemiologist come to such different conclusions about why heart disease befalls one individual or group and not others, and, in particular, the kinds of roles that race, class, and gender play in distributing health and illness? Where do their ideas about disease causes, risks, and determinants come from? What consequences do these ideas have for how we as a society understand health disparities and act to mitigate them? In turn, what particular policies and interventions are seen as rational, legitimate, and effective courses of action? And how are these processes of rationalization, legitimation, and validation accomplished? This book seeks to answer these questions by critically analyzing ideas about what causes disease alongside ideas about where health inequalities come from.

Explaining Disease, Accounting for Disparities

In order to examine conceptions about what causes disease and health disparities, we need to take a closer look at epidemiology, the science of disease distribution, determinants, and frequency. Its core concerns are with the patterns of health conditions in human populations and with the factors that influence those patterns. Epidemiology thus plays a critical role in shaping our understanding of health and its variation, and in framing public health policies. Epidemiology as a set of social practices both emerges out of and contributes to systems of social classification by race, class, sex, and gender. These classificatory and meaning-making practices are numerous, diffuse, and unremarkable, almost to the point of being invisible. In this way, race, class, and gender become part of our everyday logic or "'common sense'—a way of comprehending, explaining, and acting in the world."[1]

At multiple nodes of epidemiologic knowledge production—grant applications, data collection instruments, statistical software, and journal publications—and in multiple activities such as articulating research questions, collecting and analyzing data, interpreting results, and disseminating findings, epidemiology continually yet often imperceptibly legitimates particular definitions of race, class, and gender and systems for categorizing those differences. Using such classificatory schemes, epidemiology provides readily available explanations for illness outcomes and, in so doing, validates those classifications and categories as objects of biomedical inquiry and scrutiny. These explanations then direct future scientific practices and health-related resources along racialized, classed, and gendered lines. In this fashion, common, mundane, on-the-ground scientific work routinely, yet often invisibly, makes claims about which

social differences matter and how. In short, as the basic science under-
pinning public health programs, many clinical interventions, and public
guidance on avoiding disease, epidemiology engages in the production
and adjudication of authoritative claims of how differences matter in
heart disease. And it does so in the name of disease prevention and management, the optimization of health and well-being, and the maximiza-
tion of the value and utility of a populace.

In this book, I focus on the epidemiology of heart disease. On a macro
level, cardiovascular diseases—a class of conditions that affect the heart
or blood vessels and include hypertension, coronary artery disease, and
stroke—have long been the leading cause of mortality in the United
States[2] and worldwide.[3] For instance, in 2009, cardiovascular diseases
were responsible for one of every three American deaths, and coronary
heart disease for one of every six American deaths. Upward of 15.4 million Americans are estimated to suffer from coronary heart disease and
almost 78 million from hypertension, or high blood pressure.[4] Projec-
tions show that by 2030, an additional 8 million will develop coronary
heart disease and 27 million more will have hypertension.[5] These conditions are extraordinarily costly. Coronary heart disease accounted for an
estimated $83.6 billion in health care expenditures in 2007 (a 44 percent
increase since 1997[6]) and an additional $68 billion in lost productivity.[7]
Estimated direct and indirect costs in 2008 for high blood pressure were
$50.6 billion.[8] By 2030, projected total costs for coronary heart disease
and hypertension are expected to rise to $223.8 billion and $245.2 billion, respectively. It is clear that cardiovascular diseases exact the greatest
economic toll of all other health conditions: The combined $143.0 billion
spent in 2008 on medical care for heart conditions and hypertension
far eclipses the $74.3 billion and $72.2 billion spent on trauma-related
disorders and cancer, the next two costliest conditions.[9]

Epidemiologists have been studying the patterns of heart disease for
many decades. As a result, there is a vast body of knowledge to consider.[10]
For example, black women and men die from coronary heart disease at
higher rates than whites, even after adjusting for income level. In 2008,

mortality rates (per 100,000 population) for this condition were 161.7 for white males and 183.7 for black males, 91.9 for white females and 115.6 for black females. Mexican Americans also suffer from higher rates of heart disease mortality than non-Hispanic whites.[11]

Epidemiologic research has also shown that the prevalence of hypertension is disproportionately high among African Americans, Mexican Americans, and American Indians. In fact, African Americans' levels of hypertension are among the highest in the world. They are also increasing: The prevalence of high blood pressure among blacks increased from an average of 35.8 percent in 1988–94, to 41.4 percent in 1999–2002. Blacks develop hypertension earlier in life than do whites, and their average blood pressures are also higher. Consequently, sequelae of hypertension also affect blacks far more: Compared with whites, they have a 1.3 times higher rate of nonfatal stroke, 1.8 times higher rate of fatal stroke, 1.5 times greater rate of death from heart disease, and 4.2 times the rate of end-stage kidney disease. One condition that results from both hypertension and coronary heart disease is congestive heart failure; according to one study, the occurrence of heart failure before age 50 is twenty times more common among blacks than whites.[12] As expected, then, death rates from hypertension are starkly unequal: In 2008, mortality (per 100,000 population) from high blood pressure was 16.5 for white males, 50.3 for black males, 14.5 for white females, and 38.6 for black females.

This pattern of early onset and higher and earlier mortality among blacks is seen across all cardiovascular diseases. One study found that the disproportionate rates of cardiovascular diseases in blacks compared with those of whites start in young adulthood and increase with advancing age, resulting in 28 percent of all cardiovascular-related deaths among blacks occurring before age 65, versus only 13 percent of such deaths among whites.[13]

Significant differences by class and by sex also exist in the epidemiology of cardiovascular disease. Among men 25 to 64 years of age, heart disease mortality for those with incomes less than $10,000 was 2.5 times that for those with incomes of $25,000 or more. Moreover, neighborhood measures of socioeconomic status were also inversely related to fatal coronary heart disease among black and white women and men, but this association was larger for women than for men.[14] Among people with lower educational and income levels, not only is hypertension more prevalent, but also on average, their blood pressure measurements tend to be higher than of those with more education and household income.

Finally, although the epidemiologic wisdom is that women develop heart disease some ten years later than men, the intersecting dynamics of race, social class, and age on women of color and poor women seem to significantly attenuate and even reverse much of this presumed "sex advantage." For instance, hypertension is more prevalent among men up until about age 55, but thereafter it is more prevalent among women.[15] There are also indications that the influence of class on heart disease is more pronounced for women than for men: The poorest women aged 25 to 64 years were 3.4 times more likely to die from heart disease than those with the highest incomes; this income gradient is much steeper for women than for men.

Altogether, epidemiologic data has built a mountain of evidence that persistent, severe, and consequential inequalities in cardiovascular health exist. These inequalities represent only part of what physicians and health policy scholars W. Michael Byrd and Linda Clayton call "an American health dilemma," a phrase that echoes Gunnar Myrdal's historic characterization of the chasm dividing whites and blacks in the mid-twentieth-century United States.[16] But accepting that health disparities exist only further begs the question of what kind of problem they are. Epidemiologic studies have tried to account for inequalities in heart disease by pointing to at least four possible explanations. The first attributes cardiovascular disparities to the uneven distribution of modifiable risk factors, such as hypertension, obesity, lack of physical activity, diet, smoking, and diabetes. And indeed, the prevalence of these risk factors has been shown to differ by race-ethnicity, social class, and gender.[17] Second, unequal treatment of heart disease and its risk factors is seen to result in unequal cardiovascular health status. An impressive number of studies have in fact documented racial and sex differences in care.[18] Third, possible physiological and genetic differences are hypothesized to account for some health disparities, particularly by race-ethnicity and sex and, indeed, are sometimes considered the key to understanding the causes of complex health conditions like heart disease.[19] Finally, some groundbreaking efforts are currently underway toward more explicitly structural and theoretically informed explanations of how social determinants might be associated with inequalities in heart disease.[20]

But what of those afflicted with heart disease? While the lay people[21] I spoke to as part of my research may have a less formalized and systematic picture of health disparities, the appearance of illness in their own bodies usually initiates a flood of questions: Why me? Why this disease? Why now? Those who must live with diagnosed disease also pay attention to the health of those around them and are often highly cognizant of the unequal toll that cardiovascular and other chronic diseases have taken on their families and communities. They question the distinctive and disproportionate risks to which they and others like them might be exposed. Like epidemiologists, then, lay people's attempts to make sense of where, when, why, and who heart disease strikes are quests for ways to explain and account for the causes and determinants of the disease and their distribution across populations.

Clearly, the nature of the "problem" of health disparities and of the roles that race, class, and gender play in generating them can be and are understood in multiple ways. These ways of knowing are consequential. The conceptions of human differences they admit, the definitions of the problem they promote, the solutions they promulgate, and, crucially, their status as legitimate modes of knowing in our knowledge-stratified society have deep implications for our negotiations, contestations, and organization of health inequality. It is therefore important to highlight here the recent explosion of research, policymaking, and public attention to the causes of health inequalities. The problematization of health disparities and the mandate for a governmental response are now fairly well institutionalized. In 1993, the National Institutes of Health (NIH) established an Office of Research on Women's Health and the National Center on Minority Health and Health Disparities. In 1998, the Clinton administration launched the President's Initiative to Eliminate Racial and Ethnic Disparities in Health under the auspices of the Department of Health and Human Services Office of Minority Health, which was continued under the George W. Bush administration. In 2010, as part of the Patient Protection and Affordable Care Act, the National Center on Minority Health and Health Disparities transitioned to become the National Institute on Minority Health and Health Disparities (NIMHD). Institute status gives NIMHD a more prominent presence within the NIH structure and authorizes it to plan, coordinate, review, and evaluate all minority health and health disparities research activities conducted and supported by the NIH institutes and centers. *Healthy People 2010*, a document that outlined health and prevention objectives for the United States for the first decade of the twenty-first century, included eliminating racial and ethnic disparities in health as one of two overarching priorities. In *Healthy People 2020*, the goals with regard to health disparities have been reframed, to achieving health equity, eliminating disparities, and improving the health of all groups.

But the larger issue of how to think about human differences in health also reverberates throughout multiple other institutional domains. A failed California ballot initiative illustrates how accepted logics about the relevance of human differences for health have entered into the political sphere. In 2003, the American Civil Rights Coalition, headed by Ward Connerly,[22] successfully placed Proposition 54, titled the Racial Privacy Initiative, on the October 2003 California ballot. The Racial Privacy Initiative, which ultimately did not pass, would have amended the state constitution to bar state agencies from collecting, analyzing, sorting, or acting on any data on race, ethnicity, or national origin. Curiously, however, it made a key exemption for medical research subjects, allowing state agencies to continue to classify and analyze them by race, ethnicity, and national origin.[23] Apparently, its sponsors felt that medical research—in contradistinction to other institutional practices—should be assertedly race-conscious rather than colorblind.

Contentious debates about the meaning and medical significance of race and the politics of representation in medical research have been ongoing for decades.[24] As the sociologist Steven Epstein has explored, a steady stream of clinical research began to raise the issue of the appropriate place of "race" in health and biomedicine, giving rise to what he calls a new common sense and "biopolitical paradigm of inclusion-and-difference" for medical research.[25] Recent findings over potential differences in the efficacy of pharmacological therapies and in the use of various heart disease–related treatments[26] have raised impassioned arguments over definitions of racism, the nature of race in biomedicine, and the suitability of "racial profiling" in medical research and treatment,[27] spilling over into mainstream media.[28] And in the genomic era, while debates about the relationships among genetics, race, and ancestry remain quite public, many have argued that all the while, scientists have continued to embed genetic understandings of racial differences into their daily practices.[29] Such ongoing and recurring contestations underscore the nagging questions that surround the meanings of race and whether and how it should be used in health research and medical care.

Particular understandings of sex and gender have, like race, imbued medical research. In 2001, the Institute of Medicine (IOM), a part of the National Academy of Sciences, released its report on sex differences in health.[30] Provocatively titled *Exploring the Biological Contributions to Human Health: Does Sex Matter?*, the IOM Committee on Understanding the Biology of Sex and Gender Differences concluded that sex differences rooted in biology did indeed matter, and it proposed numerous recommendations to remedy what it saw as a deficit of research into the mechanisms and origins of such differences. But aside from brief discussion of the conceptual and linguistic conflation of "sex" and "gender" and the need to clarify their distinctions, no mention was made of gender.

Studies of the consequences of hormone replacement therapy (HRT) constitute one extremely active area of medical research that bears on our understandings of the health effects of sex. In little more than a decade, there has been a complete sea change in medical views on the safety and efficacy of HRT for disease prevention. Prior to 1998, the epidemiologic and clinical bandwagon was that hormone replacement would not only make postmenopausal women feel better but would also protect them from a panoply of conditions, including heart disease. Since then, however, a flurry of clinical trial results indicates that, at best, these claims have been exaggerated, and, at worst, such advice in fact placed women at increased risk for multiple conditions, including some of those that HRT was thought to prevent.[31] In 2003, for example, *The New England Journal of Medicine* published final results from two clinical trials of hormone replacement therapy among older postmenopausal women which showed that HRT in fact slightly elevated the risk of heart disease.[32] In the face of such unanticipated findings, it would seem that the stability of the biological construction of sex differences should be threatened. Yet, in 2006, a special issue of the *Journal of the American College of Cardiology* concluded that the pathological processes and manifestations of heart disease differed systematically for women than for men.[33]

Institutional efforts to shape the research agenda and encourage particular approaches to studying health disparities provide another window into what kinds of explanatory accounts for the health impacts of human differences are valued and legitimated. In 2000, the Office of Behavioral and Social Sciences Research at the NIH convened a conference to critically examine research on the social and cultural dimensions of health. The final conference report featured key recommendations to improve social science research and integrate health research across multiple levels of analysis. In response, two new funding programs were established. The first supported methodology and measurement research—into research design, data collection techniques, measurement, and data analysis techniques—in the social and behavioral sciences.[34] The second funding program supported research on basic social and cultural constructs and processes used in health research, including "the implications of different conceptualizations and measurements of social stratification systems and processes . . . for understanding health at the individual and higher levels of aggregation (e.g., community)." It was also intended to fund explorations into the social etiology of health and illness "to improve understanding of how macro-level (societal) factors, such as social policies, structures, and cultural norms, are linked to micro-level (individual) factors, such as a person's behaviors, and ultimately to health."[35] Yet another funding program, which came as a result of a 2006 NIH-sponsored conference on behavioral and social sciences research contributions to understanding and reducing health disparities, was designed "to encourage behavioral and social science research on the causes [of] and solutions to health and disabilities disparities in the U.S. population."[36] In 2008 and in 2012, the NIH convened a Summit on the Science of Eliminating Health Disparities, to showcase emerging science that can inform policies and programs to reduce health disparities.

While these last examples could be read as conceptually and institutionally significant moves to rethink and diversify the ways in which we study and understand disease causation and health disparities, there is throughout an overwhelming emphasis on the continued production of expert knowledge. To be sure, multi- and interdisciplinary research, "community consultation," and community-based participatory research were encouraged, but there was no explicit acknowledgment that lay people too understand the origins of their own conditions in potentially illuminating ways. This is true also of the epidemiologic and medical research described above: Embedded therein is an unspoken assumption that authoritative knowledge about disease causes and health inequalities is the province of credentialed professional experts.

But this need not be the case. Numerous scholars have grappled with the complex issues of knowledge and expert–lay engagement in various ways.[37] Hilary Arksey, for example, found that one lay group organized by those suffering from repetitive strain injury (RSI) collected their own statistics regarding prevalence, developing an expertise with which to challenge the medical establishment.[38] More generally, she argues, lay persons have the potential, through their practical experience and "insider" knowledge, to exert influence in medical fact–building around RSI, though their claims are vulnerable to co-optation by credentialed medical experts. The sociologist Phil Brown coined the term "popular epidemiology" to describe the collection, analysis, and utilization of data by community activists and families affected by toxic waste.[39] These efforts "repeatedly differ with [those of] scientists and government officials on matters of problem definition, study design, interpretation of findings, and policy applications."[40] Significantly, popular epidemiology, in contrast to mainstream epidemiology, emphasizes social structural factors as centrally implicated in disease causation. Brown also outlines how lay and professional "ways of knowing" vary in their positions regarding value-neutrality, standards of proof, and uncertain and emerging diseases and conditions. Finally, Steven Epstein uses the term "lay experts" to refer to AIDS activists who acquired the vocabulary and frameworks of biomedicine and parlayed other significant social and cultural resources to become genuine participants in the design and execution of clinical trials.[41] These studies thus examine lay engagements with scientific communities in cases where a small number of "auto-didacts," in Epstein's words, within social movements absorb enough of the jargon and concepts of the relevant science to forge and force connections with the credentialed establishment and to position themselves as credible interlocutors. That is, the grounds upon which lay people can be understood to possess "expertise," in the extant literature, are based upon their scientization—their acquisition and mobilization of the concepts, frameworks, and vocabularies of scientists themselves.

But for these notable exceptions, however, a conjoint consideration of lay *and* expert knowledge has been understudied. This is the case despite a widespread call in science and technology studies to analyze expert–lay relations.[42] This book seeks to answer this call, to take seriously the notion that knowledge production—whether through scientific methods or lay experience—is suffused with social and political concerns. Thus, to explore the multiple ways in which we think about and understand the causes and origins of health inequalities, I interviewed both epidemiologists who research heart disease and people of color who live with it.[43] I also conducted ethnographic observation and informal interviews at epidemiologic conferences where results of studies were shared and discussed. And I analyzed papers, commentaries, and editorials published in major epidemiology journals. In this book, I outline the major dimensions of a deep divide that I found between epidemiologists' and lay people's ideas about human differences and their consequences for heart disease. The conceptual chasm revealed by the two vignettes in this Introduction's opening is, I argue, representative of fundamental disagreements about the nature of social difference, their significance for health and disease, and the validity and credibility of different forms of knowledge.

The Science–Lay Divide: Individualized Differences versus Embodied Inequalities

As the chapters that follow demonstrate, I found that epidemiologists ritualistically included various measures of difference in their research to limit or describe study samples and to stratify, adjust, and interpret results. In so doing, investigators infused such human features as race, ethnicity, social class, sex, and gender with particular meanings and definitions. With respect to race, they interpreted the meanings of racial differences through a *cultural* prism. Like the epidemiologist I encountered at the outset of this Introduction, they tended to attribute racial disparities to "cultural" or "ethnic" differences, related to the customary values and practices of a racially or ethnically defined social group. Whites remained essentially acultural. When it came to social class, epidemiologists often agreed with the lay people in my study that its health effects are produced by differential access to resources and opportunities, social environments, living conditions, and the stress of chronic deprivation. Yet, at the same time, epidemiologic conventions for measuring economic status predominantly involved individual-level variables that only hinted at the complex social processes that govern and produce class stratification. Finally, regarding sex and gender, epidemiologists viewed sex as a crucial axis of analysis because of its definition as a *biologically* meaningful distinction, while gender—as a reference to the *social* distinctions and relations among groups based on sex—was almost completely ignored. I found epidemiologists to be overwhelmingly concerned with "the estrogen connection"—with explicating the potential (and often presumed) links between women's exposure to endogenous estrogen and their lower incidence of heart disease.

In contrast to epidemiologists, the African Americans, Asian Americans, and Latinos with heart disease whom I interviewed articulated complex and nuanced understandings of the intersecting relationships between group status, relations of power, and well-being. They considered the health effects of racial, class, and gender differences as mediated through profoundly and intrinsically *social* processes. In their view, race, class, and gender operate together to structure their everyday experiences and life chances that, in turn, affect their risks for disease. While the meanings they assigned to human differences were highly variable, lay people talked about the risks posed by race, class, and gender in terms of the consequences inequality had on their sense of self, everyday interactions, and the economic and environmental conditions of their lives. For them, the health effects of racial difference stemmed from the material and interlocking consequences of racial inequality. Their racialization as members of specific racial groups structured and ordered their everyday experiences and conditions of life that had, in their view, direct implications for their cardiovascular risk. Lay people, like epidemiologists, saw both sex (as a biological attribute) and gender (as a system of social arrangements, processes, and practices) as binary in nature. However, they starkly disagreed with scientists in their belief that the cardiovascular risks differentiating women from men were based in gendered inequality rather than in sex differences. And with respect to class, lay people parted ways conceptually from epidemiologists by continually returning to the refrain that social class was intimately intertwined with the dynamics of race.

This underscores a broader divide I found between lay people and scientists on the issue of intersecting dimensions of inequality. In short, many lay participants saw social experiences, institutions, and structural arrangements organized along intersecting racial, class, and gender lines.[44] They spoke, for example, of how access to educational opportunities was highly constrained by their race, class, and gender and how this then shaped their economic trajectories throughout life. They described racial and gender segregation in the labor market and the gendered division of reproductive labor. The multiple means through which differences were made meaningful, and their interactional and institutional consequences for the social worlds of people of color, in turn exacted costs to their health. These lay perspectives were rooted in views of society as hierarchical and of positions within that hierarchy as *relational*— that one's conditions of life and well-being are indelibly shaped by the histories of social relations *between* one's own and other groups.

Along all three dimensions of human difference, then, what lay people perceived to be the systematic stratification of everyday experiences and conditions of life became transposed in epidemiology into a set of individualized, discrete, sociodemographic variables of racial categories, socioeconomic status, and sex. That is, epidemiology devolves complex, intersecting, and relational inequalities of race, class, and gender into individual-level and highly reductionist measures of standardized racial categories, socioeconomic status (as measured by income, occupation, and/or education), and sex, respectively. (In this book, therefore, I use the terms "race," "class," and "gender" when referring to those social relations of power, and "racial categories," "socioeconomic status," and "sex" to refer to the individualized, reductive measures of epidemiology.) Through such individualizing and devolutionary practices, I argue, epidemiologic knowledge furthers biomedicalization—the expansion of the jurisdiction of medicine through means that are often simultaneously scientific, technological, economic, and organizational.[45] More specifically, epidemiology participates in *stratified biomedicalization*, which emphasizes the selective and strategic nature of biomedicalization, its unequal (and sometimes unintended) effects across populations, and how these may exacerbate rather than ameliorate social inequalities along many different dimensions.[46] Here, cardiovascular epidemiology is an example of stratified biomedicalization because it categorizes, selectively monitors, and attempts to regulate and intervene on bodies and groups defined as "different" in disproportionate ways. This epidemiologic way of knowing turns these bodies and groups into scientific objects of scrutiny, triggers the use of clinical and other medical practices on them, and places them within specific social and organizational arrangements such as public health and health promotion programs targeting "at-risk" populations. These disparate disciplinary and normalizing practices in turn reinforce biomedical and commonsense logics about differences and disease. As a result, the conceptual divide that exists between scientific and lay understandings of race, class, gender, and cardiovascular risk has enormous consequences for clinical practice, public health, and health policies, as well as societal ideas about race, class, and gender.

The Social Production of Scientific Credibility

As readers have probably already surmised, however, the science–lay divide and epidemiologic biomedicalization are not simple stories of scientific myopia circumventing "real," authentic experience, or of scientific "discovery" and authoritative expertise invalidating anecdotal, "subjective" perception. First, there was significant heterogeneity and complexity *within* the epidemiologic and lay accounts of heart disease risk and causation that I gathered during the course of my research. Individuals from both participant groups often expressed outwardly contradictory views within the same interview, holding simultaneous beliefs about the health effects of human differences that seemed paradoxical. But what may appear to be conceptual confusion is actually a reflection of the mutable, multivalent, and intensely personal and political nature of race, class, and gender. In this book, I try to highlight this complexity and heterogeneity.

Second, the fault lines run not only between what epidemiologists versus lay people believe, as might be expected, but also between what epidemiologists *think* from what they actually *do* as scientists. In fact, there was at times a somewhat surprising amount of agreement between researchers' reflections on the meanings and implications of human difference and those of people of color with heart disease. For example, I found that both groups of participants repeatedly raised concerns about the problematic measurement of race, its ambiguous meaning in a world of multiraciality and shifting racial categories, and the debatable utility and significance of findings of racial differences for clinical and public health. The epidemiologists and lay people I spoke to also shared relatively similar views on the significance of social class for health: that class shapes life experiences and conditions that in turn stratify people's abilities to care for themselves and to control their exposures to disease risks. On the other hand, while both epidemiologists and lay people agreed on the "naturally" dichotomous nature of sex and gender (that there are two and only two mutually exclusive categories), their understandings of the pathways through which those categories shaped health were vastly different. Yet my analysis shows that, despite such variations in how race, class, sex, and gender were *conceptualized*, social differences were incorporated into epidemiologic *practice* in a highly ritualized manner, uniformly and routinely included as individual-level, standardized, sociodemographic variables in research.

In fact, the custom of including racial categories, socioeconomic status, and sex in epidemiologic studies was so taken for granted that in presentations and conversations about their methods, researchers often referred simply to "controlling for the usual suspects" as a shorthand gloss for the practice. This "usual suspects" approach encompasses both a kind of conceptual devolution—wherein complex, manifold social processes are flattened into individual-level characteristics—and methodological routinization as a standard operating procedure. That is, the "usual suspects" approach has become a black box, to use a metaphor originally from cybernetics that refers to the practice of visually representing complex processes as a box with only the inputs and the outputs specified, without the need to detail the contents of the box itself. The science studies scholar Bruno Latour argues that black boxes are created when many elements and processes are made to fit together into a machine or assembly that in fact acts as one.[47] The black box metaphor is often used in situations wherein scientific claims and procedures are perceived as facts and routines, despite their often having a whole history of debates and controversy.[48] Thus factness, ritualization, and taken-for-grantedness are actually achieved, rather than being presumed to reflect the natural order of things. Yet in the case of my research, a number of epidemiologists object to the practice of the "usual suspects" on fairly fundamental grounds, despite its pervasive and even obligatory nature in their discipline.

Why, then, has the inclusion of these individualized measures of difference become so black-boxed, even when the contents of the black box, so to speak, are under dispute? I argue that it is because the "usual suspects" approach has become integral to the construction of scientific credibility and the management of uncertainty. The value of epidemiology as a scientific discipline is seen, both inside epidemiology and beyond, to depend upon its ability to achieve and maintain credibility. More specifically, the social and scientific trustworthiness of epidemiology rests upon scientists' successfully complying and coping with a number of political, methodological, and economic requirements and constraints. These include imperatives for exhaustive measurement, regulatory mandates for diverse study samples, and the need to deal with inadequate theoretical models and data. Any failure to meet these requirements seriously undercuts epidemiologists' ability to make and defend their scientific claims. In fact, epidemiologists face scrutiny and judgment on a number of fronts. First, as part of a professional scientific community, epidemiologists are acutely cognizant of how their fellow scientists regard their work. Also, epidemiologists have come to occupy a very public role as expert authorities on disease risks and determinants. And finally, they have to be accountable to their funders in order to continue to receive the resources necessary to do research. The epidemiologists in this study managed the varying uncertainties that threatened to undermine the integrity of their research by fulfilling specific methodological, political, and economic contingencies important to these constituencies, thereby maintaining the kinds of scientific and social credibility called for on each of these fronts.

Thus I found that the "usual suspects" approach offered epidemiologists the best available, "good enough" tool to deal with the most common sources of uncertainty. The "usual suspects" approach persists as a standard operating procedure in epidemiology because it promotes the production of credible epidemiologic claims. But in so doing, this ritualized inclusion of individual-level, demographic variables has important consequences for research on the etiology of heart disease. First, it institutionalizes the understanding of what I and the lay participants argue are *social* differences as *individualistic* ones. Second, these individualized variables all too often serve as a first *and* final explanation for group differences seen in health status and disease outcomes. That is, they provide a readily available account for why such differences exist, in ways that deflect the focus of epidemiologic investigation *away* from race, class, and gender as causal forces in and of themselves. And finally, the "usual suspects" approach encourages an atomistic and piecemeal treatment of race, class, and gender—as *independent* and *discrete* explanations for disease variations, rather than as *interdependent, synergistic, and intersecting* dimension of inequality. Because of the need to produce and sustain credibility, the heterogeneity, complexity, and even uncertainty that exists both between and among epidemiologists and lay people are black-boxed, and social relations of power are made orderly and socially and scientifically intelligible through their transposition into standardized variables of race, socioeconomic status, and sex. In the process, this black box comes to be seen as robust even when its content is not; epidemiology endorses and promotes its use, even as individual epidemiologists take issue with it. Thus, the story of the science–lay divide that this book tells includes an account of how the practices and infrastructures of epidemiologic work and, importantly, standard definitions of what counts as legitimate and "doable"[49] research are co-produced[50] along with epidemiologic conventions regarding individualized measures of social difference and biomedicalizing ideas about the health effects of those differences. In truth, the gulf between scientific, expert ways of knowing heart disease and lay perspectives on its causes is as much a hierarchy and an uneven playing field as it is a divide.

A Look Ahead

The research on which this book is based was conducted using several methodologies. I conducted participant observation at conferences where epidemiologic studies are presented, such as the American Heart Association Scientific Sessions, the American College of Cardiology Annual Meetings, and the American Heart Association Cardiovascular Disease Epidemiology and Prevention Conferences. I also collected data via participant observation at various health education events, such as lectures and symposia on heart disease open to the public. I conducted in-depth interviews with a purposive sample of epidemiologists who had published and/or were involved in studies investigating racial, socio-economic, and gender differences in heart disease. I also interviewed a convenience sample of people of color (African Americans, Latinos, and Asian Americans) residing in the larger San Francisco Bay Area who had been diagnosed with heart disease. I asked all the participants to give themselves pseudonyms. In addition, I changed the names of all other people, places, and institutions mentioned in the interviews to protect the identity of the participants. I use "Dr." to indicate epidemiologists, and I use "Mr." and "Ms." to indicate lay participants. And finally, I analyzed literature published since 1985 on the practice of epidemiology. A more extensive description of research methods can be found in the appendix.

My investigation was both guided by and reflects on several theoretical commitments that, while distinct, are interrelated in ways that I wanted to explore further. Throughout my analysis I rely on concepts of biopower and biopolitics and examine how redefined ideas of the state, sovereignty, power, and subjecthood coalesce in debates about health

disparities and their sources. I also wanted to empirically examine theories of intersectionality to better grasp how interlocking systems of
oppression shape both the distribution of life chances and the risk of
risks, as well as the production of authoritative knowledge about disease
causation and health inequality. Finally, I was deeply influenced by the
concept of social conditions as fundamental causes of disease and wanted
to extend, through my empirical investigation, our current understanding of what those fundamental causes are and how they operate. These
three sets of commitments constitute the conceptual foundations for this
book, and I provide an overview of each of them in chapter 1.

To set the stage for the remainder of this book, chapter 2, "Disciplining Difference: A Selective Contemporary History of Cardiovascular
Epidemiology," offers a history of cardiovascular epidemiology in our
contemporary era. Drawing on secondary sources as well as on interviews and observational data, I trace the emergence of the current ruling
paradigm of disease causation—the multifactorial model—and examine
its theoretical tenets and implications for the study of social disparities
in cardiovascular disease. I then describe several key events in the development of cardiovascular epidemiology. Over the course of this history,
epidemiology as a discipline has increasingly articulated its public role as
the official producer of scientific knowledge on disease determinants, and
the rational arbiter of prevention advice. In so doing, I argue, epidemiologic knowledge has come to have a kind of everyday salience as a form of
expertise with which people now regularly engage, interact, and negotiate.
Moreover, epidemiology has always influenced and been shaped by social
ideas about human difference, from its historical concerns with particular
subpopulations (people of color, immigrants, the poor, and women) to
the contemporary study of health disparities. I then turn to an analysis of
several conceptual and methodological dilemmas in epidemiology that
are especially acute in the study of racial, class, and sex/gender differences,
such as the problem of establishing causality and the resulting reliance
on observational studies. The chapter closes with a critical review of the
typical approaches in epidemiologic research on heart disease disparities.

In chapters 3 through 5, I explore the ways in which epidemiologists and people of color with heart disease understand the roles of race, gender, and class differences in heart disease. I analyze the varied meanings of race, class, and gender and how they are mobilized, deployed, and interpreted in epidemiologic and lay accounts of cardiovascular risk and incidence. The meanings of such social differences are neither intrinsic nor self-evident. Rather, as epidemiologists and lay people invoke notions of race, ethnicity, class, socioeconomic status, sex, gender, and so on in claims about disease causation, they continually redefine and negotiate the meanings they attribute to these social features, and the differences they make in heart disease.

Examining the *meanings of* "difference" shows us how "difference" is *made meaningful*; that is, exploring how race, class, and gender are defined tells us something about how they function and are made to do work within systems and relations of power. Such differences are therefore "real" in the sense that they are consequential—such social constructions form the basis for intersecting processes that exert concrete and material though changing and complicated effects on people's sense of self and of group identity, their life chances, and their experiences. Because of the authority accorded to epidemiology as a scientific discipline, it authorizes ideas about what kinds of differences matter, how they matter, and how they should be defined. Thus, epidemiologic conceptualizations of race and its health effects have a powerful capacity to shape what we believe to be true about individuals and groups of different races, and whether and how we act upon these beliefs.

As such, chapters 3 through 5 argue that epidemiology functions as a biopolitical project, a key contemporary site of biopower, and an active participant in the construction of biomedical differences and their social organization in interlocking relations of power.[51] Epidemiologic research taking place every day authorizes particular schemes for categorizing human beings and the surveillance activities, health policies, and clinical practices built upon such classifications. Scientific categories and constructions of difference help to organize governmental efforts to administer and regulate the health and vitality of individuals and populations. Moreover, as the boundaries between the worlds "inside" and "outside" science become increasingly porous, and the culture of biomedical science increasingly contributes to popular culture, conceptions of bodily "differences" like those constructed in cardiovascular epidemiology critically inform those mobilized in everyday life. Thus these chapters explore the question of how differences *are made to matter* in epidemiology—how epidemiologic methods of *sorting* people become part and parcel of efforts to *stratify* them, and how, in turn, stratification processes depend upon sorting mechanisms.

But at the same time, alongside epidemiologic classifications exist people's own understandings of the ways their race, class, and gender do or do not influence their health. The ways in which they make sense of heart disease constitute complex processes that draw upon many sources, including but not limited to scientific ones. I consider how lay participants in my research view the usefulness or relevance of epidemiologic knowledge about "risky differences" and how their social contexts and experiences shape their integration and negotiation of that knowledge in their everyday lives.[52] Furthermore, the experiences and knowledges of individuals with heart disease provide alternative, intersectional understandings of how myriad processes through which their race, class, and gender are embodied come to have consequences for their health. The experiential knowledge of people of color who live with heart disease—as individuals implicated by intersecting axes of power like race, class, and gender—thus serves as a critical contribution as well as potential counterpoint to "expert" epidemiologic knowledge.

As we shall see, considerations of race, class, and gender cannot be neatly divided into three separate, successive chapters. Instead, both epidemiologists and lay people of color living with heart disease invoke combinations of these dimensions of difference in ways that indicate the conceptual complexity of their interactions and intersections. So throughout chapters 3 through 5, I describe how these differences are invoked in multiple, intertwining, and conjoint ways and analyze what such invocations indicate about how various groups see the nature of difference, inequality, and their influences on health.

Chapter 3, "The Contested Meanings and Intersections of Race," takes up the often fraught issue of race, which, in epidemiology, is most often measured by self-classification into one of the racial and ethnic categories standardized by the U.S. Office of Management and Budget. I found that epidemiologists readily expressed profound uncertainties about the meanings of race, its appropriate measures and interpretations, and its implications for disease prevention and public health policy. Yet my analysis also shows that it is ritualistically included in their research. In so doing, epidemiologists implicitly infused "race" with multiple meanings and definitions. Most predominantly, they interpreted the meanings of racial differences through a cultural prism. In contrast, people of color with heart disease tended to articulate how social inequalities along racial, class, and gender lines structured their everyday experiences and life chances that, in turn, affected their health. Race was experienced as a master status, shaping social encounters and educational and economic opportunities in ways that exacted a toll on their psychic, mental, and bodily health. But race was also experienced as intersectional as well, inextricably intertwined with experiences of class and gender; thus chapter 3 tries to capture these experiences of intersectional inequality.

Chapter 4, "An Apparent Consensus on Class," turns to considering the issue of class. In contrast to the very divergent scientific and lay perspectives on race, I found a good deal of consensus on the significance of class differences for health. Both epidemiologists and people with heart disease unequivocally pointed to structural dynamics of class inequality—its effects on differential access to resources and exposures to myriad health risks—in their causal accounts of heart disease. The appropriate conceptualization of class was seen by both groups as indisputably about differences that are social in nature. At the same time, however, epidemiologists were inclined to invoke individualistic explanations for socioeconomic differences that indict health behaviors and the cultural milieus within which they are presumed to arise. They also invariably expressed concern over confounding between class and race and how best to separate their effects through statistical techniques. Lay people of color, on the other hand, tended to emphasize racial and class stratification as intersecting and mutually dependent processes.

In chapter 5, "The Dichotomy of Gender," I position gender as an interesting counterpoint to race and class. Importantly, neither epidemiologists nor lay people questioned that gender and sex are binary in nature, and self-evidently so. Within epidemiologic circles, the notion of gender differences in heart disease as rooted in biology was completely uncontroversial. The biological distinctiveness of heart disease in women versus men was considered the natural order of things. In contrast, though, I found that lay people very rarely invoked biological differences of sex. Instead, working-class women of color in particular referred to interlocking dynamics of race, class, and gender that stratified their educational opportunities and structure a racially and sex-segregated labor market. Those employment opportunities available to them were largely restricted to low-paying jobs, with little potential for advancement, minimal job stability, and little power over their hours, pace of work, or the nature of the work process. Such occupational stratification, along with a disproportionate share of childrearing responsibilities (what feminist scholars have termed "reproductive labor"),[53] represents, in these women's eyes, critical sources of cardiovascular risk that entwine gender with race and class in interlocking systems of inequality. Therefore, it is in also in this second sense that gender can be seen as dichotomous, invoking oppositional understandings of its nature—as biological versus social—and consequences for health that cleave along a science–lay divide.

In chapter 6, "Individualizing 'Difference' and the Production of Scientific Credibility," I move from the issue of how epidemiologists *conceptualize* the meanings of human differences for heart disease to consider how they *manage* those differences in their everyday scientific practices, and *why*. Using interview and observational data, I explore the ritualized conceptual and methodological devolution of racial, class, and gender differences—the "usual suspects" approach—and analyze how it is integral to the construction of scientific credibility, even as a growing number of epidemiologists question this practice at a fairly fundamental level.

Finally, in the Conclusion, I summarize the key arguments and frame the implications of my findings for health policy and for future research and scholarship in health disparities, expert–lay relations, inequality, and power. Because epidemiology is the science of choice for public health policy and decision making, we must understand and take into account the conditions under which that kind of knowledge is being produced. Conventions and techniques which satisfy a number of methodological, political, and economic contingencies that must be met in order to achieve and maintain scientific credibility constrain epidemiology's ability to elucidate how relations of power act as fundamental causes of disease, placing people defined as different "at risk of risks." That being said, however, there is burgeoning interest in and effort devoted to understanding the *social* determinants of health, the so-called unnatural causes of disease, as one television series puts it.[54] Indeed, the divisions explored in the chapters to come run not just between epidemiologists and lay people as between what epidemiologists *think* and what they actually *do* as scientists. Many of them would in fact agree with lay people's accounts of heart disease, which support the notion that conditions of social inequality function as fundamental causes of disease, by stratifying life chances, resources, and the conditions within which health can be promoted, maintained, and/or undermined. Yet the credibility-generating effects of epidemiologic conceptions of difference—as individual-level risk factors—cannot be ignored. Consequently, I conclude that more comprehensive answers to the question of how difference matters require different ways of obtaining those answers and different ways of producing knowledge, and thus alternative definitions of credibility and expertise.

1

The Politics of Disease Causation

In order to interrogate, account for, and make sense of the politics of disease causation, I rely on several sets of concepts and theoretical arguments: biopower and biopolitics, intersectionality theory, and fundamental causality. This chapter's intent is to provide a selective review of the works, concepts, and arguments I have found most valuable and to offer a taste of how I use them to think with throughout this book. While to date these literatures have not regularly been brought into conversation with one another, I hope to show that doing so helps to articulate a set of questions that can bring to light how the politics of causation operate to shape the distribution of health across populations, the knowledges we use to make sense of that distribution, and the means by which those knowledges might be revised to intervene in health inequality more productively. The sections of this chapter can be read modularly, as different parts of the toolkit that I use to situate my inquiry and analysis.

First, a quick discussion of what I mean by the politics of disease causation. On the one hand, I argue in this book that epidemiology is a technique of biopower, the fusion of disciplinary knowledge with power to govern the health of bodies and populations. Yet I am also interested in how the individuals implicated by epidemiologic power-knowledge see themselves not only as a focus of regulation but also as members of groups immersed in complex relations of power and capable of questioning scientific knowledge about health and illness. In multiple ways, these forms of disciplinary knowledge, governance, and contestations of scientific knowledge are all centrally concerned with disease causation. Interventions to optimize health and struggles to challenge them rest on how different groups understand the risks and determinants of disease. These claims about the causes of disease—and about their differential distribution—both shape and are shaped by social, cultural, and organizational conditions and relations of power that together constitute what I consider the politics of disease causation. To help me interrogate the politics of disease, I therefore turn to three arenas of scholarship: biopower and biopolitics, intersectionality, and theories of fundamental causality.

Biopower and Bipolitics: Differentiating and Normalizing Power-Knowledge

One of the foremost ways in which I understand epidemiology is as a technique of biopower and form of power-knowledge that serves to identify, differentiate, and normalize groups and human populations. Foucault charts the emergence of biopower from a state power solely based on sovereignty and the right to take life or let live, to one that also lay increasingly in "the right to intervene to make live"[1] or to let die. According to Foucault, growing governmental concern with the surveillance and regulation of bodies and populations in the seventeenth century led to the development of expert fields of knowledge and the refinement of diverse and efficient techniques of human control that coalesced to bring "life and its mechanisms into the realm of explicit calculations and made knowledge-power an agent of transformation of human life."[2] Foucault describes biopower—this power over life—as consisting of a continuum between two poles: a disciplinary power or anatomo-politics, and a regulatory power or biopolitics. Anatomo-politics targets "the body as a machine: its disciplining, the optimization of its capabilities, the extortion of its forces, the parallel increase of its usefulness and its docility, its integration into systems of efficient and economic controls."[3] Biopolitics, in contrast, focuses on populations, on "the species body, the body imbued with the mechanics of life and serving as the basis of the biological processes: propagation, births and mortality, the level of health, life expectancy and longevity."[4] Together, this bipolar technology—this interplay between technologies of discipline and technologies of regulation—"succeeded in covering the whole surface that lies between the organic and biological, between body and population."[5]

Along the way, Foucault makes several interrelated arguments that are particularly relevant to the project of this book. First is his tracing of the emergence of the *population* as an increasing concern of modern states. The health, growth, life expectancy, and vitality of populations—as phenomena in and of themselves—become economic, social, political, and administrative problems of governments. Second, Foucault asserts that circulating between the two poles of biopower is the element of the *norm*, "applied to both a body one wishes to discipline and a population one wishes to regularize. The normalizing society is therefore not . . . a sort of generalized disciplinary society . . . [but] a society in which the norm of discipline and the norm of regulation intersect along an orthogonal articulation."[6] A third point of significance is Foucault's use of the term "discipline" to refer to both expert fields of knowledge and to techniques of control and regulation—or, in his phrase, "power-knowledge." Disciplines "create apparatuses of knowledge, knowledges and multiple fields of expertise. . . . The discourse of disciplines is about a rule: not a juridical rule derived from sovereignty, but a discourse about a natural rule, or in other words a norm. Disciplines will define not a code of law, but a code of normalization."[7] The focus thus remains on "the 'how' of power,"[8] instantiated not only in formal rules and rights but also in the production of discourses and regimes of truth, "infinitesimal mechanisms . . . techniques and tactics . . . how these mechanisms of power . . . have been and are invested, colonized, used, inflected, transformed, displaced, extended, and so on."[9]

In conceptualizing epidemiology as a technique of biopower, then, I am emphasizing its constitution and operation as a discipline—a domain of power-knowledge—that acts along both poles of disciplinary and regulatory power, on individual bodies and whole populations. Because of its preoccupation with the incidence and distribution of disease determinants in populations, epidemiology has been critical in facilitating the emergence of the notion of the population and its mobilization as an object of concern and intervention. Through its concepts, practices, techniques that identify and quantify patterns of health and illness, measures of central tendency, and distributions and deviations of susceptibilities, epidemiology creates norms—it "is, inevitably, a normalizing science."[10] It both disciplines individuals through its discourses of risk and practices of surveillance, and regulates populations by providing the apparatuses and means to produce biopolitical objects of knowledge and targets of control such as rates of birth, death, disease, and risk factors.

Foucault's elaboration of biopower is also distinctly important here because it is the primary site in which he reflected publicly on the significance of race and racism for modern governmentality. Toward the end of *The History of Sexuality*, Foucault begins to hint at the ways in which he saw the regulation of sex in the nineteenth century become "anchorage points"[11] for different varieties of racism, including eugenics. Racism, however, becomes much more central in his 1975–76 Collège de France lectures (compiled in *Society Must Be Defended*) as a means to answer the question of how power over life can be at once to make live as well as to let die. As he reasons,

What in fact is racism? It is primarily a way of introducing a break into the domain of life that is under power's control: the break between what must live and what must die. The appearance within the biological continuum of the human race of races, the distinction among races, the hierarchy of races, the fact that certain places are described as good and that others, in contrast, are defined as inferior: all this is a way of fragmenting the field of the biological that power controls. . . . Racism also has a second function. . . . On the one hand, racism makes it possible to establish a relationship between my life and the death of the other that is . . . a biological-type relationship: "The more inferior species die out, the more abnormal individuals are eliminated, the fewer degenerates there will be in the species as a whole, and the more I—as species rather than individual—can live, the stronger I will be, the more vigorous I will be. I will be able to proliferate." . . . The death of the other, the death of the bad race, of the inferior race (or the degenerate, or the abnormal) is something that will make life in general healthier: healthier and purer.[12]

While Foucault is clear to say that racism preexisted biopower, he proposes that the emergence of biopower, with the concomitant question of differentiating between lives to be fostered and those deemed unworthy, draws racism into the administration and management of life. Disciplinary control of bodies and regulatory power over populations— and their techniques of surveillance, measurement, hierarchization, and judgment—all place normalization as a central process of biopower. And, Foucault argues, "in a normalizing society, race or racism is the precondition that makes killing acceptable."[13]

This "modern, 'biologizing,' statist form"[14] of racism that is Foucault's particular interest draws on evolutionary discourses as it creates internal enemies (rather than enemies from without) against which society must defend itself:

What we see as a polarity, as a binary rift within a society, is not a clash between two distinct places. It is the splitting of a single race into a super-race and subrace . . . a battle that has to be waged not between races, but by a race that is portrayed as the one true race, the race that holds power and is entitled to define the norm, and against those who deviate from that norm, against those who pose a threat to the biological heritage. . . . At this point . . . we see the appearance of a State racism: a racism that society will direct against itself, against its own elements and its own products. This is the internal racism of permanent purification, and it will become one of the basic dimensions of social normalization.[15]

Effectively, what then follows from state racism is that "the state is no longer an instrument that one race uses against another: the state is, and must be, the protector of the integrity, the superiority, and the purity of the race."[16] But at the same time, as Ann Laura Stoler asserts, Foucault's lectures also show his grappling with reinscriptions of race as well as disjunctures in racial grammar and forms of racism: "What concerns him is not modern racism's break with earlier forms, but rather the discursive *bricolage* whereby an older discourse of race is 'recovered,' modified, 'encased,' and 'encrusted' in new forms."[17]

Foucault's arguments about the exercise of biopower therefore centrally implicate racialization processes and racism, in ways that have contemporary resonance for thinking through epidemiology's role in disease stratification and in the production of knowledge about racial difference and racialized populations. Many contemporary observers have turned to Foucault's concept of biopower—and his accompanying concerns with racism, hierarchy, and the power of the state—to understand the modern preoccupation with the sciences of life itself and to analyze their operation, interventions, and consequences. For instance, Steven Epstein conceives of the shifting politics and practices of racial, ethnic, and gender inclusion and representation in health research from the mid-1980s onward as the emergence of a new biopolitical paradigm. He defines biopolitical paradigms as "frameworks of ideas, standards, formal procedures, and unarticulated understandings that specify how concerns about health, medicine, and the body are made the simultaneous focus of biomedicine and state policy."[18] Monica Casper and Lisa Jean Moore use biopolitics, understood as "the social practices and institutions established to regulate a population's quality (and quantity) of life,"[19] to interrogate the politics by which some bodies are made visible and celebrated, while others are erased and/or denied. The concept of biomedicalization, developed by Adele Clarke, Jennifer Fishman, Jennifer Fosket, Laura Mamo, and me, is fundamentally hinged on the notion of biopower and on Foucault's insights more generally.[20] With biomedicalization theory, we emphasize not just control over but also *"transformations of* medical phenomena and of bodies, largely through . . . technoscientific interventions not only for treatment but also increasingly for enhancement. The panoply of biomedical institutions is itself being organizationally transformed through technoscience, along with biomedical practices . . . and the life sciences and technologies that inform them."[21] And Adriana Petryna uses biopower to analyze "life politics after Chernobyl"—that is, the complex and ever-shifting scientific, social, and financial arrangements of Soviet and post-Soviet responses to the 1986 nuclear reactor explosion at Chernobyl.[22] In these responses, Petryna notes that "state power is as concerned with making bodies and behaviors ever more predictable and knowable as it is with creating . . . spaces of nonknowledge and unpredictability. The biology of populations is held in question; the government of life is unmoored."[23] Against a backdrop of limited access to health care and widespread impoverishment, scientific research and legal procedures combined with an economy of claims and compensation to provide the grounds for biological citizenship: the "demand for but selective access to social welfare based on medical, scientific, and legal criteria."[24]

Finally, Nikolas Rose argues for an analysis of the biopolitics of the twenty-first century through examining five sets of "mutations": molecularization or a "style of thought" that sees the molecular level as the site of intervention, manipulation, and recombination; optimization, the mandate to "secure the best possible future"; subjectification or the recoding and reshaping of "what human beings are, what they should do, and what they can hope for"; expertise referring to the rise of new subprofessions that exercise power over the management of life; and bioeconomics driven by the identification or creation of biocapital, fueled by investments in hope and optimality.[25] Importantly, Rose sees biopower as "more a perspective than a concept: it brings into view a whole range of more or less rationalized attempts by different authorities to intervene upon the vital characteristics of human existence."[26] When using this perspective to analyze the contemporary situation in the West, Rose concludes that

> the transformed biopolitics of the 21st century . . . is a biopolitics organized around the principle of fostering individual life, not of eliminating those that threaten the quality of populations; it is a biopolitics that does not operate under the sign of the sovereign state; it is a biopolitics that does not seek to legitimate inequality but to intervene upon its consequences. Crucially, it is a biopolitics in which references to the biological do not signal fatalism but are part of the economy of hope that characterizes contemporary biomedicine.[27]

Rose points out that in biopower today, "though death suffuses it" and it "has its circuits of exclusion, letting die is not making die," biopower operates "according to logics of vitality, not those of mortality," as "the government of life."[28] All of this, Rose argues, provides grounds for some optimism, given that we are all "biological creatures, and that each such creature exercises a demand on each other simply by being a creature of this sort."[29] In part, it is this tension between biological commonality and biological difference that this book seeks to interrogate.

All of these more contemporary engagements with the Foucauldian notion of biopower find resonance in this book. Like Epstein, I am concerned with how racial and gender inclusion in biomedical research and practice makes certain claims about the nature of those social differences in the consequences for bodies and for population health. These consequences are differential and stratified,[30] as Casper and Moore point out and as argued by the concept of stratified biomedicalization. As in the case of state responses to Chernobyl, this book explores what questions about bodies and behaviors are asked and made knowable, and what questions remain unknown and unasked. Both Petryna and Rose mobilize the figures of the "citizen" and the "subject" to think about how claims for care can and are made at the same time that expectations and obligations of what human beings are, what they ought to do, and how they ought to live are being reshaped. The chapters that follow will similarly explore the questions about disease causation that are asked and that remain unasked, and how these encapsulate ideas about what claims for health, behaviors, and social environments can be made and to whom.

Intersectionality: Theorizing Complex
Differences and Inequalities

Intersectionality is the conception of race, class, and gender (as well as other inequalities) as intersecting relations of power, bases for identity, and dimensions of hierarchical difference. It encompasses a theoretical and empirical commitment to assert and explore the mutual constitution of race, class, and gender in social interactions and institutions. While the idea of intersecting dimensions of inequality and difference has a long history, intersectionality as a concept or theoretical rubric was first widely circulated by the work of Kimberle Crenshaw.[31] Among feminist scholars, intersectionality has now taken on the status of a "basic paradigm"[32] (and even a "buzzword"[33]), coalescing into a framework or approach based on some key assumptions.[34]

Central among these is the assertion that categories of social identity are not discrete dimensions of social life and that any one category is no more important than any other. Social categories are historically, geographically, and locally specific, such that members of a social group, their experiences, and the meanings that identity holds for them are deeply heterogeneous. Categories are simultaneously identities as well as what Spelman calls interlocking matrices of power and oppression, wherein the meanings and consequences of human differences are predicated upon one another.[35] Therefore categories of identity or difference cannot be seen as additive; intersectionality analysis instead attempts to understand social locations, experiences, and processes that shape the intersections of multiple axes of inequality. Finally, by uncovering the operation of intersecting relations of power and their consequences for the material well-being, lived experiences, and life chances of those who occupy marginalized as well as privileged positions, intersectional research works intentionally to change the status quo and advance social justice.

An intersectional approach attempts to analyze social relations and processes across multiple domains and levels of social action. In the sociologist Lynn Weber's[36] useful schema, these social domains and their associated institutions include, first, the *ideological*—those institutions that produce and distribute ideas and knowledge, shaping cultural beliefs, public images, and even scientific knowledge about dominant and subordinate groups. Second, institutions in the *political* domain "creat[e] and enforc[e] laws and government structures that define citizens' and noncitizens' rights, responsibilities, and privileges,"[37] and, I would add, the boundaries of belonging and exclusion that separate citizens—not just in the legal but also in the social and cultural sense—from noncitizens. And third, the *economic* domain maintains control over the production and distribution of such valued goods and resources as wealth, education, employment opportunities, income, information, and health care.

Rather than consider the ideological, political, and economic as specifiable domains of social life, however, I find it more useful throughout this book to see these as overlapping means of action and influence. Intersectionality's emphasis on conjoint meaning-making *and* institutional practices echoes Omi and Winant's conceptualization of racial formation as a means to understanding how the concept of race continues to play a fundamental role in structuring and representing the social world. They define racial formation as the "sociohistorical process by which racial categories are created, inhabited, transformed, and destroyed."[38] According to their approach, this process of racial formation is the ongoing, unfolding outcome of "racial projects" in which human bodies and social structures are represented and organized, that "connect what race *means* in a particular discursive practice and the ways in which both social structures and everyday experiences are racially organized."[39] They argue that the interpretation of experiences in racial terms and the framing and shaping of social structures along racial lines mutually reinforce representations of difference and their institutionalization in the social order.

While intersectionality theory takes a wider lens than Omi and Winant's focus on race, I appreciate their articulation of coincident, synergistic representational and material processes. The mutual reinforcement of ideas about human differences and their material consequences in and for institutional practices underscores the simultaneously ideological, political, and economic social relations in health care and the biomedical sciences—the particular concerns of this book. Health care and biomedicine can no longer be thought of simply as an institutional or economic sector but instead are increasingly and pervasively ever-present throughout social life and our daily existence, creating and circulating new, recycled, and revised ideas about social groups and human differences. These ideas maintain preexisting and establish new bases of group belonging and the accompanying responsibilities of social and cultural citizenship—this, to me, is part of the essence of biopolitics and biopolitical governance, as detailed above. Finally, health care and biomedical knowledge are valued resources; they are social and economic goods in and of themselves. Their unequal distribution has material consequences for individuals' and groups' economic well-being (as when untreated chronic illness leads to disability and loss of employment), and, in turn, health is itself the product of economic patterns of intersecting inequalities, as this book will show. In the complex institutional practices and social interactions that constitute the domains of health and biomedicine, race, class, gender, and other interrelated systems of power define and shape patterns of behavior and beliefs. In so doing, they reproduce and remake inequality in intersecting ways.

Despite (or perhaps because of) this rich theoretical complexity, many have observed that putting intersectionality theory to methodological and empirical use is difficult.[40] By interrogating the very nature of categories and categorization itself, intersectionality theory questions the groups and group attributes commonly used to articulate the scope of a research inquiry, structure comparative data analyses, and characterize samples and study results. Yet intersectionality theory also clearly defines a particular research agenda focused on problematizing the "who" that is being studied, keeping issues of power and relations of domination and subordination at the center of the analysis and calling for social change. Weber provides a cogent expression of both what an intersectional analysis argues and how it is to be done that is worth quoting at length:

[Intersecting systems of oppression] are (1) historically and geographically contextual (2) socially constructed (3) power relationships that operate at (4) macro social-structural and micro social-psychological levels and are (5) simultaneously expressed . . .

1. *Historically and geographically contextual:* . . . analyses focus on specific times and places and avoid the search for common meanings of race, class, gender, and sexuality that would apply in all times and places . . .

2. *Socially constructed:* . . . Although they may have biological or material referents, race, class, gender, and sexuality are not fixed properties of individuals nor of materially defined groups. Their meaning can and does change over time and in different social contexts . . .

3. *Power relationships:* Race, class, gender, and sexuality are power relationships of dominance and subordination, not merely gradations along a scale of resources—who has more than whom—or differences in cultural preferences or gender roles. They are based in relationships of exploitation of subordinate groups by dominant groups for a greater share of society's valued resources. They change because oppressed groups struggle to gain rights, opportunities, and resources—to gain greater control over their lives against dominant groups who seek to

maintain their position of control over the political, ideological, and economic social domains . . .

4. *Macro social structural and micro social psychological levels:* These power relationships between dominant and subordinate groups are embedded in society's *macro* social institutions and in the *micro* face-to-face interactions that constitute the everyday lives of individuals. Specifying the linkages between these two levels is a key component of a race, class, gender, and sexuality analysis . . .

5. *Simultaneously expressed:* Race, class, gender, and sexuality *operate simultaneously* in every social situation. At the societal level, these systems of social hierarchies are connected to each other and are embedded in all social institutions. At the individual level, we each experience our lives based on our location along *all* dimensions, and so we may occupy positions of dominance and subordination at the same time.[41]

This agenda, as offered by Weber, helps to articulate the project of this book. On the one hand, the historical and geographic specificity of intersectionality [(1) in the above], the socially constructed nature of dimensions of inequality (2), and their simultaneous expression (5) altogether mean that heterogeneity, contradiction, and complexity characterize how social situations, identities, and experiences are intersectional. Yet on the other hand, the meanings of race, class, gender, and so on are not created *de novo:* Their imbrication in power relationships (3) and at the social structural and social psychological levels (4) suggests that the meanings and consequences of social inequalities exhibit a patterned durability, though they do change over time. Capturing the enduring as well as heterogeneous nature of inequality and transformations over time and across space is part of the intent of this book. In essence, this follows the sociologist Patricia Hill Collins, who argues that intersectionality works best as a conceptual framework "describing what kinds of things to consider than as one describing any actual patterns of social organization . . . an interpretive framework for thinking through how intersections of race and class, or race and gender, or sexuality and class, for example, shape any group's experience across specific social contexts."[42] In Collins's view, intersectionality should be used as a heuristic device to think through the ways in which social institutions, organizational structures, patterns of social interactions, and other social practices at multiple levels enable, actualize, exemplify, and explicate how social phenomena like race, class, and gender mutually construct one another. I am therefore interested here in analyzing and understanding the simultaneity of these axes of "difference" in lived experience, and the fluid ways in which they overlap, intersect, and operate antagonistically or synergistically.

In doing so, I take an approach to complexity that the sociologist Leslie McCall characterizes as in between "intercategorical" and "anticategorical" approaches.[43] As she explains,

> On the one hand, some feminist scholars explicitly use categories to define the subjects of analysis and to articulate the broader structural dynamics that are present in the lives of the subjects. . . . On the other hand, scholars also see categories as misleading constructs that do not readily allow for the diversity and heterogeneity of experience to be represented. . . . The point is not to deny the importance—both material and discursive—of categories but to focus on the process by which they are produced, experienced, reproduced, and resisted in everyday life.[44]

That is, while I provisionally adopt categories of race, social class, and gender to illustrate the patterns of inequality and their effects on health that I see in participants' narratives about heart disease, these same narratives also push me to question the integrity, uniformity, and validity of those very categories. The broad organization and day-to-day experiences of social groups are, as McCall describes, "irreducibly complex—overflowing with multiple and fluid determinations of both subjects and structures—to make fixed categories anything but simplifying social fictions that produce inequalities in the process of producing differences."[45]

In sum, I use intersectionality to attend explicitly to the *relational* and *patterned* yet *fluid* nature of power and its *simultaneous* impacts on structural and institutional as well as interactional, psychological, and identity aspects of lived experience. Thus, in the narratives about the meanings of race, class, and gender for heart disease that I describe in this book, I specifically point to how and where scientists and lay people see (or don't see) the linkages between macro-level structural processes and their everyday existence, and how these are rooted in relationships between socially constituted groups that both are embedded in *and* exceed those categories. That the connections between inequality and health are intersectional, categorically patterned yet complex, relational, and expressed on multiple levels of social organization, experience, and meaning-making is, as we shall see, a key aspect of the science–lay divide. Intersectionality theory therefore enables an analysis of the biopolitics of heart disease causation: Ideas about human differences emerging from relations of power are tied to ideas about what places people at cardiovascular risk, which are in turn taken up in scientific and biomedical knowledges and interventions and acted upon and contested by lay people with heart disease.

Fundamental Causality: Social Inequality and the Social Production of Disease

A third animating framework for analyzing claims about heart disease causation and how difference matters is the fundamental cause perspective. Fundamental causality offers a deeply sociological and potentially theoretically powerful explanation of health disparities and their multicausal and durable nature. It takes up longstanding though marginalized traditions in the study of health and disease that integrate sociological concerns with epidemiologic approaches.[46] The core proposition of this theory, according to the sociologists Bruce Link, Jo Phelan, and their colleagues,[47] is that certain social conditions constitute fundamental causes of disease. By "social conditions," they refer to "factors that involve a person's relationships to other people. These include everything from relationships with intimates to positions occupied within the socioeconomic structures of society . . . factors like race, socioeconomic status, and gender . . . [and] stressful life events of a social nature."[48]

These social conditions have a fundamental relationship to health because they involve access to resources whose risk-avoiding and disease-ameliorating benefits accrue disproportionately for the socially and economically privileged. These resources include knowledge, power, money, social connections, and prestige; they profoundly shape people's ability to avoid risks and to minimize the consequences of risk exposure and disease once they occur. They are broadly serviceable, flexible, multipurpose, transportable from one situation to another, and therefore have wide-ranging utility and serve as the general means by which individuals make their way in the world. These socially distributed resources act at both the individual and contextual levels:

At the individual level, flexible resources can be conceptualized as the "cause of causes" or "risk of risks" that shape individual health behaviors by influencing whether people know about, have access to, can afford, and receive social support for their efforts to engage in health-enhancing or health-protective behaviors. In addition, resources shape access to broad contexts that vary dramatically in associated risk profiles and protective factors. For example, a person with many resources can afford to live in a high SES [socioeconomic status] neighborhood where neighbors are also of high status and where, collectively, enormous clout is exerted to ensure that crime, noise, violence, pollution, traffic, and vermin are minimized, and that the best health-care facilities, parks, playgrounds, and food stores are located nearby. Once a person has used SES-related resources to locate in an advantaged neighborhood, a host of health-enhancing circumstances comes along as a package deal. Similarly, a person who uses educational credentials to procure a high-status occupation inherits a package deal that is more likely to include excellent health benefits and less likely to involve dangerous conditions and toxic exposures. In these circumstances, the person benefits in numerous ways that do not depend on his or her own initiative or ability to personally construct a healthy situation; it is an "add on" benefit operative at the contextual level.[49]

Fundamental causality asserts that these resources forge concurrent and multiplicative links with multiple different risk factors and multiple disease outcomes that may shift over time. In this way, the causal linkages and pathways between social conditions and outcomes, and even the disease outcomes themselves, may change or shift in salience without altering the underlying fundamental relationship between those social conditions and health. This perspective argues that, at the end of the day, public health interventions at the individual, risk factor level are inefficient and will have only limited success, as many of the fundamental causes of heart disease lie further upstream in the social inequalities that give rise to those risks. Attempts to mitigate those social inequities would then likely yield considerable downstream benefits in prevented morbidity and mortality and reduced disparities in heart disease as well as other health conditions.

Fundamental cause theory helps to explain the circumstances under which health disparities wax and wane. As Link and colleagues note, "When innovations beneficial to health are developed in our society, their implementation necessarily occurs within the context of inequalities in knowledge, money, power, prestige, and social connections."[50] As knowledge is produced about the health effects of a risk factor, or as new risks or treatments arise, those able to command the most resources are in a better position to take advantage of this new knowledge, avoid risks, and access treatments. That is, those who are already advantaged benefit disproportionately from improved capabilities to prevent and control disease. Indeed, "it is our enormously expanded capacity to control disease in combination with existing social and economic inequalities that create health disparities by race and SES."[51] Multiple studies have confirmed this fundamental cause claim that new health-related knowledge and innovations—like Pap tests, mammography, and statins, the growing ability to manage some diseases, and the finding that hormone replacement therapy increases the risk of breast cancer[52]—all disproportionately accrue to those who are better off. Through this stratification of the uptake and subsequent benefits of newfound abilities to control disease and enhance health, existing social and economic inequalities are repeatedly *reproduced* to cumulatively build deepening patterns of morbidity and mortality.

The notion of fundamental social causes provides a conceptual stance from which to analyze claims about the nature and effects of racial, class, and gender differences on heart disease. What is striking in my interviews with lay people is the degree to which the fundamental cause perspective resonates in their accounts of race, class, and gender and the role they play in heart disease. Their accounts support the notion that social inequality stratifies life chances, resources, and the conditions within which health can be promoted, maintained, and/or undermined. Their narratives echo the World Health Organization's definition of health, broadened to encompass not only well-being itself but also the "prerequisites for health—what people need to make health possible—freedom from fear of war; equal opportunity for all; satisfaction of basic needs for food, water, and sanitation; education; decent housing; secure work in a useful role in society; and political will and public support."[53]

But in this regard, those diagnosed with heart disease push beyond some of the implicit limitations of fundamental cause theory: Rather than emphasize distributional differences in resources, as that theory does, lay people spoke more explicitly about power relationships as central to health disparities. That is, it is *relations of power* tied to the representation and organization of race, class, and gender that are seen by lay people as fundamental causes of disease, placing those defined as different "at risk of risks." In this way, lay accounts echo two prominent themes in intersectionality scholarship. First, they argue that the social locations of multiply oppressed groups provide a unique location from which to understand systems of inequality.[54] Second, they move away from a focus on individuals and instead examine how relations of power and hierarchies of privilege are organized, sustained, and reproduced to stratify life chances.[55]

I take up these arguments extensively in chapters 3 through 5. But before doing so, some introduction to the discipline of epidemiology—which stands at the heart of the biopolitics of disease causation—and its history is in order. Understanding epidemiology's emergence, the ways in which it has been positioned and mobilized as the official producer of knowledge about health, and some of the claims about human differences that are embedded within its methods will help to explain its centrality in governing populations and as an object of uptake and/or scrutiny on the part of individuals and social groups. This is the objective of chapter 2, to which I now turn.

2

Disciplining Difference

A Selective Contemporary History of
Cardiovascular Epidemiology

This chapter provides a contemporary history of cardiovascular epidemiology, drawing mostly on secondary sources, supplemented with ethnographic data collected from epidemiologic conferences and interviews
with epidemiologists. It emphasizes the contemporary social and historical developments most pertinent to the conceptualization and study of
individual and population differences, particularly those of race, class,
and sex/gender. I also include conceptual, methodological, and epistemological debates circulating both within and outside the world of epidemiology that are relevant to research on human differences. This history
underscores the social and cultural shaping of epidemiologic practices
and their significance for our current state of official knowledge on cardiovascular disease causation and risks.

As a discipline, epidemiology is at a historic moment in its development:
Social and genetic epidemiologists are mobilizing new conceptual models,

methodological tools, analytic techniques, greater interdisciplinary collaborations, and explicit scientific and political commitments to further their respective research agendas. In so doing, they are reshaping the relationships among the profession of epidemiology, other disciplines, individual scientists, and the public. The existence of such theoretical, methodological, epistemological, and political heterogeneity complicates any exploration of the discipline of epidemiology. As Dora Roth explains, epidemiology "is regarded as a distinct and independent science (or discipline) not because it deals with special problems or because it has acquired a unique content, but because it has developed specialized procedures of investigation and application."[1] Departments of epidemiology exist throughout academic institutions in the United States, numerous professional associations and academic journals have been established, and funding agencies have provided broad support for epidemiologic research. All of these indicate the taken-for-granted assumption that epidemiology is a legitimate scientific approach to an ever-larger body of problems. Epidemiology is widely considered to be an authoritative mode of knowledge production on health risks and disease as well as a tool for policymaking. Cardiovascular epidemiology in its own right has become a credible and consequential source of scientific and popular knowledge about heart disease, and a key site in which conceptions of race, class, and sex/gender are shaped and invoked.

In the following section, I lay out the argument that the epidemiology of cardiovascular inequalities is a contemporary manifestation of biopower and domain of power-knowledge, but one that must work to maintain its public authority and credibility in the face of scientific and social disputes. I next provide a chronicle of the more recent history of cardiovascular disease epidemiology in the United States, focusing on the period from 1947—widely considered to be the debut of modern cardiovascular epidemiology—to the present. Specifically, I examine the emergence and consequences of the basic theoretical paradigm of epidemiology—the multifactorial model of disease causation—and its implications for the routinization of the measurement of race, socioeconomic status, and sex.[2] In the final sections of this chapter, I describe the subsequent burst of activity in cardiovascular epidemiology that served to place millions of individuals and multiple communities under the epidemiologic gaze and that provided the scientific basis for the making of claims about the nature of cardiovascular risks. I explore debates over the credibility of epidemiologic science that mark its relationship with the public and configure how the discipline and its practitioners consider research on health inequalities. This analysis illuminates the social conditions that structure contestations over the conceptualization, measurement, and interpretation of racial, class, and sex/gender inequalities in heart disease incidence and distribution.

Biopower and the Epidemiologic Gaze

The development of epidemiology more broadly and that of cardiovascular epidemiology in particular are part of a unique set of historical, social, political, cultural, and technoscientific contexts. Epidemiology has roots that reach as far back as Hippocrates[3] but came of age approximately in the past century and a half. It emerged out of the same crucible that produced the development of bureaucracies and technologies for classifying and enumerating, the rise of statistical thinking and the social authority of quantification, the emergence of a scientifically rooted medical profession, and concerns to intervene in the public's health.[4] However, according to Olga Amsterdamska, noted sociologist and historian of science and medicine, "the first explicit and extensive efforts to define epidemiology as a science and to demarcate it from other neighboring fields date from the period immediately following World War I."[5]

Epidemiology's core concerns are with the patterns of health conditions in human populations and with the factors that influence these patterns. A fundamental project of epidemiology is to develop predictive models of health status.[6] As such, epidemiology ultimately aims to apply its quantitative technologies and products to the governance of collective and individual health and the factors and behaviors that determine them. That is, epidemiology performs cultural work by tying together statistics about individuals and populations with particular conceptions of the "problem" of health, disease, morbidity and mortality.[7] In a word, the kind of cultural work that epidemiology does is what Michel Foucault calls biopower.[8]

Biopower, as described in chapter 1, is the mutually productive combination of power and knowledge, in which apparatuses and technologies exert diffuse yet constant forces of surveillance and control on human bodies and their behaviors, sensations, physiological processes, and pleasures. New disciplinary bodies of knowledge concerned with problems of population such as birthrates, longevity, and public health[9] began to construct and establish what was considered normal and pathological across wide-ranging spheres of life.[10] Such knowledge fixed and rendered individual differences "scientific," arraying individuals around constructed notions of the norm and pinning them down in their particularity. Individuals became cases to be studied, enabling the refinement of more diverse and efficient techniques of control based upon the regulation, quantification, judgment, and hierarchization of human bodies.

Reflective of the preoccupations of modernity, epidemiology thus came to serve as an instrument of normalization; that is, it served not only as a form of representation but also as a means of instrumental control.[11] As the historian Theodore Porter observes, "[M]easures succeed by giving direction to the very activities that are being measured. In this way individuals are made governable. . . . Numbers create and can be compared with norms, which are among the . . . most pervasive forms of power in modern democracies."[12] Weighted with the power of scientific reason and rhetoric, epidemiology became a significant tool for the disciplining of individuals and populations, for the exercise of power over behaviors and bodies, and for arbitrating contestations over different forms of knowledge and their legitimacy.

Dominant Paradigms of Disease Causation:
The Multifactorial Model

By the turn of the twentieth century, the germ theory—the notion that diseases had specific, singular causes in the form of microorganisms—had become the ruling paradigm for understanding disease causation in the West.[13] Throughout the first half of the twentieth century, however, the credibility of the germ theory was gradually eclipsed by the epidemiologic transition: the shift from the predominance of infectious to chronic diseases like stroke, cancer, and most notably, heart disease. The germ theory's monocausal understanding of disease proved insufficient to account for the increased etiologic complexity and long latency of these new leading causes of death. Also, at the time of this transition, these chronic illnesses were understood to be degenerative, inevitable manifestations of the natural aging process.[14] However, rising rates of chronic diseases in the industrialized West suggested that they were instead the outcome of multiple, specifiable, and changeable factors that might therefore be prevented. In epidemiology, such hypotheses eventually coalesced into the multifactorial model of disease causation.

In the multifactorial model, the incidence of chronic illnesses like heart disease is viewed not as a random phenomenon, nor as the inevitable outcome of aging, but as linked to identifiable factors of susceptibility and exposure. The multifactorial model posits that most of these illnesses are the result of multiple causes, determinants, and risks, involving complex "webs" of interactions among agent, environmental, and host factors.[15] This is the dominant conceptual framework—the foundational assumption—underwriting the epidemiology of chronic disease.[16] Thus, contemporary epidemiology understands the health status of individuals to be the outcome of their particular constellations of health risks and exposures, not in a deterministic but rather a probabilistic fashion.

The shift in focus from infectious to chronic disease after World War I occurred at the same time that governments in the West began taking on a greater role in health care and medical research. The state's increased need for information on population health, and for ongoing surveillance of morbidity and mortality, in turn benefited epidemiologists whose proficiency with statistical models proved crucial to understanding population health.[17] Thus the interwar period saw the synergistic development of and dependency upon epidemiology, with an emergent emphasis on the complex web of causes contributing to disease incidence. The rise of a statistically minded epidemiology provided techniques through which multiple "risk factors"—social, environmental, and behavioral variables statistically associated with disease incidence—could be studied and analyzed.[18] These new methods were critical to identifying, establishing, and legitimating associations between predisposing factors and disease incidence. The epidemiologic study of heart disease in particular emerged as a central player, shaping the development of this maturing discipline and both reflecting and contributing to the normalization of the notion of the "risk factor."

The Emergence of Cardiovascular Epidemiology: The Framingham Study

The era of the epidemiologic study of heart disease in many ways began in 1947, when researchers at Harvard Medical School joined with officers of the U.S. Public Health Service to initiate a study in the town of Framingham, Massachusetts, located about twenty miles outside of Boston.[19] The initial objectives of the Framingham Study were to develop and test methods for the early detection of heart disease and to screen an asymptomatic population to determine rates and incidence of the disease.[20]

In 1949, the just-created National Heart Institute (now the National Heart, Lung, and Blood Institute) took over the Framingham Study.[21] With this transfer came several revisions to the study objectives and methods.[22] First, the goals of the project shifted to identifying factors, including "bodily traits, [and] life habits,"[23] that predisposed individuals to coronary heart disease. Specific hypotheses were formulated for testing, including the increase of coronary heart disease with age, male sex, hypertension, elevated blood cholesterol levels, tobacco smoking, habitual use of alcohol, lack of physical activity, increased body weight, and diabetes. Based upon these newly articulated hypotheses, data collection procedures and instruments were revised to gather information including various bodily measurements; blood pressure; consumption of coffee, tea, alcohol, and tobacco; other dietary factors; physical activity; medical history; blood and urine chemistries; electrocardiograms and X-rays; measurements of pulmonary function; work status and other sociodemographic data.

The investigators subsequently had to reconsider the basis for sample selection. Felix Moore, who became director of biometrics at the National Heart Institute, concluded that the study sample needed to be more representative of the town's population if incidence rate estimates and associations of heart disease to hypothesized risk factors were to be reliable and applicable to other regions and populations in the United States. Consequently, a random sample was drawn up and participants were recruited accordingly. Volunteers were also accepted, but their data were kept in a special category, as their characteristics might differ systematically from those of participants who were randomly selected. All told, 5,209 Framingham residents, both men and women, were recruited into the sample. (Several additional cohorts have subsequently been recruited to the study, including the original participants' children [the Offspring Cohort] in 1971, their spouses [New Offspring Spouse Cohort] in 2003, and the grandchildren of the original participants [Generation Three Cohort] in 2001.[24])

Over the past six decades, the Framingham Study has produced some of the most notable medical findings related to cardiovascular risk and the progression of heart disease. It identified the major heart disease risk factors—high blood pressure, high blood cholesterol,[25] smoking, obesity, diabetes, and physical inactivity—and the influence of age, sex, menopause, and psychosocial factors.[26] The contributions of the Framingham Study to the theoretical and methodological development of epidemiology are also highly significant. The epidemiologist Mervyn Susser argues that it was one of two major historic epidemiologic events (the other being the linking of lung cancer to cigarette smoking) that firmly established the multifactorial paradigm with its attention to potentially modifiable environmental factors.[27] The Framingham Study is often held up as an exemplar of epidemiologic research and as the model and prototype for a prospective cohort study,[28] a specific and (from that point forward) widely used study design in which a group of individuals is followed over a period of time to observe who develops the condition in question.

The prospective cohort study was a critical conceptual and methodological development. As the science and technology studies scholar Anne Pollock observes, "[S]tudying healthy populations—rather than ones selected because they already had a particular disease of interest to investigators—was an innovation that reversed the lens of pathology . . . [a] shift from seeing the body as inherently healthy in need of occasional intervention . . . to one always at multiple risk for disease."[29] Indeed, as the first site in which the term "risk factor" was used instead of "cause,"[30] the Framingham Study served to verify and integrate the very concept of risk factors into modern medicine.[31] Thus while people were no longer seen as vulnerable to inevitable processes of degeneration, they were viewed as always potentially at risk and therefore in need of surveillance, screening, preventive services, and other medical interventions. Crucially, as the historian Robert Aronowitz points out, the risk factor approach did not so much displace existing models of disease as supplement them with new procedures for quantifying variables and establishing their relationships to illness.[32] Thus Framingham served to demonstrate the utility of new methods of epidemiologic research, the ability of such studies to produce knowledge that could enhance the public's health, and the legitimacy of a new perspective on disease progression. As a pioneer of a new paradigm of clinical surveillance and intervention, the Framingham Study stretched research much earlier into the formation of disease than ever before.

However, upon closer examination, the story of the Framingham Study is not so neat. In many ways, the study breached many of the foundational principles and rules for the conduct of a study that epidemiologists now take to be inviolate.[33] For example, the basic objectives of Framingham were revised after the study and data collection had begun.[34] As originally envisioned by the study's founders in 1947, its purpose was to establish the incidence of heart disease among the general population. However, when the National Heart Institute took over the study in 1949, its rationale shifted to determining factors influencing the development of heart disease. Only at this point was a required sample size estimated and data collection protocols and instruments accordingly revised; these continued to be modified over the years. However, recruitment efforts were not successful in gaining the participation of sufficient numbers of potential respondents selected at random, and the sample was therefore supplemented by volunteers. Yet, most descriptions of the Framingham Study in epidemiology textbooks and other accounts elsewhere omit these alterations, while others defend the methodological integrity of the study. For example, Thomas Dawber, a principal investigator of the Framingham Study in its earlier years, argues that with the modified objective of determining which differences among groups played a role in incidence, random sampling and high participation rates were no longer imperative:

> Random sampling is not essential if the purpose of an epidemiologic study is to compare subgroups of the population determined by specific characteristics. The primary concern should be that the population contain sufficient numbers of subjects of these characteristics to enable comparison.[35]

In part because of these methodological workarounds, conclusions drawn from the Framingham Study have always been dogged by questions about their generalizability and the representativeness of the sample. While the study did include almost equal numbers of women and men and some attempts were made to measure indicators of socioeconomic status, concerns were raised about refusal and retention rates as well as the inclusion of only white individuals. Indeed, many questioned whether the study's estimates of incidence and risk were reliable enough to be applied to other populations. Yet, according to Dawber,

> there appears to be good reason to accept the Framingham findings as a reliable estimate of the actual incidence of the various disorders, with some obvious exceptions: there were too few black residents of Framingham to provide sufficient incidence data; the makeup of the white population was not completely representative of the U.S. white population; and there were

more participants of Italian extraction than would be found in most communities in this country. However, unless national origin plays an important role (which apparently it does not), the data reported may be considered reasonably representative of the North American white population.[36]

This conclusion seems curious, in that "national origin" (or "Italian extraction," as it was termed in data collection instruments and some publications) among whites was summarily dismissed as playing a role in coronary heart disease incidence,[37] whereas the importance of "race," defined here as a black–white binary, was in comparison unquestioned. Given the relative lack of knowledge about racial disparities in heart disease incidence and risk at that time, the taken-for-granted significance of race is striking.[38]

Given these problems, along with the initial lack of recruitment procedures including eligibility criteria, data collection methods, and details of how the data were to be analyzed, Susser argues that the Framingham Study would never have been funded in today's political, economic, scientific, and regulatory contexts.[39] Indeed, in 1995 the Framingham investigators had to add the Omni Study, a cohort of minority residents, in order to comply with the new 1994 mandate that National Institutes of Health–funded research on human subjects include representation by minorities and women.[40] Nonetheless, the "successes" of Framingham served to establish the now-dominant conviction that the determinants of heart disease can legitimately and usefully be thought of as constellations of measurable risk factors, that the varying prevalence of these risk factors across populations explains the varying incidence of heart disease, and that prospective studies produce sound epidemiologic data and scientifically defensible results.

Expanding Epidemiologic Surveillance and Biomedicalizing Difference

Since the Framingham Study, numerous cohort studies, involving scores of communities and millions of individuals, have been launched to investigate etiologic factors of cardiovascular disease.[41] These massive epidemiologic projects were part of a larger phenomenon in the United States to produce quantitative criteria for public decisions, aided by the success of quantification in the social, behavioral, and medical sciences alongside the emergence of a "culture of evidence."[42] Also, in the postwar period in the United States, the rise of laboratory-based medical sciences instigated efforts within epidemiology to redefine its own bases of scientificity, in part by presenting its statistical research designs as experimental and reframing communities as metaphorical laboratories.[43] Long-term studies of communities therefore afforded a way for epidemiology to remain scientifically and socially relevant.

Cohort investigations of communities other than Framingham began in Tecumseh, Michigan, in 1957 and in Evans County, Georgia, in 1960. Other community-based studies include the Honolulu Heart Study, started in 1965 with a sample of Japanese American men (N=8,000)[44] who enabled the investigation of cultural, dietary, and immigration factors in the development of heart disease.[45] Beginning in the 1980s, several cohort studies were initiated that involved multiple recruitment and research sites. For example, the Atherosclerosis Risk in Communities Study (ARIC) began in 1987 (N=16,000), with sites across the United States, and a significant subsample of African Americans.[46] The Coronary Artery Risk Development in Young Adults (CARDIA) study was initiated in 1984 with a sample fairly evenly divided among blacks and whites, and women and men from four urban areas (N=5,100).[47] In 1989, the Cardiovascular Health Study began among a randomized sample of elderly people (N=5,000) in four clinical sites. More recently, the Multi-Ethnic Study of Atherosclerosis (MESA) was initiated in 1999 to observe and identify subclinical characteristics and risk factors of cardiovascular disease; approximately 28 percent of the cohort is African American, 22 percent Hispanic, and 12 percent Chinese American (N=6,500).[48] Other efforts to focus more exclusively on the cardiovascular risk factors among women and people of color have accelerated and include the Nurses' Health Study, begun in 1976 with a sample of female nurses

(N=122,000);[49] the Strong Heart Study, launched in 1989 among Native Americans (N=4,500);[50] the Women's Health Initiative, which in 1993 started recruiting women from multiple racial and ethnic backgrounds (N=205,000);[51] and the Black Women's Health Study, initiated in 1995 (N=65,000).[52]

Some of the core epidemiologic claims about cardiovascular risk produced by these observational studies helped establish key risk factors.[53] For instance, in the 1960s through the early 1970s, epidemiologic research first indicated links between diet, serum cholesterol levels,[54] Type A behavior,[55] and coronary heart disease. In the American Heart Association (AHA) Pooling Project, scientists from the AHA Committee of Epidemiological Studies–Subcommittee on Criteria and Methods decided to minimize the perceived uncertainties of an increasing number of small epidemiologic studies on coronary heart disease by conducting a statistical summary of risk factors and individual coronary heart disease risk from several select cohort studies. The Pooling Project firmly ascertained the quantitative relationships between cholesterol, blood pressure, smoking, and coronary heart disease risk, and its publications[56] "had a major strengthening effect on the risk factor concept as the basis for preventive action."[57]

The following decade was marked by the emerging understanding of the contributory role of lipids and lipid fractions,[58] insulin, and alcohol consumption in cardiovascular risk. In the mid-1980s through the 1990s, interest in Type A behavior shifted to attempts to dissect component effects of hostility and anger[59] and the risks associated with restricted social networks and social support.[60] The importance of obesity and body fat distribution, and the role of diet, particularly the effects of antioxidants and different kinds of foods, were further elaborated.[61] Now, genetic epidemiologic research into genetic polymorphisms potentially linked to heart disease has begun in many of these cohort studies, including ARIC, CARDIA, MESA, and the Strong Heart Study. This time period also witnessed the growing understanding of the importance of risk factor clustering—that certain susceptibilities often travel together and have both independent and synergistic effects on one another and on the cumulative risk for heart disease.[62] Metabolic syndrome is probably the most commonly recognized of these clusters. It consists of central obesity (excess weight around the middle and upper parts of the body) and insulin resistance (wherein the body uses insulin less effectively, leading to elevated levels of fat and blood sugar), along with other risks such as physical inactivity and inflammatory factors in the blood. Insulin resistance is itself a constellation of interrelated risk factors and markers that include abnormal cholesterol levels, hypertension, and obesity; metabolic syndrome is also referred to as insulin resistance syndrome or Syndrome X.[63]

What are now considered to be the main, established risk factors for coronary heart disease include cigarette smoking, high blood cholesterol, high blood pressure, diabetes, sedentary lifestyle, and obesity. These factors also constitute the primary elements that go into clinical risk assessments. Male sex, family history of heart disease, and increasing age are also widely recognized as risk factors. However, these known risk factors altogether account for only approximately 40 percent of the cases of heart disease; that is, more than half of the individuals who have heart disease have none of these factors.[64] Thus ongoing epidemiologic research is also examining a slew of newer risk factors—such as homocysteine, inflammatory factors, C-reactive protein, and fibrinogen (all chemicals or proteins found in the blood), among others—for their effects on the incidence and progression of cardiovascular disease, and for their predictive value in identifying who will eventually develop heart disease.

Under the intense surveillance of epidemiologic cohort studies, individuals classified as distinct groups and populations characterized by particular risk factors become sites for the further production of epidemiologic knowledge on cardiovascular risk. Indeed, often asymptomatic risk factors are seen as diseases in and of themselves, producing new classes of patients and changing our norms of what constitutes legitimate targets for medical intervention to include those that derive their meaning from their probabilistic associations with disease.[65] When demographic and behavioral factors are implicated in producing more frequent adverse outcomes, as is often the case, standards of conformity and deviance are created.

Moreover, the power of these knowledge claims and acts of judgment about health risks is magnified by the mask of scientific neutrality, generated through the constitution of epidemiologic knowledge and the rational, statistical arbitration of risk. As Porter notes, the validity of epidemiologic calculations, embodied in their seeming abstractedness and scientific objectivity, serves as "an agency for acting on people, exercising power over them. . . . Numbers turn people into objects to be manipulated."[66] Individual bodies are constructed not as the potential objects of medical control, but as the *de facto* objects of epidemiologic surveillance, under the current assumption that almost all bodies have one or more health risk factors.[67] Epidemiology's classificatory practices thus confer scientific legitimacy on the enterprise of risk assessment and management, imparting an aura of rationality to what are thoroughly social, power-laden, and ultimately hierarchical discourses, institutions, and practices.

These governing and disciplining knowledges and technologies of epidemiology reflect and sustain longstanding public health and biomedical concerns to categorize and pathologize populations by race, class, and gender.[68] Such efforts do not go unresisted, however; there is a strong though often obscured history of counter-hegemonic understandings of the health effects of race, class, and gender. Many social movements have contested the dominant politics of disease causation and health care, even going so far as to set up alternative health systems that they believe took better account of the role of social difference and inequalities in the production of health.[69] But even against the backdrop of this resistance, the epidemiologic gaze continued to sharpen its focus, such that scrutiny has converged upon select groups whose members manifest or embody a disproportionate share of the "problem" of heart disease. Based on the multifactorial model, epidemiologic research seeks to identify characteristics of the "host" which increase the likelihood that a category of individuals defined by those characteristics will develop some condition or disease. As the social studies of biomedicine scholar Catherine Waldby explains,

> This conceptualisation of disease aetiology means that epidemiological science can only proceed through the specification and classification of sub-populations. If the social topography of disease is taken to indicate a pattern of disease aetiology constituted at least in part through host factors, then hosts must be categorised according to these factors.[70]

Thus, the conceptual framework of the multifactorial model, which posits that differences in host characteristics contribute to disease, enables the biomedical relevance of racial, socioeconomic, and sex/gender classifications and their inclusion as flattened, reductionist variables in epidemiologic research. Conventional epidemiologic practices categorize the population at large into more specific classifications of higher- and lower-risk groups. The focus is thereby narrowed on sub-populations—often characterized by sociodemographic dimensions of race, socioeconomic status, and sex—that represent apparently more pressing concerns. (Indeed, Pollock argues that the very emergence of modern cardiology was deeply intertwined with efforts to differentiate and construct distinct racial and class groups.[71]) In so doing, however, epidemiology has run into a series of issues that I explore next.

Conceptual, Methodological, and Political Contestations within Epidemiology

Currently, the production of epidemiologic knowledge continues to escalate, and the public and policymakers increasingly turn to its findings for guidance on risk identification, assessment, and management. At the same time, the reliability, utility, and relevance of epidemiology has been subject to ever closer scrutiny both within the epidemiologic community and from without. In particular, debates over the front and back ends of the epidemiologic research process—setting the agenda and research questions, and the interpretation and application of results—can be especially intense.

However, epidemiologists, like many other scientists, feel that public doubts about the utility of their discipline stem from the public's fundamental misunderstanding of the objectives, interpretations, and inherent limitations of the scientific arbitration of risk. For example, the then-editors of the *New England Journal of Medicine*, Marcia Angell and Jerome Kassirer, found fault with the press for its reporting of epidemiology and with members of the public for their "unrealistic expectations" of what modern medical research can do for their health. They assert that "the public at large needs to become much more sophisticated about clinical research, particularly epidemiology."[72]

Such representations of a misguided public echo the science studies scholars Alan Irwin and Brian Wynne's observation that the dominant ideology regarding the public's understanding of science assumes that lay people desire and expect certainty. The public is therefore seen as incapable of confronting "science's 'grown-up' recognition that risk and uncertainty are intrinsic to everything."[73] However, within critical social studies of science, normative assessments of the public's "misinterpretation" and "ignorance" of scientific objectives, methods, and results are considered to be framings of the "problem" that are socially constructed and power-laden. Such claims serve to fortify the demarcation between "expert" understandings and analyses of risk and disease and what the "lay" public is able to grasp, thereby sustaining the social credibility and authority of science.[74] Indeed, qualitative field research indicates no such naïveté and instead shows that individuals and groups are quite sophisticated and sometimes more aware of the ambiguities and contingencies of scientific knowledge than scientists are forthcoming about them.[75]

In this vein, public doubts about the utility and credibility of epidemiology implicitly and explicitly question the ability of cardiovascular epidemiology, as currently practiced, to address the kinds of issues that some argue matter most for public health. The taken-for-granted nature of the multifactorial model, the risk factor approach, and other aspects of the contemporary epidemiologic paradigm seem to have been disrupted to some extent. There is no longer the undisputed confidence that standard techniques will provide plausible and reliable answers to questions of disease etiology and risk reduction. Moreover, challenges such as the persistence of social inequalities in heart disease incidence and outcomes are proving increasingly pivotal to the public's as well as scientists' assessments of the efficacy of epidemiology. At their core, these contestations speak to the changing social conditions within which epidemiology plays an increasingly visible role yet paradoxically also comes under increasing fire. As such, epidemiology as a discipline constitutes a significant site of both public and professional surveillance, participation, and intervention.

In the following sections, I examine some of these contestations, using ethnographic and interview data, as well as findings from a content analysis of literature on epidemiologic theories, methods, and the state of the discipline. These debates involve some of the key concepts and discourses in epidemiology, including notions of causal inference, validity, and units of analysis. Although on their surface these debates appear to be highly technical, they go to the core of how scientific and social credibility are intimately intertwined, and they prove to be particularly consequential for the study of social inequalities in heart disease.

The Problem of Causal Inference

A major fissure within epidemiology and source of critique from without has to do with resolving the issue of causal inference, or the ability of a study to make claims about potential disease determinants or causes from the data. The choices of study design and methods are absolutely critical. Evolving alongside advances in basic and clinical research, epidemiology has developed a well-understood hierarchy of research models and kinds of data based upon the perceived relative validity of the answers each provides. This hierarchy embodies, in a sense, the epidemiologic conventional wisdom on the ability of various kinds of study designs to make scientifically supportable claims about causality. At the apex of this hierarchy

is the randomized controlled trial, in which the exposure to some suspected causal factor is applied to a randomly selected experimental group
of research participants, while it is replaced with some kind of placebo or
alternate intervention for the other, control group.[76] This design enables
the assumption that the experimental and control groups are quite likely
to be "otherwise equal" with the sole exception of the exposure or risk
factor under study. This assumption in turn permits the inference that
any observed effect must be due to the independent contribution of the
experimental intervention. This ability to experimentally and deliberately
control the exposure independently of other factors and the random selection of who is to be exposed are widely represented as making the randomized trial the most powerful research tool for ascertaining causation.
Indeed, I found that in scientific meetings, public lectures on heart disease
risks and causes, interviews with epidemiologists, and in epidemiology
textbooks, these features of clinical trials are repeatedly noted in order to
bolster the legitimacy of their conclusions.

On the other hand, observational data of the kind generated in large
quantities by heart disease cohort studies,[77] like those described earlier
in this chapter, are regularly depicted as coming in a poor second. In
fact, observational data are often viewed as suspect in that they can lead
to misconceptions about disease etiology and risk that sometimes prove
to be obdurate, even in the face of later, "more accurate" clinical trial
data that counter observational findings. For example, epidemiologists I
interviewed frequently note that data from observational studies of the
effects of hormone replacement therapy on heart disease risk led to the
belief that it reduced cardiovascular risk for postmenopausal women.[78]
Yet this conventional wisdom was subsequently contradicted by data
emerging from several large, highly reputed clinical trials. Respondents
thus repeatedly caution that findings from observational studies must
be viewed as provisional answers and not definitive, "conclusive" ones,
which can be obtained only through randomized controlled trials.

However, assessing causation in chronic conditions like heart disease
involves substantial uncertainties on pivotal issues such as the timing and

nature of exposures, long incubation periods, the progressive nature of the disease, and the multiple co-factors involved in pathogenesis.[79] For example, many of the risk factors under study in cardiovascular epidemiology, such as sedentary lifestyle, obesity, and high cholesterol, take years to produce results large enough to be measured. Moreover, these risk factors often interact with one another, complicating attempts to ascertain causes, mediators, and effects. Such uncertainties further undermine the ability of studies to make causal claims in the case of complex, chronic diseases.

Moreover, statistical association is not the same as a causal relationship. Although historically in the development of epidemiology, statistical methods enhanced the scientific status of the discipline and the plausibility of its flagship disease model—multifactorial causation—critics point out that at the end of the day, epidemiology rarely is able to say that risk factor X is a cause of disease Y. In fact, exactly what is meant when the term "risk factor" is invoked is ambiguous; it can refer to cause, association, predisposition, or susceptibility. This embodies, as Aronowitz notes, both the limitations and the attraction of the risk factor logic[80] that characterizes a great deal of cardiovascular epidemiology. While the precise meaning of a statistical association is highly ambiguous, scientists can avoid having to equivocate among one meaning or another. Instead, risk factors can be defined "by utilitarian or empiric criteria,"[81] simply by their demonstrated statistical relationship to heart disease. Indeed, the multifactorial model could be construed as "an objective model of disease causation with no beginning or end—just multiple, interacting associations . . . an empirically driven and often mechanismless multicausality. . . . Whatever worked in a model was potentially causal. . . . It was left to statistical techniques to sort out the relationship among factors."[82] Thus, in settling questions of causality—the very reason why such studies are presumably launched in the first place—epidemiologic research frequently falls short.

In addition, the factors of most interest here—racial, class, and gender differences—cannot be randomly "assigned" to individuals as can a drug or a low-fat diet. Moreover, even if they could, it could not be done so independently of other factors that would make the experimental and control groups "otherwise equal."[83] One's race, class, and gender permeate and indelibly shape so many other aspects of life potentially related to cardiovascular health that it would be impossible for groups to be "otherwise equal." This thereby violates a key assumption that helps to validate inferences of causality. Thus, not only feasibility but also epidemiologic validity becomes problematic in the quest to address issues of social inequalities and their consequences for cardiovascular health through clinical trial research. Observational research, then, represents the next best solution.

But in relying on observational studies, epidemiologic research on the roles of sociodemographic inequalities in heart disease incidence and distribution encounters other methodological quandaries that have hampered its ability to state with confidence the conclusions of a study and its implications. Such research depends upon the reliable collection of myriad factors that influence cardiovascular health. Through the application of multivariate statistics (an analytic analogue to the theoretical framework of the multifactorial model[84]), it is assumed that the contributions of each epidemiologic variable—including categorical race, socioeconomic status, and sex—to the outcome can be independently calculated. However, the impossibility of disentangling the effects of one variable from those of another, and from other aspects of life that may affect heart disease incidence, means that the assumption of "independent" variables is again violated.

Disputes about Validity

A second methodological quandary that epidemiology runs into, particularly when investigating inequalities in heart disease, is the problem of validity. In designing a study, there is always some amount of tradeoff between what are termed "internal" and "external" validity. Internal validity is closely related to the issues of causal inference discussed above. It refers to the extent to which conclusions drawn from the data in fact reflect the normative "reality" of the group being studied per se and are not the outcomes of biased or chance observations. This aspect of epidemiologic research is often encapsulated in calculations of a study's statistical significance, confidence intervals, and so on. External validity, in contrast, refers to the degree to which the conclusions drawn about the group under study can be applied to other groups and populations; this characteristic bears on concerns about a study's generalizability.[85] Thus the selection of a study sample that is heterogeneous, while enhancing its external validity because the sample mirrors more closely the natural variability within the general population, may threaten its internal validity because so many differences exist within the sample that it is difficult to tease out which play a role in the outcome of interest. On the other hand, the selection of a more restricted sample has the potential to strengthen its internal validity, but at the expense of its generalizability.

Because of this seemingly unavoidable tradeoff, research on samples that are diverse along sociodemographic lines may be viewed as scientifically suspect in terms of their internal validity. On the other hand, studies of groups that are limited by racial category, socioeconomic status, or sex—samples, in effect, defined by their "difference"—are viewed as circumscribed in their applicability to other groups. Working on the assumption that results without internal validity are of little use to either the group being researched or to other populations, many epidemiologists tend to give up external validity for internal validity, creating a body of knowledge based on fairly circumscribed and homogeneous samples.

The use of complex social variables like racial categories and socioeconomic status[86] will always, to some extent, be plagued by questions of scientific validity (the extent to which they measure what they set out to measure), and reliability (usually judged by the degree to which measurements can be replicated across space and time). Within epidemiology, stable and quantifiable markers that reside in the biological body are constructed as more definitive and accurate indicators of risk and effect, or, as one epidemiologist put it, as more likely to be "really measuring what you want [them] to measure," and therefore less threatening to internal validity. Causal claims are thus seen as far more legitimate when they emerge from studies using biologically manifested measures. Epidemiologists I interviewed who use or had considered using measures of racialized or gendered experience or class-based exposures that went beyond the conventional indicators recounted the subtle pressures they felt to "prove" the scientific acceptability of such measures. These epidemiologists perceived being "disciplined" by their colleagues and by epidemiologic convention, and socialized as scientists to choose instead biological indicators perceived to be more reliable because they are viewed as more replicable.[87] Epidemiologic research on the causes of social inequalities in heart disease, then, often falls short of ideal standards of measurement and validity in this regard.

Critiques of Conceptual and Methodological Individualization

In addition to these methodological concerns of validity in the epidemiology on racial, socioeconomic, and sex differences, a host of broader, more fundamental epistemological debates figure prominently in the often fractious world of epidemiology. A primary point of contention is the devolution of the focus of epidemiologic concepts and practices to the individual. Because most epidemiologic findings emerge from research in which the unit of analysis is the individual, processes and dynamics of disease risk and causation are systematically reduced to the level of the individual, simultaneously simplifying a complex world into smaller, presumed independent units of observation.[88]

The image of a complex and interconnected "web" of both causal and protective factors that together determine an individual's health status tends to concentrate attention on those risk factors *closest* to the outcome of interest. These typically translate to the direct biological or behavioral risks addressable at the individual level.[89] Nancy Krieger, a prominent social epidemiologist, for example, finds that at critical shifts in the historical development of epidemiology, practitioners were exhorted to focus on identifying "causes" most amenable to medical intervention as close to the specified outcome as possible, given that "'even knowledge of one small component may allow some degree of prevention.'"[90] Even so-called psychosocial and social-behavioral variables—such as health-seeking behaviors, social support, and lifestyle factors like exercise, diet, and smoking—are measured at the individual level. Underwriting such methodological practices is the notion that these factors, despite their occasional designation as "social" variables, are individually mediated, the independent characteristics and behavioral choices of decontextualized individuals. Some epidemiologists thus argue that these practices implicitly assume that characteristics of one's social environment, as incorporated in the multifactorial model, are exogenous to the individual—that one's circumstances are taken as a given, as if individuals were dropped into a set of conditions that are not socially constructed or patterned.

Moreover, the kinds of interpretations conventionally given to statistical associations between risk factors and measures of race, socioeconomic status, and sex serve to further reinforce the "individualization of risk," perpetuating the notion that risk is individually, rather than socially, determined.[91] For example, the recognition that rates of sedentary lifestyle or physical activity vary systematically by race, income, education, and sex[92] is often interpreted to be the consequence of the lifestyle choices and risk management routines of individuals.[93] At other times, studies examining rates of physical activity adjust or control for racial category and socioeconomic status or compare across racial and socioeconomic categories,[94] often with little discussion or explicit study of the complex social contexts and causes leading to sedentary lifestyles. The first convention clearly individualizes the risk of physical inactivity, fostering "blame the victim" assumptions, while the second often can leave the impression that such associations are to be expected given the populations in question, playing into common racial and class stereotypes.

Conventional epidemiology therefore remains predominantly concerned with the identification of individual-level risk factors,[95] earning it the label of "risk factor epidemiology." Such consequences further concretize the notion that non-intersectional and individualistic constructions, such as racial classifications, socioeconomic status, and sex, additively help "explain" the distribution of health and illness, pushing aside uncertainty and ambiguity over what *exactly* about one's race, class, sex, or gender shapes risk for chronic illness and how these mechanisms operate in concrete practice.[96] There is an inherent contradiction here: Race, class, and gender are not attributes of individuals but refer to relations among socially defined and differentiated groups. Thus an epidemiology of individuals and their risk factors will not be able to account for such group-based processes and relationships. All of these slippages and conceptual imprecision, some epidemiologists argue, produce an overly simplified, reductionist, and therefore inaccurate and scientifically invalid picture of disease causation and risk vis-à-vis such categories.

Thus, many social epidemiologists—who represent an important subfield within the larger discipline—advocate fundamental conceptual and methodological shifts that require the incorporation of variables at the group level into the analysis of individual-level health outcomes.[97] Social epidemiologists argue that social relations may affect individual health outcomes independently from individual factors,[98] an epidemiologic analogue to the sociological proposition that individuals are shaped not only by their personal characteristics but also by the characteristics of the social groups to which they belong. As Krieger asserts,

> the essential claim is that understanding patterns of health and disease *among* persons in these groups requires viewing these patterns as the consequence of the social relationships *between* the specified groups. . . . This perspective . . . asks how individuals' membership in a society's historically-forged constituent groups shapes their particular health status, and how the health status of these groups in turn reflects their position within the larger society's social structure.[99]

Social epidemiologists thus promote the thesis that disease is *socially* produced and that the relative positions of socially designated *groups* and the structural processes and institutions that maintain such positions are highly consequential for their health. A more comprehensive understanding of disease etiology must therefore include the investigation of social, cultural, and political forces as causes of illness as well as the biological ones, and of group-level dynamics as well as individual characteristics.[100]

Though the inclusion of both individual- and group-level factors in epidemiologic studies may appear at first mention to be a relatively innocuous practice, it in fact challenges many of the discipline's standard operating procedures and assumptions about the scientific validity and legitimacy of different types of research and data. With the "individualization of risk"[101] and the focus on individual factors and outcomes, group-level data is perceived by traditional epidemiologists to be less useful in contributing to etiologic understanding. Further, such data can even be viewed as somewhat suspect in that they can indicate associations between some variable and outcome that may not bear out at the individual level. The lore of epidemiology is in fact littered with famous examples of such "ecological fallacies."[102] Common epidemiologic practice usually proscribes mixing individual-level with community- and macro-level variables, because numerous statistical complications can arise, rendering problematic the drawing of causal inferences from such multilevel data.[103]

However, social epidemiologists counter that while such concerns are indeed valid, "the complexity of developing theoretical formulations that relate multiple levels . . . is likely to be a better reflection of reality than the simpler multicausal models prevalent today."[104] The epidemiologists Mervyn and Ezra Susser,[105] for example, argue for moving beyond the multifactorial framework of disease causation to a causal model based on the metaphor of Chinese boxes, a set of boxes of differing sizes that nest within one another. The essence of this new paradigm is that disease causation occurs on multiple levels, and the integration of these levels is critical to investigating and solving a designated problem. In using this conceptual framework then, "hypothesis, design, and analysis would always keep in focus the object of viewing all the relevant levels as a whole. Each level is seen as a system in itself that interacts with those above and below it."[106] Social epidemiologists also express great interest in plumbing mathematical modeling and statistical procedures designed to account for complex, fluid, and dynamic systems that are being used in other disciplines, including econometrics, climatology, and the study of global warming.[107]

The epidemiologist Ana Diez-Roux also proposes that alternate types of causation be considered:

> These include not only causal determination (determination of the effect by an external cause, as in "among susceptible individuals, smoking causes lung cancer") and statistical determination (as in "x percent of persons with high cholesterol will develop a myocardial infarction"), which are the types of determination commonly implicit in epidemiologic research, but also other types of determination such as reciprocal causation and structural or holistic determination. . . . Reciprocal determination (determination of the consequent by mutual action) would be present if, for example, a person's consumption of "unhealthy" foods is influenced by the types of foods available where he or she lives, and if in turn food availability is influenced by consumption in the area. Holistic determination (determination of the parts by the whole) would be present if a person's risk of adopting a certain behavior were influenced by the prevalence of that behavior in the social group to which he or she belonged, or if a person's risk of disease depended on the degree of social inequality in his or her society.[108]

The concepts of reciprocal and holistic determination aim to consider the contextual and social conditions and situations within which people live and work and allow for synergistic and more complex relationships between individuals' traditional risk factors and their social, cultural, and material communities and environments. Such new definitions of causality are potentially important to the study of sociodemographic inequalities in heart disease, as they provide fresh conceptualizations of those cardiovascular risks that are frequently mobilized in explanations for racial, class, and gender differences, as discussed in the Introduction and in chapters 3 through 5.

Finally, social epidemiologists emphasize the distinction between the question of why some individuals are at higher or lower risk than others and that of why some populations *as a whole* are at higher or lower risk. The work of the epidemiologist Geoffrey Rose[109] has been theoretically influential in formulating a different set of etiologic questions based upon this distinction. Rose points out that the set of factors which explains why a particular individual has a disease may be very different from society- or population-wide forces that produce a populace with a particular distribution of risk for that disease. Relatively rare factors may explain the risk distribution of *individuals* while widespread and common factors can account for the distribution among *populations*. The former approach is characteristic of conventional risk factor epidemiology, while the latter articulates a population-based strategy.

Conclusion

As a basic science of public health, epidemiology has had to deal with a public that is increasingly diverse, more demanding that science acknowledge and account for its diversity, and at times openly skeptical of the utility and credibility of epidemiology as a relevant and beneficial scientific discipline. Critiques and commentaries on mainstream epidemiology, both from within and from outside the profession, have occasioned much contestation and debate, even earning the label of "the epidemiology wars."[110] Great divides exist on what is considered causally "fundamental": Some argue that social, political, and structural influences underlie individual and biological causes of disease.[111] Others argue that all levels of causation—social structural, individual, and genetic— matter, and that it is meaningless to designate one as more important than another.[112] And finally, still others simply observe that the balance in the epidemiologic knowledge currently being produced and in the body of epidemiologic literature as a whole needs to be tipped more toward the consideration of societal and structural factors, as currently it tends to favor the individual and micro levels.[113]

Certainly there is much contestation within the epidemiologic community over whether more, better, or radically different theoretical and methodological explications can strengthen the discipline and perceptions of its utility and credibility. Simultaneously, there is considerable deliberation about how epidemiology can achieve its goal of determining disease mechanisms and improving public health, and what kinds of scientific, methodological, and/or conceptual endeavors might accomplish this.[114] Debates over whether deep and fundamental changes to the practice of epidemiology may be in order have filled the pages of leading epidemiology journals, the hotel hallways and ballrooms of epidemiologic conferences, and the narratives of cardiovascular epidemiologists interviewed.

Mervyn Susser, for example, attributes the present "stagnation and inertia" of epidemiologic science to the ultimate failure of the dominant conceptual paradigm—the taken-for-granted multifactorial model of causation—to further illuminate chronic disease etiology and stimulate new thinking in epidemiology.[115] Instead, he argues, "The dominant risk factor black box obscures our vision and impedes our capacity to deal with the near future."[116] As indicated by the deficiency of current epidemiologic knowledge and procedures, "the signs are ominous that we are nearing its displacement by a new era. . . . [W]e need either to adopt a new paradigm or face a sort of eclipse."[117] Raj Bhopal, in his review of epidemiology textbooks, argues that their heterogeneous vocabulary to describe concepts and methods, and differences in perspectives on the purposes and scope of epidemiology, can be read as Kuhnian indications of an evolving discipline or signs of an imminent paradigm shift.[118] Others suggest that epidemiology may already be in transition "from a science that identifies risk factors for disease to one that analyzes the systems that generate patterns of disease in populations . . . from relationships between exposure and disease variables to the analysis of systems that give rise to exposures and through which those exposures act to cause disease."[119] But the fact that at least within the epidemiologic community, these debates largely revolve around issues of science—its concepts, models, methods, and the like—reflects Porter's observation that

> scientific knowledge is most likely to display conspicuously the trappings of science in fields with insecure borders, communities with persistent boundary problems. . . . Science is indeed made by communities, but communities that are often troubled, insecure, and poorly insulated from outside criticism. . . . The enormous premium on objectivity in science is at least partly a response to the resultant pressures.[120]

Whether epidemiology is to be transformed by approaches infused with new theoretical frameworks or by renewed commitments to conventional definitions of scientific rigor and validity, or by both, or by altogether other forces, social and cultural analyses of science argue that scientific disciplines do not "progress" on some linear path or by intellectual considerations alone.[121] Ultimately, no amount of methodological reform can "rid" epidemiologic knowledge of the social and political concerns of the actors who construct it and the broader social, cultural, and political situations within which they must do so.[122] Instead, social, cultural, political, and economic forces and the content and conduct of science must be viewed and analyzed as mutually shaping and constituting one another. This co-production of science and society can be especially visible and acute when considering the nature and influence of human differences on human health, as the chapters that follow will show.

3

The Contested Meanings and Intersections of Race

In this first of three chapters on the meanings of difference, I show the complicated and highly contested terrain of epidemiologic and lay considerations of race and its intersections with class and gender. This terrain is deeply divided, in that scientists in my study tended to attribute racial disparities to cultural differences, while those living with heart disease foregrounded the *structural*, *relational*, and *intersectional* processes of racialization to make sense of their risks. It is no wonder, then, that the lay people I interviewed consistently critiqued conventional racial and ethnic categories used in epidemiology, as well as in everyday life, for their inadequacy in capturing the complex meanings of race and its implications for cardiovascular health. However, this dissatisfaction with racial categories is in fact shared by the epidemiologists I spoke with, and there are also many contradictions and rifts among *both* the scientists and people with heart disease in how they thought about, understood, and mobilized notions of race.

In this chapter, I first describe epidemiologists' and lay people's discontent with racial classification, with special attention to a subtle but significant distinction in the source of their dissatisfaction. For their part, scientists expressed frustration with categories that have uncertain and leaky boundaries; lay people, in contrast, critiqued the act of categorization itself. I then move on to the contours of the science–lay divide by showing how scientific and lay talk and thoughts about race are the most at odds with each other, and in ways that underscore differences not just in the content and meaning of race, but in their very conceptions of how inequality—of which race is only one dimension—is lived. Scientists were often quite adept at talking about the health implications of race in a piecemeal, separable, factorialized kind of way. For them, race was most frequently constructed as cultural difference, and occasionally as biological difference. In contrast, race for lay people had a kind of all-encompassing property to it that intertwined and interlocked with family economics, attributions of class, feminized labor, segregation and neighborhood environments, educational opportunities, and so on. That is, in a word, they understood inequality to be *intersectional*, as the last sections of this chapter will show.

By detailing the routinization of racial categories in epidemiologic science and its inclusion of "race" as an individual-level, culturally mediated trait, this chapter shows how epidemiology neglects the intersectional social, political, and structural processes and relations of power that operate as significant determinants for cardiovascular risk and health. In so doing, epidemiology effects a stratified form of biomedicalization that attends to some aspects of racial difference and some pathways through which race shapes health, while excluding others from scientific inquiry and policy intervention.

Racial Classification: Lived Identity
versus Scientific Categorization

In epidemiologic research in the United States, race is conventionally measured by self-classification into one (or sometimes more) of the racial and ethnic categories now standardized by the U.S. Office of Management and Budget[1]: American Indian or Alaskan Native, Asian, Black or African American, Native Hawaiian or Pacific Islander, White, and Hispanic or Latino.[2] Epidemiologists regularly use these categories to limit study samples or to adjust study results, under the assumption that systematic differences in the relationship between dependent and outcome variables may exist between different races. But when asked to reflect on their experiences of racial identification, the lay participants I spoke with pointedly critiqued scientific attempts to measure and use race as a variable in epidemiologic research on several counts. What follows is an examination of both scientists' and lay people's reactions to racial categorization processes.

My interviews with lay people living with heart disease underscore the power of social inscription and categorization in shaping how lay participants racially classify themselves. Many interviewees spoke passionately about the eclipsing influence of others' perceptions in forming and naming racial identity. For example, Carmen Hernandez described herself as "a mixture . . . of Indian blood . . . African blood and some white blood" but identified as a "Latina of Mexican, Colombian descent" and explained why she sees herself as such:

> My feeling is more that I lean more toward the minority part of . . . my background, than I do to the white part—to a certain extent partly because that's how I've been treated. I've been treated as what they call a "Hispanic" woman. . . . And when the dominant culture tells you you're Hispanic, that encompasses a lot of things. . . . A lot of people have seen me as that, not necessarily because I profess myself as that, but because they simply see me as somebody who is different.

Diane Jamison, an African American woman who developed hypertension in her early thirties, also echoed the primacy of racial inscription over self-identification in shaping the lived realities of individuals. In expanding on this point, she used both herself and the multiracial professional golfer Tiger Woods as examples:

[Tiger Woods] was trying to acknowledge all of his different ethnic backgrounds, and I was thinking to myself, that's true, we all have different things in our background. But because you look like an African American person, you're going to move through the world like an African American person, and your experience is going to be that of an African American person. . . . I mean, when he won the Masters [Golf Tournament, in 1997], they were like, "Well, are they going to have collard greens and sweet potatoes?" . . . It never goes away! . . . You can identify all kinds of ways, but the truth of the matter is that the world looks at you the way you look, and that's where they put you. . . . My grandfather's white. It doesn't make a difference in my life because I'm looked at by the world as an African American person. . . . On those boxes where you can choose "mixed race," . . . I totally get the concept, but let's face it, you move through the world the way you look.

Or, as Rudolfo Barrister anguished, "I can't look at myself outside of being told that I'm black in the social circles in which I move. Even in the black social circles, I'm reminded of blackness, as if it is something you can *touch*! I don't see myself as a skin color! But I'm told that that's the way I *must* see myself." Despite Mr. Barrister's own multiracial heritage (one grandparent is Cherokee, another is white) and despite his feeling that he lacks the cultural ties to call himself African American, he concluded, "I'm *compelled* to feel black—or subordinate, I should say."

Ms. Hernandez, Ms. Jamison, and Mr. Barrister argue that in their lived experience, racial self-identification—the preferred method of epidemiologists—is not a meaningful way to measure race if the intent is to examine the impacts of race on their conditions of life. Instead, the racial or ethnic categories that are placed upon them by others more directly structure their everyday experiences and their material and social environment. These participants emphasize that race becomes consequential through the social significance that is invested in it and imposed *by others*, rather than its being an attribute self-selected by an individual presumably free to choose, a model that current epidemiologic practice implicitly embodies.

Lay people's discussions of social inscription parallel in many ways contemporary sociological understandings of race. The sociologist Patricia Hill Collins, for example, writes: "Individuals cannot simply opt in or out of racial groups. . . . Within unjust power relations, groups remain unequal in the powers of self-definition and self-determination."[3] The philosopher Iris Marion Young similarly observes that "one *finds oneself* as a member of a group, which one experiences as always already having been."[4] Seemingly ready-made and neutral demographic categories serve to veil historically constructed infrastructures of social relations governed by racial hierarchy, marginalization, and exclusion. By arguing that racial categories are in fact ascribed characteristics, participants with heart disease point to how representations of those who inhabit such categories in turn lead to particular social and institutional practices. This is precisely the core argument of the sociologists Michael Omi and Howard Winant's notion of racial formation, that race is "made real" through the linkages forged "between the discursive and representational means in which race is identified and signified on the one hand, and the institutional and organizational forms in which it is routinized and standardized on the other."[5] Racial formation is thus a matter of both cultural representation and social structure, both macro-level social processes and micro-level interactions. And as I discuss later in this chapter, lay people argue that through mechanisms of racial formation, attributions of race in fact shape cardiovascular health.

A second lay critique of the scientific measurement of race is the assumed normativity of whiteness. Mr. Barrister's sense of otherness to himself—reminiscent of the double-consciousness W. E. B. Du Bois noted a century ago[6]—distinguishes his self-awareness from that of a white man: "I don't even know how to begin to imagine putting someone in my shoes. . . . But then I don't think that a white man ever thinks that. He has no cause to begin to think about being a member of . . . a subordinate group." Here, Mr. Barrister points to one of the privileges of whiteness: As a category that is socially constructed as unmarked, whiteness comes to serve as an unquestioned and unreflexive norm. Ms. Jamison reflected on this explicitly in the context of scientific research:

> Why is it that whites are considered as what's the norm . . . and everyone else is a deviant? I've always wondered, why is that? . . . Why aren't Asians the base group? . . . Why [are] whites . . . considered so race-neutral? . . . In my opinion the way that studies are done and the way things are done, it's like they [white people] are the ones who are normal and they're the ones who are like the prototype, so anything that deviates from that is something that needs to be studied.

Here, Ms. Jamison notes the unique and invisible luxury of the dominant racial group: to remain unnamed, unscrutinized, and normalized. Her comments underscore how the routine practice of equating whiteness with normality, far from being limited to just scientific research, resonates with and reinforces social representations of racial otherness.[7]

In short, the conventional racial and ethnic categories commonly used in epidemiology do not account for lay people's complex experiences of racial identification. The seeming demographic neutrality of bureaucratic racial categories obscures processes of social inscription, and the profound consequences of how people are labeled, and by whom.

Many of the cardiovascular epidemiologists I interviewed, however, did acknowledge being deeply troubled and confused about the meanings of race, its appropriate measures and interpretations, and its implications for heart disease prevention and public health policy. These scientists viewed both conceptual and methodological ambiguities as plaguing scientific methods of studying race. One predicament researchers singled out as being especially problematic is the measurement of race, particularly with reference to who gathers that data, and how. Epidemiologists cited examples of studies and databases in which information on race was collected not through self-report but through research staff's ad hoc judgments about appearance, language, and/or surnames. They also criticized the aggregate nature of conventional racial categories, in which groups with distinct cultural roots, economic circumstances, and social histories are lumped together. While the epidemiologists I interviewed complained about this most frequently for Asian Pacific Americans and Latino/Hispanic Americans, it is arguably also a problem for any of the other racial classifications commonly used in research. While such racial categories may be scientifically routinized, some epidemiologists pointed out that they tend to shed little light on, and can actually confound, the investigation of group differences in health.

Many of the epidemiologists I interviewed also viewed the fluidity and sensitivity of racial categories to social and political forces as scientifically troubling—categories can appear, disappear, and change meaning in response to the vicissitudes of the social, cultural, and political moment. In epidemiology, variables are most conveniently managed and least subject to measurement error or bias when they are stable and constant and therefore replicable and comparable over time and from study to study. But in the case of racial characteristics, as one epidemiologist described, researchers can invest significant effort in carefully designing procedures to categorize and select which groups to include, only to be undone by sociopolitical changes: "You could come up with a wonderful study question, wonderful survey, and you go to your study population and—whoops, it's changed!" Therefore, while modifying racial categories according to the current historical context may be desirable from a social and political point of view, from the perspective of doing science, such instability renders race ill suited as a scientific and epidemiologic variable. In short, both groups of participants actually agreed that current racial categories by themselves leave much to be desired, though for different reasons.

In turn, epidemiologists also expressed serious misgivings about the validity of racial categories and measures. This involves a more or less technical issue of potential misclassification or measurement error: whether the recorded race of an individual accurately reflects her/his "actual" race. But researchers also saw such concerns as raising fundamental epistemological questions about the nature of race itself, wondering, for example, what "race" means in a multiracial world, what phenomena exactly are being captured in the variable of race, and then how to interpret the racial differences that are found. Such questioning of the conceptualization of race has even been codified in a "Statement of Principles: Epidemiology and Minority Populations" by the American College of Epidemiology, a major North American professional association:

> The ability to define issues and problems along the lines of racial and ethnic classifications becomes more difficult. . . . The matter of defining and characterizing who are in these populations and what specific aspects of being "minority" pose health risks is becoming more and more complex. Social changes complicate the ability to separate disadvantages based on economic or political status from those associated with racial or ethnic variation that is related to cultural or even biological factors. Growing recognition of diversity within global categories such as "Black" or "Hispanic" as well as the reality of growing diversity within these populations are rendering these designations decreasingly useful for defining culturally or biologically homogeneous groups.[8]

Indeed, epidemiologists I spoke to critiqued the measures and meanings of racial categories, enumerating doubts about the clarity and stability of categorical boundaries and the degree to which racial categories can serve as reliable tools for health research and interventions. People of color with heart disease, on the other hand, took issue with the very notion of categorization itself, questioning how classification can take account of deeply social processes of ascription and the power to define racial otherness.

Moreover, despite scientists' variable acknowledgment of the ambiguity and insufficiency of their methods of racial categorization, my analysis of epidemiology in *practice* shows that such categories were almost ritualistically included in research. Both participant observation and interview data indicate that race was routinely and often uncritically used to limit or describe study samples, as well as to stratify and adjust results.[9] One researcher referred to the inclusion of race as just something that everyone has to do—"everybody *has* to measure race." In interviews, epidemiologists often referred to the "holy trinity" of race, sex, and age as variables that are absolutely requisite in statistical analyses. In presentations of research methods and results, multiple scientists I observed referred simply to controlling for "the usual suspects," "traditional risk factors," or "traditional demographic risk factors" as shorthand glosses for the routine adjustment for race and other individual characteristics. This matter-of-fact and habitual mention of including and controlling for race without explicit rationalization indicates a practice that once may have come with articulated justifications, but that is now so taken for granted that it is perceived as a standard operating procedure with which epidemiologists must comply.

According to my interviews with epidemiologists, the ritualized incorporation of race into cardiovascular epidemiologic research is motivated by multiple factors. These include the pressures of identity politics, bureaucratic mandates to include racial minorities and considerations of race in research,[10] an acknowledgment of the need for culturally tailored health interventions, and some limited recognition of the significance of race in shaping health outcomes. There was the generalized sense that racial groups differ in multiple and epidemiologically significant ways. But at the same time, however, as I argue in chapter 6, the inclusion of race in such research is also driven by the very nature of science itself as a ritualized practice, with its needs for replicability, comparability, and standardization. As a result, scientists habitually invoked race and made use of racial categories but without delving into its complex social and structural dynamics. In so doing, investigators implicitly infused "race" with multiple meanings and definitions. As I explore in the following sections, they occasionally invoked biological notions of race but much more frequently conceived of race as cultural difference. I explore each of these scientific understandings of race in the following two sections and juxtapose them with lay accounts of the significance of race for health.

Race as Biological Difference: Genetics
versus Multiple Forms of "Heredity"

In the relatively few instances in which I heard and observed racial disparities in heart disease conceptualized as rooted in biological differences, epidemiologists tended to speak of those biological differences in terms of genetics. Lay people, on the other hand, incorporated multiple and alternative ideas about what, along with genetic material, is actually inherited from generation to generation.

Even though a few epidemiologists explicitly disavowed any biological basis for race, and others simply avoided invoking such understandings of racial difference, some others did mobilize conceptions of biology and genetics, especially when discussing the future of scientific research on racial health disparities. For example, several spoke of the potential of genetic epidemiology and studies using biomarkers to reveal "deeper" or "underlying" sources of racial differences in heart disease and its risk factors. One epidemiologist, when asked about the future of etiologic research on racial disparities in heart disease, responded that "the exciting stuff that's going on [is] in genetics. . . . They're literally identifying alleles every couple of weeks." Another affirmed, "I'm sure there are some real racial differences that have to do with genetic differences" and went on to caution that in order to be able to uncover such differences, we "certainly [have to be] able to have an honest discussion of these things." Moreover, in my observations of presentations of epidemiologic research at scientific meetings, findings of racial differences were often interpreted as the outcomes of, and clues to, possible genetic differences between racial groups. In addition, epidemiologic studies that investigated genetic determinants were often designed as a comparison of the frequencies of particular mutations between two or more racial/ethnic groups.

The scientific construction of racial difference through a biological lens relegates matters of racial inequalities in heart disease to the function of genetics and physiology. Effective reduction then is seen in terms of intervening in individual bodies, rather than changing social and environmental conditions. In so doing, cardiovascular epidemiology works to legitimate popular conceptions of racial differences as biological difference, thereby funneling resources toward intervention at the individual level.

A few people of color with heart disease also invoked biological constructions of racial differences in heart disease, with such expressions as "it's in the genes," "it's a faulty gene," "there's a hereditary factor," and "the problems that I have are inherited." A number of them invoked sickle cell anemia as a parallel example of a genetically transmitted disease. However, most lay participants, even as they mobilized biological notions of race, did so with a significant conceptual twist. They understood "heredity" as involving the intergenerational transmission of not only genetic material but also aspects of diet, knowledge, and other health-related behaviors, which epidemiologists commonly classify as "culture." For example, Bonnie Joe, an African American woman with severe heart disease, reasoned that biological differences existed between races in part because cultural practices over time create different kinds of bodies; in her explanation, she compares herself to me as examples of this:

> You just can't put us together and make us be the same, because we're not. . . . You can't treat us all the same. You came up on a rice diet. . . . A lot of your diet was with rice, right? Because this is your culture. We come up with corn bread. . . . So everybody come up differently, so your inside is used to something different.

Mr. Barrister argued similarly:

> I feel very strongly that the food pattern, the diet of the black or the African American person, had an awful lot to do with it . . . because the slaves, for example, were not given any consideration as far as their diet was concerned—they had to make do with the leftovers . . . the undesirable part of the animal. . . . And over the years, I don't doubt for a moment that this has been built into the biology of being black. . . . I hate to deal in stereotypes

but . . . I can imagine that over a few centuries of people eating the same thing over and over again are going to build in biological changes that will be passed down to . . . the succeeding generations.

Thus Ms. Joe and Mr. Barrister incorporated other historically rooted, socially and culturally mediated risks that they believe change bodies over time in ways that can then be passed down from generation to generation. Such a complex construction of racial difference as "biological" difference points to how participants with heart disease view the nature of biological and heritable risk as cumulative and sedimented across multiple generations. Thus while lay participants speculate that biological differences may account for some of the disparities among racial groups in cardiovascular risk and incidence, their genetic discourses are intertwined with alternative definitions of "heredity."

Race through the Cultural Prism

Throughout my research, scientists frequently mobilized "culture" as a means to account for cardiovascular inequalities by race; in contrast, the presence of notions of culture in lay interpretations of those same inequalities was much less common. In particular, I argue that epidemiologists invoked culturalist understandings of race—that is, a particular idiom of culture that refers to behaviors and traits seen as intrinsic to racial and ethnic groups—whereas lay people understood culture to be the complex product of history, both individual and collective. Thus the notion of equating a set of cultural ways with a racial category, or decontextualizing them from biography and social history—as epidemiologists were wont to do—makes little sense to those who occupy those categories.

By far the construction of race most routinely invoked by epidemiologists was that of "cultural difference": Researchers repeatedly referred to differences of a "cultural" or "ethnic" nature, ones they perceived to be related to the customary beliefs, norms, and practices of a racially or ethnically defined social group. In such culturalist explanations and interpretations of race, there were multiple nuances to the kinds of claims being made. There was an understanding that race could be equated with or linked to culture, and that the primary reasons for the existence of racial disparities in heart disease are differential cultural behaviors and beliefs seen as intrinsic to ethnic groups. For example, one epidemiologist noted, "Race/ethnicity . . . means their culture, their background, their thinking process, how they make decisions. And it's not just diet, not just genetic. It's environmental." Another researcher concurred: "You have the genetics, but far more important is the shared environmental factors that boil down to cultural habits of how they eat, whether they exercise, those kinds of things."

In these ways, racial differences in cardiovascular risk and disease were viewed and constructed through the prism of culture and imbued with causal reasoning that referred to "ethnic" customs and ways of life. Race was seen to be a methodologically legitimate, though imperfect, proxy for cultural differences hypothesized to be significant for heart disease, through their shaping of health-related behaviors and beliefs. In so doing, epidemiologists often assumed that such practices could be simply "read off" of an individual's or group's racial identification—that is, that culture was based *in* race. Yet for individuals like Rudolfo Barrister (whom we met earlier in this chapter) who deny any African American racial or cultural affiliation, epidemiologic research would likely presume that the way he is racially categorized reliably predicts his health-related behaviors.

Even those epidemiologists who acknowledged the possibility of such erroneous extrapolations still worked from the assumption that race and ethnicity—at the moment—are significant because they correspond in some systematic way to "cultural" behaviors. Two epidemiologists I interviewed, for example, spoke of the rising incidence of heart disease that comes with the acculturation of immigrants to the United States and their second-generation offspring. These epidemiologists noted that as newcomers and their descendants conform to Western ways of life and "pick up our nasty habits," as Dr. Karen Verceau put it, their rates of cardiovascular risk increase to levels similar to those of native-born individuals. Dr. Verceau raised the notion of dietary differences—a staple in the culturalist construction of race—and argued that "when people have a common diet . . . the differences between ethnic groups were quite a bit reduced." Dr. Carolyn Munson described the increasing multiraciality—and multiculturalism—of children today: "They're just a combination of cultural, ethnic, racial backgrounds. When this generation starts having their children, people are going to get further and further away from one culture." On the one hand, epidemiologists' observations of such phenomena allude to the possibility that race and ethnicity might become less relevant over time as culture, diet, and other health-related behaviors become more globalized, as immigrant populations are increasingly assimilated, and as rising intermarriage among ethnic groups creates generations of multiethnic, multicultural children. But on the other hand, discussions of the *future* declining significance of race for cardiovascular disease were underwritten by notions that its *current* relevance is largely attributed to cultural distinctions.

The popularity among epidemiologists of culturalist constructions of racial difference can be attributed to several aspects of the concept of "culture" that contribute to its social and scientific utility: its conceptual flexibility, its discursive opposition to biology, its tangible nature, and its resonance with health promotion ideologies. First, the concept of "culture" allows a wide range of behaviors, habits, preferences, and practices to be defined as such and encapsulated under the rubric of research into cultural difference. Culture is seen as a fluid and malleable concept, eminently adaptable to different objectives and lines of research.

Second, cultural practices were seen as a politically acceptable way to talk about differences among "ethnic" groups without insinuating that "races" differ in some biological way. As seen above, epidemiologists readily counterposed cultural differences in explicit opposition to genetic explanations of racial difference. Instead, aspects of the cultural "environment"—that is, what exists *outside* the body—were framed as important determinants of cardiovascular health, thus discursively distancing claims of cultural variations from the political dangers of essentialist claims of intrinsic, inherent differences.

Third, cultural readings of racial difference were perceived as tangible and "factual" in that they were descriptive of outwardly observable habits and customs thought to pose different kinds of cardiovascular risks and benefits for different cultural groups. Indeed, it is in part because such practices were seen as scientifically observable, empirically verifiable, and thus "real" that epidemiologists perceived cultural conceptualizations of race as less contestable and politically controversial. This is the sense in which an individual's race is seen as an epidemiologically useful and necessary proxy variable, because it captures at least some of the multiple ways in which cultural beliefs and practices might influence health. Moreover, the inclusion of race or ethnicity affords epidemiologists the convenience of including only one widely standardized and all-inclusive variable in lieu of many untested and perhaps overly specified ones.

Finally, culturalist constructions of race resonated particularly well with health promotion and risk reduction mandates. Viewing race through the prism of culture provided an extremely convenient entry point for targeting risky lifestyle behaviors, such as diet, which are a focus of heart disease research and the mainstay of prevention discourses. Ms. Joe recounted her experience as a research subject:

[The study's investigators] were showing a film on these people that they had in the study, and they were showing white people and how they ate and they showed the black people and how they ate. And when they were showing the black people and their diet, it was so funny to them. And that pissed me off, okay?! I mean, it just pissed me off. This is the way we eat. There's nothing funny about it.

Thus participants with heart disease offered examples of how conceptions of race-based risk and pathology are embedded within epidemiologic research: Constructions of *cultural* difference function to stigmatize racially defined groups and, at their core, uphold essentialist notions of *racial* difference.

Not all epidemiologists, however, were wholly satisfied with the construction of race as cultural difference, even as they invoked it. In fact, about half of those interviewed expressed one or more reservations about the dominant understanding of race as rooted in differential cultural behaviors and beliefs. For example, some observed that taking into account all of the behavioral risk factors for heart disease—the very ones often tied to race and ethnicity—does not account for all of the differences between racial groups. Others also noted there are enough statistical paradoxes, where heart disease prevalence goes in the opposite direction of what risk factor prevalence would indicate, to create significant uncertainty about the claim that racial differences can be attributed largely to cultural ones. One researcher was very clear that even though differences in risk factors and behaviors can be *statistically associated* with racial and ethnic origin, to say that one's race is *causally and directly linked* to those behaviors is meaningless. Rather, she stressed, race serves in these instances as a crude and imperfect proxy for a multitude of economic, cultural, and other dynamics.

Despite such qualifications, however, constructions of race as culture were widespread and strongly aligned with observations of racial disparities in risk factor prevalence. Epidemiologists I interviewed and observed therefore saw behavioral differences as a convenient and relatively uncontroversial target for explanatory research into racial gaps in cardiovascular disease rates. Because behavioral risk factors often carry connotations of culture, ethnicity, and other dynamics commonly perceived to be related to race, cardiovascular risk and prevention discourses almost tautologically became racialized. Such discursive representations of race cycled back into research as epidemiologists, familiar with the conceptions of race as culturally mediated differences in risk behaviors, treated risk factor levels as explanations for racial disparities in incidence. In turn, any disparities that were found were often attributed to those differences in risk behaviors, confirming, in a circuitous fashion, the legitimacy of cultural understandings of racial difference and the racialization of risk discourses. Thus the cultural prism, with its conceptions of the effects of race on cardiovascular risk and its focus on risk behaviors, creates self-authenticating practices that triangulate with one another.[11] That is, lines of research strengthened and reinforced the loop of logic through which race and certain racial groups became targets of scrutiny and potential intervention. Under this reasoning, constructions of race as cultural differences in risk factors become legitimate, standardized ways to think about the role of race in health, displacing other modes of conceptualization. In short, then, "culture," as differential risk behaviors, is constructed as a scientifically legitimate causal agent for heart disease.

The culturalist lens of epidemiology echoes the ethnicity paradigm of race that dominated the period of the 1930s through the 1960s, in which "ethnicity" coexisted with and sometimes displaced "race" as a descriptor of difference.[12] Omi and Winant argue that belonging to an ethnic group came to be understood in behavioral rather than biological terms; however, as the sociologist Ruth Frankenberg points out, one could easily argue that biology continued to underwrite conceptions of ethnicity.[13] Numerous scholars critique the ethnicity paradigm on the grounds that, in its reliance on group norms to explain differences in outcomes, sociopolitical dynamics and structural contexts get "ruled out at the level of assumptions."[14] Frankenberg observes that in its rhetoric of essential sameness, the ethnicity paradigm evades issues of power: If different racial groups are basically the same underneath but vary in their values and degree of assimilation into the American majority, any failures to achieve social equality must therefore be the fault of people of color themselves.[15]

Representations of pathological cultural practices linked to specific racial/ethnic groups seemed to have some conceptual power to shape the interpretations that people of color I interviewed gave to their experiences. When I asked Mr. Barrister about what causes hypertension, he immediately began to talk about the "so-called soul food" of black Americans as "probably the number one cause." Diet was also the first factor that Sarah Quincy, an African American who also has hypertension, mentioned: "I think it could be the diet, since it runs in families and usually you eat the way your parents [were] brought up eating. . . . I think that's why it's passed down through generations." These frequent causal attributions to eating practices and preferences reflect and adopt conventional biomedical perspectives on dietary risk factors.

However, what is also significant is that lay people complicated simplistic notions of dietary risk. For example, Ms. Joe, whose parents were sharecroppers, described this at length:

> As I look back on my life and I remember the diet that we came up on— like I say, we were poor. My mama had fourteen children. . . . And my father did sharecropping. And you know they never made any money because the people the land belonged to—those are the ones that made the money off of it. You just got a little to get your bills paid and maybe get you some food for the winter, until you could grow . . . some more food the next summer. . . . We couldn't afford to buy like regular cooking oil like we do now, so they used hog fat. . . . So that was pure cholesterol. . . . A lot of our diet was fat because we couldn't afford the other things. . . . The meat— they would pack it with salt, you know, to keep it from going bad. . . . So we [were] raised up on a high-salt diet with a lot of fat in it and the starchy foods. . . . So, as I look back over my life at that time, I think that's what might have caused [hypertension and heart disease].

Echoing other African American informants, Ms. Joe made clear that in addition to immediate economic constraints, her diet was shaped in large part by cultural tastes and preferences that themselves emerge from a history of racism. In their view, generations of making do amidst the dire deprivation of slavery, and the material inequalities imposed by residential, educational, and occupational segregation, lie at the root of many contemporary dietary practices and preferences that are now seen to impose differential risks.

Cigarette smoking is another cardiovascular risk factor typically seen as a habit tied to racially and culturally defined groups, in particular to Asian and Pacific Americans. But in her analysis, Geline Laroya, a Filipina with hypertension, described how cigarette smoking was actively promoted in the Philippines by the global reach of the tobacco industry: "The demand was developed, the availability. The Philippines is . . . a dumping ground of international companies. . . . Tobacco companies deliberately dump lots of products into the Philippines." She implicated the purposeful and calculated strategies of transnational corporations to cultivate nicotine addiction and generate demand for their commodities by promoting brand name recognition in overseas markets like the Philippines. While such risk factors as diet and smoking, from an epidemiologic standpoint, would be racialized as culturally mediated behaviors, lay participants instead argued that larger structural forces influence the "lifestyle choices" of different groups.

To be fair, culturalist constructions of race in cardiovascular epidemiology often seemed to be motivated by the desire to account for cultural diversity. But the selective embrace of cultural and other relatively apolitical parameters of difference—without tracing or acknowledging their often structural and historical roots—tends to uphold extant social hierarchies. The interpretation of racial differences in health as stemming predominantly from "ethnic" variations presumes that such variations are the result of cultural preferences. However, as their discussions of diet and smoking illustrate, participants with heart disease contextualized such cultural behaviors as the outcomes of responses to more structural barriers and processes.

Lay participants highlighted another critique of the cultural prism, pointing out that people within a racial or even ethnic group may not share the same cultural practices. For example, while Sharon Chavez identifies as Latina, when I asked what that means to her, she explained:

It just means my heritage. I mean, my family's been here for a bunch of generations, so I'm pretty much Anglicized. . . . You know, I'm just another person. . . . I'm not like ethnocentric or religious or anything . . . only thinking of myself as Hispanic and only associating with Hispanics, and only doing things that would be considered Latino or whatever. . . . And I speak English, and I don't eat a lot of sauces and fried foods. I don't know. I don't run to church every Sunday. . . . I'm not, you know, like close-knit family. I'm just a person.

Here, Ms. Chavez searched about for behaviors and beliefs that she felt exemplified what it means to be Hispanic or Latino and against which she can compare her own sense of ethnic affiliation (and notably, when she did so, she came up with a list of fairly common stereotypes). Since she did identify racially as Latina, this identification describes an aspect of herself that is technically true—that is, in accordance with standard demographic classifications of her "race" or "ethnicity." However, dominant assumptions about what that entails in terms of cultural behaviors do not accurately capture her everyday way of life. To her, the meaning of "being Latina" is constructed as the enactment of particular cultural and social aspects of life. In contrast, Ms. Chavez's racial identification is "just . . . [her] heritage" and plays a minimal role in shaping her daily life. Underwriting dominant perspectives on the links between race, ethnicity, and health is the understanding that they are made via cultural *practices*—that is, actual activities and things people do—that together, constitute a *lived* racial or ethnic identity.

This then raises a concern with respect to epidemiologists' understandings of race as culture. Researchers' use of race as a methodologically legitimate proxy for cultural differences, and their mobilization of "culture" as the predominant way to understand racial variations, implicitly presumes a uniformity of culture from shared racial affiliations. But this ignores the experiences of individuals like Ms. Chavez and Mr. Barrister, who do not or only minimally engage in practices and beliefs that epidemiologists define as "ethnic" and "cultural" and potentially related to health. Moreover, such perspectives neglect heterogeneity within racial categories that tend to aggregate groups with distinct cultural roots, economic circumstances, and social histories.

This is *not* to say that some behaviors and practices commonly viewed as culturally rooted do not play a role in cardiovascular risk, because undoubtedly they do. Paying attention to and including culturally mediated behaviors in their studies of heart disease etiology thus does important scientific work for epidemiologists. A culturalist conception of race has the upsides of its conceptual flexibility, its tangible nature, its relative convenience as an epidemiologic variable, and its etiologic significance. Yet what epidemiologists gain from the cultural prism comes with important tradeoffs in terms of a fidelity to *how* culture actually operates in lived experiences of disease risk and incidence, and *for whom*. When epidemiologists treat race-as-culture as static, separable from and stripped of its historical contexts, and thus as curiously intrinsic to racialized individuals, they effectively ignore the actual variability in and historical fluidity of cultural behaviors and beliefs. When I critique the routine attribution of racial difference to cultural difference and the pathologization of "cultural" behaviors, it is because these scientific practices neglect the social structures and relations of power that give rise to and sustain such cultural differences and, in so doing, misrepresent their fundamental and underlying causes.[16] In contrast, lay participants, while acknowledging the relevance of behavioral risk factors in causing heart disease, were inclined to contextualize cultural preferences and behaviors as the fluid products of social, economic, and political life, shaped and organized by representations of race.

The Health Consequences of Racism and Intersectional Inequalities

In contrast to the omnipresence of *culturalist* interpretations of race in epidemiology, *structural* constructions of race abound in the narratives of those living with heart disease. Lay participants in my research were far more likely than epidemiologists to attribute the cardiovascular effects of race, in conjunction with class and gender, to numerous interactional experiences and structural dynamics that can be understood as intersecting and interlocking systems of inequality. In this case, most of the lay participants frequently articulated how, in multiple sites and facets of their lives, their racialization as members of particular racial, class, and gender groups structured and ordered their everyday experiences and conditions of life. These experiences in turn had consequences for their health. The connections lay people drew between their group status and position and their health histories significantly echo calls for the greater consideration of intersectionality in health research.[17] While their understandings of race were highly variable, expansive, and even contradictory and paradoxical, participants with heart disease tended to invoke intersecting social forces and experiences as members of specific race-class-gender groups when talking about their cardiovascular risks. I contend that the linkages which many lay participants saw between their experiences of classed and gendered racialization and their heart disease underscore how intersecting power relationships function to stratify cardiovascular health. With respect to race, those structural and relational factors mentioned most frequently as being consequential for heart disease include the effects of racial hierarchy on their sense of self and everyday interactions, and on their economic and environmental conditions of life.

The Health Effects of Racial Ascription in Everyday Interactions

First, lay participants described a pervasive, oppressive sense of double-consciousness[18] as contributing to their cardiovascular risk. Consider Mr. Barrister and his inescapable sense of otherness as he felt forced to see himself as others saw him: "I can't look at myself outside of being told that I'm black. . . . I'm told that that's the way I *must* see myself." He related how this double-consciousness "limited and proscribed" his interactions with others. When I asked him in the interview whether his life experiences affected his health, he returned to this sense of racialized otherness and replied:

> Yes, I think it has, because it's conditioned everything that I am, unfortunately. . . . I can certainly say it has affected [me] because these things

stress me out. . . . It's really difficult. . . . It's affected everything. . . . You can't relax. . . . You always have to have a mask. . . . Your emotions are negatively affected *day in and day out* by the fact that you are black, and not a single day goes by that you're not reminded of this. . . . So, yes, everything is affected. My health is generally affected by the fact that I'm black.

Mr. Barrister clearly connected his heart disease to the burdens of racialization, which he experienced as unavoidable and pervasive.

Several of the participants with heart disease had grown up in the South during the decades following World War II and spoke extensively about the virulence of racism in the Jim Crow era. For example, Rahel Clayton, an African American woman born and raised in the South, was diagnosed with hypertension at the age of twenty-three. When I asked her what she believed had caused her heart disease, she responded, "It could be a lot of things. It could be stress. It could be environment. . . . I think all of us are part of our environment. . . . You have to be black in order to know. . . . I don't think you would ever know unless you've been there." In reflecting on her "environment," she remembered that her grandparents, who also suffered from heart disease and diabetes, "would call [white people] 'Mister' and 'Missus'. They would call my grandfather by his name. . . . It was survival for them." Such strictly policed rules of interracial interaction were an endemic part of the social organization and patterns of race relations in the segregated South. This rigidly enforced racial etiquette[19] reflected and sustained racial distinctions and hierarchy, constantly legitimated unequal power relations in everyday interactions, and was used as a means of social control. When I asked Ms. Clayton what she thought contributed to her grandparents' heart disease, she responded,

They suppressed a lot of things. . . . It was like, "You can't say this, you can't say that." . . . I'm sure that they suppressed a lot of their feelings because they could not speak out for what they believed in. . . . I really think that stress—you know, just not doing what you want to do, having to answer to someone else—plays a big part.

As for her own hypertension, Ms. Clayton maintained that her life-long experience of racialized interactions "affected a lot of things. I think it affected me as a person. . . . It does make you feel different because . . . being raised in the South, you can't do things that you see, you know, other kids do. . . . It was always like this suppression. There was a suppression. You suppressed your feelings."

Many other lay participants described similarly difficult compromises they had had to make between their desire to fight back and resist such treatment, and their need to survive. Carmen Hernandez, for example, identifies as a Latina and was diagnosed with high blood pressure fifteen years ago, at the age of forty-four. When I asked why she thinks she developed hypertension, she related that her physicians had told her it was directly associated with her weight and her sedentary lifestyle. But in her mind, she attributed her condition to "the stress that I feel in my life," triggered by her health conditions, her problematic relationship with her doctors, her low-status job, and, significantly, a lifetime of living in a racist society. She described how contemporary racism, particularly in its more covert and slippery forms, affects her:

> You always get that—at certain times when people say, "Well, you know, you're Latina. That's how you would think." . . . I usually try to take comments like that or attitudes like that with a grain of salt and say, "Well, you know, I'm not going to let that bother me. Why should I?" . . . Other times, you want to say something, and sometimes you're able to and other times you're not. . . . But my sense is that if I let it bother me too much, it's going to be harmful to me, and it's not going to change the attitude of the person who's doing it. . . . And it's very subtle. It's not a blatant thing. . . . But it's going to happen. It happens every day and it's going to continue to happen.

When I asked her how such experiences affect her, Ms. Hernandez replied emphatically:

I think just the ways that it's made me think, to a certain extent, about myself, and even though I'm okay with who I am—you know, a Latina of mixed descent or mixed blood—when you're to a certain extent bombarded with a lot of negative attitudes and perceptions, it's going to tend to weigh on you to a certain extent. . . . I get to a point where I get very depressed and very frustrated.

Similarly, Geline Laroya, an immigrant from the Philippines who had been a highly visible political activist working to overthrow the dictatorship of Ferdinand Marcos, described how painful she found the experience of her immigration:

I remember . . . being conscious of trying to say the right things the right way . . . so that you won't cause so much attention to yourself, either to be ridiculed or to lose an opportunity. . . . Just being very different, everything about you is looked at and either questioned, praised in a condescending way or criticized in an unfair way. . . . That's stressful. . . . I think it made me quiet, you know, which was kind of weird because, here's this flaming young activist . . . and then [she] tries to disappear, you know, in, let's say, work meetings. . . . After all, you have other plans, you know. You get by that way.

When I asked Ms. Laroya whether she thought these experiences affected her well-being, she initially responded, "I never thought of it that way. . . . I guess I still have a big separation between what goes on in your daily experiences and how it affects your health." But then she continued:

In terms of stress or things like that, you know, because you force yourself to be what you are not. . . . You keep quiet when you know you're not a quiet person. . . . Simmering, right? Instead of speaking up because you don't feel safe to do so. . . . Or you calculate things—what are the tradeoffs? What are the risks?

Here, Ms. Laroya attempted to express some of the health repercussions of the constant equivocation between accommodation and resistance in her racialized interactions with others.

This theme of self-preservation that Ms. Laroya evoked was echoed by many others: Speaking out, aside from its potential material consequences, was not seen by lay participants as psychically or physically liberating but rather as stressful and tension-inducing. Race was experienced as a master status, creating interactional quandaries and shaping social encounters in ways that require constant vigilance, careful negotiation, and calculated choices about one's presentation of self. Such racialized experiences— which I argue are the manifestations of racial signification at the level of everyday life—were understood by many of those with heart disease as posing cardiovascular risks through their imposition of such bodily consequences as "stress," "suppression," and "depression."

Intersecting Inequalities in the Material Conditions of Life

Another set of factors to which many lay participants attributed their heart disease includes the health impacts of racialized economic and environmental conditions. First, many respondents recounted long and complicated histories of cyclical economic insecurity and limited educational opportunities that in turn posed risks to their cardiovascular health. In particular, working-class women of color described interlocking dynamics of race, class, and gender that stratified their educational opportunities and structured a racially and sex-segregated labor market. Those employment opportunities most available to them were generally restricted to low-paying jobs, with little potential for advancement, minimal job stability, and little power over the conditions of their hours, pace of work, or the nature of the work process. For instance, Juanita Miller was a data-entry worker; Bonnie Joe had been a seamstress; Mercedes Portes had worked as a seamstress and cleaned offices; Carmen Hernandez was an office assistant providing secretarial services for six people; Yolanda Montenegro had just started working part-time as a hotel desk clerk; and Mabel Rodriguez had worked as a housekeeper, home health aide, and a cannery worker, and in food service.

Four of these six women drew causal connections between their heart disease and their conditions of life as shaped by racial, class, and gender dynamics. For example, Ms. Rodriguez, a Mexican American woman with severe hypertension, described how hiring practices produced a racialized occupational hierarchy:

> Oh, my days, people were very prejudiced! I mean they [white people] got the best jobs. . . . It was all underneath the table. . . . Higher up, a white person rather than the Latino or black. I knew what my place was there. . . . A girl came in and was light-complected and . . . I would go in or somebody else darker than me would go in. They'd hire her. I've seen that happen. There was a lot of prejudice. It was most always swept underneath the table. Oh, we went through all that prejudice in our days. They used to call me "Mexican greaser." . . . We got the dirty jobs while the others got the clean jobs. It's always been that way.

Ms. Rodriguez speculated that if she had not been Mexican American, she would have had "different kinds of jobs and easier jobs, and a more calm life than I was having. In those days there, you couldn't even work in an office if you were Latin or black." The consequence for Ms. Rodriguez was a life of working long hours in unskilled, low-paying, and physically taxing jobs. This, combined with single parenthood, is what she believed

> developed me for having high blood pressure. . . . It was hard to take [the kids to the] babysitter, and then going to work, and then everything was rush, rush to me. . . . I started getting sick, you know. All this running around, all this worrying about money, money, money. . . . All that, I guess, brought it up on me. . . . If you have a hard life, it stays on you. . . . That's also a lot of anxiety, too . . . working in those factories. . . . Make sure that you get up in the morning, take your kids to the babysitter, wait for the

bus to get there in time to work. . . . You had to punch in for work, and if you're not there on time, two or three times, they fire you. So, all of this is too much tension for one person that's raising her kids.

The personal narratives of lay participants like Ms. Rodriguez highlight how racism and racialization, classism, and sexism intersect to define and structure the terms under which people of different classes, races, and sexes are made to do different kinds of work. These respondents argued that their limited employment options, shaped by stratified access to educational and economic opportunities, served to determine the conditions under which they developed heart disease. Significantly, these women did not reduce race and gender to issues of class, as epidemiologists often did. Rather than interpret the racial and gender inequalities they found themselves subject to as epiphenomena of more fundamental class determinants, lay people viewed racial, class, and gender dynamics as deeply intersecting and mutually constitutive.

Second, in responding to my queries about the connections between their personal circumstances and their developing heart disease, many lay participants articulated how race structured their environmental contexts in ways that not only imposed cardiovascular health risks but also limited avenues for responding to and modifying such risks. For example, some spoke about the impracticality of regular exercise in unsafe neighborhoods and amid lives with far more pressing and immediate problems than the risks of a sedentary lifestyle. David Trimble, an African American diagnosed with hypertension in his early twenties, offered this picture of the environmentally mediated effects of race on health:

Early in life, when I started knowing myself, I had to accept an oppressive type of environment, and that strengthens you. But it also weakens you. Not only as an individual, but it weakens . . . the whole race. . . . As a product of that environment, you become deprived . . . socially, economically, educationally, and in your health. . . . No matter what your station in life was, no matter what your economic social [position]—you could look at every aspect; [race] had an effect on you. You cannot say that it did not affect me. That would be a complete false thing. It does affect you. You carry a scar for life. . . . And I don't think it's speculative. I think it's actually a fact. . . . If you're a product of an oppressed environment, quite naturally you're going to have some health problems that another group of people would not necessarily have in an environment that was entirely different. When I say the environment, that takes it in as a whole. You have to take in the school system, you have to take in the housing, the availability of health facilities—you have to take all of these and put them into that pot. You just can't extract one. You have to put them all in there, and then you would see that if that environment is oppressed, the people in that environment are going to come out with some problems, not only emotionally, mentally, social problems, but they're going to come out with a multiplicity of health problems.

Here, Mr. Trimble makes an emphatic claim to authority, using his life experiences as the basis for a kind of lived and embodied expertise in the health effects of racism. He also articulates an understanding of the interlocking effects of race: It deeply affects multiple aspects of one's lived experience, and any one dynamic cannot be separated or dissected from others. Racial meanings and racialized discourses and practices construct social, economic, political, and cultural infrastructures that synergistically sustain and reproduce one another.

Finally, many of the lay participants alluded to the social–psychological toll imposed by the racialization of economic outcomes and opportunities. Diane Jamison, for example, discussed the connections between the chronic exposure to racism and cardiovascular risk behaviors:

I think that what happens is . . . when those things happen to you on a daily basis, you naturally do things that are comfortable and reaffirming to you. So, you go home and you eat food that you know is bad, but it tastes good. It makes you feel good. You go home and you may drink. . . . You may need to relax and so you're smoking. I think that because of those things, you resort to things that make you feel comfortable; even if they had bad outcomes associated, you still do it. . . . My husband used to smoke. When he would get really upset, the first thing he would do was smoke. My mom—when she's upset, she comes home and cooks a huge dinner. . . . A lot of people do that. They do things that are comfortable. . . . When you have a lot of things in your life that hurt you, you have a tendency to do it [engage in comforting but ultimately unhealthy behaviors] more often. . . . And I think that's where the direct correlation is.

Mrs. Jamison, like many others, attributed her heart disease to the psychic and emotional experience of racism and the subsequent drive to engage in unhealthy behaviors like smoking, drinking, and comfort eating as strategies for coping with and blunting the harms of racism.

It is important to note that there was significant variability among lay people's responses regarding the race–health connection. As in my exchange with Geline Laroya above, when I directly asked participants whether their experiences of racialization affected their health in any way, several asserted that it did *not* have an impact on their health. These individuals seemed to profess a kind of colorblindness or color evasiveness[20] in explaining their belief that racism did not affect their health. For example, some spoke about "turning the other cheek," not judging others on the basis of their race, and not letting others' treatment affect their attitudes and behavior. But at the same time, most of these participants readily acknowledged that their biographies were deeply shaped by their encounters with racism, and they expressed highly critical views on the impacts of racialization. And in other portions of their interviews, they passionately articulated how such experiences can explicitly, directly, and profoundly affect one's health.

Consider, for example, Joe Irving, an African American who had a heart attack and bypass surgery at the age of fifty-four. He told me that he tried to "soar above . . . the injustices" and that he "never felt belittled or put down." But when I asked why he thought African Americans suffer from heart disease at higher rates than do whites, he offered this lengthy and poignant response, centered on the denial of opportunities to women and people of color and the ensuing social–psychological harm to dignity and health:

> I would say, very easily, suppression. Blacks are suppressed, minorities are suppressed, women are suppressed. . . . Just give me a fair chance. That's all I'm asking for. . . . We should all be just given that chance. That's what's so wrong with it—not to be given that chance. . . . That's what irritates so much. That's what makes you angry, mean, nasty, and unforgiving. . . . That's all part, I guess, of the oppression thing, to be denied that chance. Sometimes not to be even heard. It's a biggie. It's got to weigh big with some people, especially if you're held back, and you feel like that's what's holding you back. . . . There are some people who just cannot shake that, you know, and it sticks in their craw, and it destroys them! . . . I can see how it could destroy people and make a difference, very easily. . . . Because that's all they've got is the opportunity. . . . And you take away that, man, and there's nothing else. . . . You miss your shot one time, you can go through life saying, "If I had just got this shot or these things happened," [even] two or three times. But these things continually happen. . . . How many times can you go through this? How many times can you turn your other cheek? How many times can [you] say, "Oh, it'll be all right. I'll get it the next time." After a while it hammers on you, it lays on you, it beats you down. It really does. And eventually maybe destroy you. . . . Is it genocide? I don't know. . . . It's the most worse thing there is, is to know that . . . your parents didn't have a chance, you didn't have a chance, and your children's not. . . . It's a *monster* thing! It's unforgivable. . . . You take that away, you destroy the people.

Mr. Irving's words paint a haunting picture of how inequality can act as a significant risk for heart disease. He and many other lay participants saw how racial hierarchy, and its deep intersections with class and gender stratification, acutely shaped their everyday interactions, the economic opportunities available to them, and the material conditions to which they were exposed. They saw how these effects of racial inequality imposed bodily consequences that produced and exacerbated their hypertension and heart disease. Thus people with heart disease formed an experiential basis from which they conceptualized, in multiple, diverse, and complex ways, their racial status and its consequences as direct cardiovascular risks. The varied means through which race is signified and made meaningful, and their interactional and institutional consequences for the social worlds of these respondents with heart disease, in turn exacted costs to their health. In this fashion, lay participants implicated their experiences as racial "others" and the multiple, intersectional effects of racial, class, and gender inequality as structural causes of heart disease.

Conclusion

In this chapter, I examined how epidemiology conceives of and regulates individuals construed to be racially different. I also explored how those living with heart disease reflect upon such constructions and navigate the disciplinary forms of biopower based upon them. In this light, the relative silence on structural causes and the popularity of cultural constructions of racial inequalities on the part of epidemiologists appear very problematic indeed, standing in sharp contrast to the experiences of those who live with heart disease. At the least, the ritualized inclusion of race as a taken-for-granted variable, as well as the continued study of race-as-culture in etiologic research on heart disease, neglects the role of race in organizing social relations of power and the effects of racialized interactions and structural racism on health. At worst, such practices displace and replace structural understandings of race with individualistic ones that ignore the ways in which relations of power are embedded within the reciprocating representations of race and the material consequences such representations have on life chances.

In so doing, epidemiology effects particular forms of stratified biomedicalization—the selective and systematically unequal ways in which biomedicine categorizes, scrutinizes, and intervenes in populations.[21] The culturalist construction of race reveals some of the precise ways in which this stratified biomedicalization works: through inclusion, exclusion, embeddedness, and in its effects. First, stratified biomedicalization occurs through the explicit targeting of racialized populations and essentializing notions of their behavior, as in epidemiology's focus on "ethnic" groups and their "cultural" behaviors. That is, biomedicalization is stratified because of the *specific inclusion* of racial deviance (from the normative "white" category) as an object requiring biomedical attention.

Second, this inclusion and attention are of a particular kind: That racial difference is understood (or at least enacted) by epidemiologists to be *culturally* mediated indicates that *structural* conceptions of racial dynamics are *strategically excluded* from consideration. Historically, culturalist constructions of race were aimed at opposing biological discourses. However, in this contemporary iteration, the cultural prism instead tends to reinstitutionalize individualized, astructural notions of racial difference. The selective embrace of cultural and other seemingly apolitical parameters of difference tends to uphold extant social hierarchies. An outcome of the biomedicalization of race by cardiovascular epidemiology is thus a relative lack of attention to structural sources of health inequality and a continued focus on the causes of and consequences to health on an individual level rather than on a group or collective one.

Third, the outwardly observable and thus seemingly "factual" nature of behavioral differences makes it exceedingly difficult—and gives the appearance of its being conceptually unnecessary—to problematize and further explore the associations between racial groups and behavioral differences. Thus the capacity of biomedicalization processes to effect a particular "definition of the situation" or framing of the "problem"—in this case, that racial disparities in cardiovascular risk are attributable to racial differences in health behaviors and beliefs—means that notions of stratification become *embedded* into our "biomedical common sense" and, increasingly, into popular logics about disease causes and solutions.

Finally, the affinity between the cultural prism and prevention discourses shows how biomedicalization can be stratified *in its effects*: Even when health promotion imperatives are not overtly racialized, their consequences are systematically uneven for different racial groups. Because risk factors often refer implicitly and explicitly to culture, behavior, and other dynamics widely seen as related to race and ethnicity, discourses about heart disease risk and prevention often invariably and cyclically become racialized. Much like *de jure* and *de facto* racism, then, biomedicalization is racially stratified both in name and in effect—in itself and in its consequences.

Epidemiology is also simultaneously a *biopolitical project* in which knowledge practices and institutions work to pathologize and regulate groups defined as racially different. The racial biopolitics of heart disease becomes embedded into the fabric of biomedical knowledge and practice. In so doing, it produces a common sense and logic about disease causation populated by atomistic individuals engaging in unhealthy behaviors, rather than the relations of power that undergird health, inequality, and knowledge. Epidemiologic representations of race-as-culture rearticulate perceived "ethnic" behaviors and beliefs as markers of risk and potential pathology and as targets for needed intervention. To be sure, some culturally mediated beliefs and behaviors have downstream consequences for cardiovascular risk, and understanding racial difference through its cultural dimensions affords epidemiologists some crucial advantages in terms of conceptual flexibility, measurability, and etiologic significance. However, such representations contribute to sociocultural views regarding "different" kinds of bodies and the ways in which individuals so marked think about themselves and their health.

As important, epidemiologic constructions of race fail to capture the full measure of complex causal pathways that people of color living with heart disease attest to. Significantly, even while lay narratives clearly point to the intersections of racial with class and gender oppression, epidemiology—as an enterprise interested in identifying discrete, independent, and individual-level effects—reiterates and reifies the notion of race as a singular dimension of human difference, rather than one that is refracted through and by class and gender, for instance. It segregates out those forms of difference perceived to be racial from others tied to class or gender. In so doing, the racial biopolitics of heart disease substantively undercuts an understanding of health inequality as intersectional. However, lay understandings of the *social* etiology of heart disease reveal how these projects of biomedicalization and biopolitics are always continually contested and negotiated, such that we cannot take for granted the authoritative status of epidemiologic science, or of its conceptions of the connections that link race to heart disease and health.

At the outset of this chapter, I alluded to the observation that of the three dimensions of difference on which this book is focused, perspectives and talk about race are among the most contentious. To begin to see this in comparison, I turn in the next chapter to how scientists and people living with heart disease conceive of social class and its implications for cardiovascular risk and health.

4

An Apparent Consensus on Class

Interviews with both groups of participants and ethnographic data from conference proceedings convey that there exists a relatively significant amount of consensus between epidemiologic researchers and people with heart disease on the relevance of social class differences for health. Both groups clearly and unequivocally pointed to class and its intersections with race and gender as significant *social* and *structural* determinants of the stratification of cardiovascular health. That is, the consequences of class differences for heart disease were seen to reside in their multiple and complex effects, in conjunction with race and gender, on people's exposures to risks and the resources they have to avoid, mitigate, and otherwise influence those risks. As I show in the first section of this chapter, understandings of the significance of class for health by epidemiologists and lay people tell us that they viewed class as structuring and organizing systems and relations of power.

However, as the second section of this chapter reveals, the two participant groups did diverge in their interpretations of the interactions between class and race. They also placed differing levels of importance on various class-based mechanisms in producing socioeconomic disparities in heart disease. Finally, the chapter ends by considering current epidemiologic conventions regarding the measurement and conceptualization of class and how they stymie efforts to understand the pivotal role of class-based structural forces in shaping cardiovascular risk. Here, I argue that an apparent consensus on the structural dimensions of the relationship connecting class to cardiovascular risk is in fact undercut by disagreements over ideas about culture and class, and meanings versus the measurement of class.

The Stratified Distribution of Resources and Risks

Epidemiologists and lay persons alike conceived of class as indisputably and manifestly about differences that are social and structural in nature. Both researchers and those living with heart disease argued that social class influences heart disease risk primarily via *structural* mechanisms, although they emphasized slightly different kinds of mechanisms. Both participant groups viewed access to resources and exposures to risks as highly stratified by class, challenging the extent to which people are "free" to pursue healthy lifestyles and sustain their own health. With varying frequency, they spoke of class as determining access to heterogeneous kinds of resources (such as quality medical services, health-related information, and nutritious foods) and exposure to multiple kinds of risks (such as economic insecurity, constrained occupational and educational opportunities, and the stress of living in hostile environments). Thus, both epidemiologists and lay experts constructed the effects of class differences in terms of the multiple connections between what class means and how social structures and everyday experiences are organized along class lines.

The first of the connections drawn was the construction of class as a determinant of access to health care. This understanding of class was pervasive in epidemiologists' accounts of cause and risk; however, it appeared only sporadically in the narratives of people with heart disease. My data show that epidemiologists widely perceived the role of access to health care in producing heart disease inequalities as clear and uncontroversial. They defined access to health care not simply as a matter of health insurance status but as effectively circumscribed by myriad other factors related to class, such as availability of time and transportation. In contrast, only three participants with heart disease mentioned issues of access—and did so only briefly—when discussing class-mediated mechanisms of cardiovascular risk. Both groups of participants agreed that social class is closely tied to the *quality* of health care to which one has access, with people of color diagnosed with heart disease further elaborating that class hierarchy systematically structures who feels entitled to and can successfully negotiate respectful relationships with their health care providers.

Second, both groups of participants also understood class to stratify access to social environments and informational resources that shape what people know about their cardiovascular health and can do to promote it. For example, Diane Jamison, the African American woman with hypertension, when asked about the health-related benefits or disadvantages that her class status affords her, enumerated:

> We have a computer at home, so I can always go online and get the latest news on what's happening. The ability to buy books and read on things. The ability to go to any doctor that we want to go to, and if we're pissed off with that one, go to another one. I mean, we really have more flexibility in where we get our services. I think that that's a major benefit of having money, that you can actually go where you need to go and where you want to go, and you're not told to go somewhere [else]. And you have more of a voice in your health. And I think that, to me, is a major advantage.

Dr. Carolyn Munson, an epidemiologist, concurred that the ability to navigate and evaluate health-related material is a crucial factor in structuring the socioeconomic gradient in cardiovascular health. Using the example of smoking, she explained how health behaviors and lifestyle habits must be viewed as mediated by the linkages between social class and educational status, and social environment and cultural milieu:

It's not just credentials. With each additional year of education, you find this gradient. . . . With each additional year of education . . . you get a decrease in risk. . . . To me the thing that makes most sense is that there's something about the skills and the resources that accumulate with additional years of education, and that with additional years of education you're not only changing how you navigate the world and the skills in which you do that and interpret it, but you're also changing kind of your social environment. . . . You're in a more educated setting around your work colleagues, for instance, or your school colleagues. . . . If you're a smoker, then along with . . . additional years [of education] . . . in your whole environment, those kinds of things go from actually being supported . . . to it being actually being easier to maintain or adopt healthy lifestyles because your social environment has changed. And also your knowledge of just the environmental influences—you're more likely to have been exposed to [the idea] . . . that most people who smoke—that's not purely an individual choice. . . . If you look at the targeting of information, where the information is distributed, the ads, you know, they're at rodeos, they're at race tracks, they're at community events where lower-income people congregate. . . . And as you become more educated, you become more cognizant of those kinds of influences and those kinds of influences are more likely to either keep you from smoking, [or] get you to stop smoking successfully. If you're higher educated and you're pregnant and you're a smoker, [you're] probably much more likely to stop smoking because you're able to either read, understand the messages about the danger to the fetus. . . . And that's the kind of thing I think that education buys you and why there's this gradient. . . . Because each piece along the way—the whole social context is changing.

Third, both epidemiologists and people with heart disease cited the chronic mental and emotional toll of economic insecurity and the constant struggle for economic survival as significant bodily stressors and important contributors to the social class gradient in heart disease. As Dr. Karen Verceau argued,

> I think the biggest issue is that when you have so many other prevailing issues—like where will the next meal come from for the children, will we have a roof over our head—what happens to you in twenty or thirty years from high blood pressure or cigarette smoking or high cholesterol seems almost irrelevant. . . . It's almost like it's a privilege of the middle class and the wealthy to be able to worry about health and the future. I personally believe everyone is interested in [and] values their health. But, when it comes to stacking up your priorities of what you're going to spend your day today on doing, it becomes very, very hard when survival is such a huge issue at hand every single day.

One of the lay participants, Sharon Chavez, compared her own life of constant financial struggle with those of people who are better off. Specifically, she argued that economic insecurity exposed her to health risks in the form of "stress" and access to health-promoting goods:

> Someone who's better educated might not have the stress or the money problems that I do. . . . Here, if you're middle class, it's really hard to make ends meet because of the price of rent and everything. I find myself increasingly going to thrift shops and garage sales instead of buying new things, and hoping I can find what I need. . . . Worrying about money is stressful. Looking for a job that isn't stressful and will help me survive financially is stressful. I'm not that knowledgeable about computers and that's pretty much a requirement for jobs these days, and I'm no longer young. . . . It's just a struggle. . . . It's going to affect my ability to choose healthy food and a good job and survive here . . . and not have to move to someplace else that's less expensive.

Even for those in less limited economic straits, such as Lee Tsan, a middle-class Chinese American woman, the need for dual incomes imposes restrictions on her ability to change her lifestyle "choices":

A friend of mine, she always said, "Oh, you shouldn't have high blood pressure. Maybe you should quit your job." She can say that because she doesn't work, and she's able to go to the gym in the morning and do workouts and then the rest of the day she just sort of relaxes and shops and picks up her son later, and that's her day pretty much, you know. So, I'm not saying that's what I want to do, but I think if I had a little more time, a little more flexibility . . . maybe to incorporate exercise into my life a little more.

Further, Dr. Max Oliver, an epidemiologist, suggested that aside from the advantages of better access to the financial, material, and environmental resources necessary to engage in behavioral risk reduction, some element of relative socioeconomic position can color individuals' reactions and receptivity to such mandates. "If you're doing well and are well off," he explained, "you're probably going to have a more positive response toward healthy dietary choices and activities, than if you're unemployed and everything is . . . objectively dismal and depressing in your life." As such, he believes that measuring one's perception of her or his socioeconomic position relative to others' may extend our understanding of how health disparities by social class are produced, rather than using absolute measures of socioeconomic status alone.

But by far, people of color with heart disease spent the most time in their interviews describing for me the intersecting, durable processes of educational stratification and labor market segmentation by class, race, and gender that interlock, compound, and overlap to produce complex risks to their cardiovascular health. Ms. Tsan works for an organization that provides services to Asian Americans and Asian immigrants, and she talked about her clients and the racialized, classed, and gendered division of labor that funnels them into occupations that pose significant risks for their health:

They work as cooks—very high pressure jobs where . . . you have to hurry up and produce the food, you know. And they are garment workers, and the garment workers often times are abused because they don't have the language capability. They don't know what their rights are as workers. And they oftentimes do what they call piece work, [in] which they have to produce a certain number of items [in] a certain time period. So they're under pressure. And I hear that a lot from the women, you know, that they can't keep up with the demand. . . . They're mostly women garment workers. There are a few men, but mostly women. The men are usually the cooks. That's the typical scenario of our patient population. Cooks and garment workers.

Other lay participants recounted complicated and long histories to explain the cyclical consequences of tenuous economic existence upon their education and myriad other aspects of their lives that together constitute risks to their cardiovascular health. For example, after graduation from high school, Carmen Hernandez enrolled in a community college; however, as she recalled:

I had to work to go to school, and I didn't have any choice—to buy my books, to pay whatever tuition was required at that time, I had to go to work. It was a very difficult time for me. . . . Then finally I decided, well, I can't go to school now because I need money, so I quit school and I worked for a few years, and then I would quit the job and I would try to go back to school . . . back and forth, back and forth.

Ms. Hernandez's ultimate inability to fulfill her academic dreams continued to be a source of great regret. She never was able to accrue enough credits to earn her college degree, and this in turn circumscribed her economic opportunities, relegating her to a low-paying job as an administrative assistant, with little control over the hours and pace of her work.

Similarly, Mabel Rodriguez had a tumultuous childhood, living with an alcoholic mother and a succession of her mother's abusive male partners. Ms. Rodriguez attended high school for several years but did not complete her high school degree. She speculated that had she been able to further her education,

> my life would have been much easier. If I had an education, I would have gone to work. I wouldn't have to go [into] laboring jobs and work like a fool, you know, for minimum wages, because in those days they didn't pay that much. . . . If I had a good education, I would never be this way. I'd be more comfortable. . . . It's hard to have something in your mind and think about what you're going to do the next day, how are you going to eat, how you're going to take care of your kids.

Thus the long-term consequences of poverty during childhood manifest in part as limited educational attainment that in turn constrains participants' abilities to earn a subsistence wage. This then creates a lifetime of chronic stress that takes its physical, mental, and emotional toll, cumulatively and synergistically, on the health of the lay participants I interviewed. From their perspectives, the conditions of life structured and imposed by their economic position, social status, and opportunities constitute significant causal pathways to bodily stress and ultimately to their cardiovascular health.

And finally, those who live with heart disease point to their environment, such as the social conditions of their housing, as another major source of psychological and physical strain. For example, Lynn Fielding, a woman with hypertension who lives in a single-resident-occupancy hotel, described the inescapable and constant tension of living in high-density housing without the luxury of privacy and space:

> Where I'm living now, I'm tense. . . . There's a lot of people [living] close to each other, and they're always in your business, or want to know what you're doing. And I feel like I don't have space . . . and then I tense up, you know. When I'm tense, it goes to my heart. . . . There's a lot of people there, the drugs, there's the screaming and yelling. . . . I'm like, "No. This is not good for my body." I'm a quiet person. I don't like a lot of junk and noise

around me. . . . I don't know how I lived there four and a half years. . . . I can't take a whole lot any more. I just can't.

In this vivid description of her living environment, Ms. Fielding expressed—and even embodied during the interview itself—the feelings of frustration, anger, and tension that it causes her. The concentration and density of people, the lack of privacy and private space that are often inevitable in such situations, and the combativeness and intrusion of her neighbors are all triggers for emotional and physical distress for Ms. Fielding. She pointed out that such exposures exacerbated her hypertension in the face of already existing risk factors and increased her dependency on her blood pressure medication.

It is as a result of these sources of class-based risk, lay people with heart disease asserted, that the stratification by class inevitably reproduces the stratification of health. Moreover, they were clear on the complex and multiple structural and institutional processes through which classed representations of subordinate groups by dominant ones are made to have material and bodily consequences. As Diane Jamison observed,

I almost feel like to a certain extent that it isn't even scientific. I think it's really just . . . the things that go on . . . in the community. I mean if you have to go to a school every day where the windows are broken out and it's cold and the cafeteria food is horrible . . . I don't care how much you meditate. I don't care how many vegetables, how many servings you eat a day, that still wears on you. . . . People have to live in a society where everyone is cared for in the same way and treated the same way. I mean, if it's okay for certain kids to go to school with, you know, one book between six kids, other kids have computers on their desks, I mean we've got to look at those kind of things. To me it's so obvious. And there's a high rate of depression—you can look around and you can see why. . . . It's just people behaving normally to really abnormal situations. Who wouldn't be stressed out? You know, who wouldn't be obese or have high blood pressure or whatever. . . . So, to me it's almost not scientific.

And, for the most part, epidemiologists seem to agree with Ms. Jamison. As one epidemiologist, Dr. Lena Kelleher, summarized:

> People of different social classes have access to different resources . . . income and wealth. It's different educational levels, social capital. It's different occupations. And all of these things are going to allow you to either purchase or know about or sort of be able to access the things that you need to be able to live well, whether it's knowledge or a safe house, or living in a safe neighborhood or having the appropriate connections, having the wealth that when something bad happens, you're all right. . . . So I think it's just all about sort of just having more resources to take advantage of what is out there to just live healthy.

Class, Race, Culture, and Behavior

But this apparent consensus on class—that its health implications are mediated largely by the stratified distribution of resources and risks—belies some disagreement between epidemiologists and lay people. In this section, I discuss the more subtle yet nonetheless deep dissension on the relationships between class, race, culture, and notions of individual responsibility. While scientists sometimes used a language of individual-level behavior and responsibility when talking about class-based dynamics, those living with heart disease insisted on situating those same dynamics within social, historical, and political contexts of inequality. Moreover, as this section shows, these contexts were seen to be rooted not just in class but also in race and gender stratification. At the same time, lay people's understandings of the specific health effects of class were heterogeneous, contradictory, and complex, so that their accounts of heart disease causation were also occasionally punctuated by more individualistic explanations as well.

Epidemiologists recognized the role of economic stratification, yet their accounts contained more reductionist perceptions of the pathological impact of individual-level attitudes, knowledge, and behavior. For example, they discussed the influence of social class, race, and ethnicity on individuals' awareness of health issues, their knowledge of when and how to engage with the biomedical system, and an agential attitude toward the consumption of health information and health care services.[1] Epidemiologists also understood class and racial differences as stemming from variations in the prevalence of risk factors—such as smoking and unhealthy dietary habits—that they theorized have something to do with lack of health education, problematic "role modeling within the family," and an aberrant cultural environment and upbringing in which such risky behaviors are tolerated and even promoted. For example, in the opening chapter of this book, I recalled my encounter with an epidemiologist who attributed disparities in heart disease risk factors between black and white women to diet, sedentary lifestyle, education, perhaps access to health care, and to "a black culture, welfare moms, or whatever, with low education who maybe missed out on the public health messages of the past ten years."

The coupling of class and racialized characteristics with the mobilization of behavioral norms and discourses of individual responsibility could also be seen in epidemiologists' discussions of heart disease interventions. For example, one related for a scientific audience the "success story" of a program to increase knowledge of the health benefits of exercise and mental "readiness for exercise" among a working-class community of Latinas. As my field notes describe:

> The presenter explains: "Low-income Latina women, even with these very extreme life circumstances, can definitely increase their exercise and fitness. Once they're informed about the importance, they're very interested. . . . The level of education and information we're starting at . . . really is shockingly low. And if you think about it, the Spanish-language media doesn't really emphasize health information in the same way that we do, and if you've not sat through all those years of elementary science education, you're really starting from a very low point. It's

really difficult to explain to somebody why it's important to lower your cholesterol when they don't understand what blood level is and what it does. So you really have to go back to the anatomy and physiology, and start from there. . . . We developed very simple, very colorful educational materials; we used a lot of . . . children's . . . materials. We had to have a lot of hands-on learning." The presenter then went on to describe how the women were "very interested" in telenovelas—Spanish-language soap operas from Mexico—adding that if we in the audience are interested in them we should tune into Channel 19 on our hotel televisions, and "you don't have to speak Spanish to know what's going on." The audience laughs at length. She continues, "So one thing that they really enjoyed doing was doing skits, where . . . we would have a role-play of how to convince their husbands that they really needed to exercise and not cook them dinner instead." The audience laughs again.

Embedded within this description of the exercise program are multiple racialized, classed, and gendered representations of Latinas as uneducated, irrational, and uniformly subject to traditional gender roles perceived to be intrinsic to their ethnic culture. This researcher did acknowledge the many barriers that the women in her study had to overcome in order to engage in regular exercise and to acquire an understanding of the relevance of exercise to their health. Yet in her presentation she chose instead to highlight that such barriers *can* be overcome and that behavioral modifications *can* be effected. Such success stories therefore served to emphasize the possibility of individual transformation and triumph over structural obstacles. These stories also functioned to underwrite the notion that the inability to change one's health behaviors is a product of individual moral failure and biomedical irrationality.

But at the same time, participants living with heart disease understood health-related habits as shaped by the consequences of diminished economic resources for escalating chronic stress, generating food insecurity, and creating deleterious social environments. Notably, they saw these diminished resources and harmful social environments as the products

of hierarchical relations between socially defined groups. Such understandings then prompted pushback against epidemiologic attributions
about health behaviors and of individual responsibility. For example, Ms.
Jamison first enumerated the ways in which she has attempted to take
heed of risk reduction mandates but then qualified this by describing the
impact of stressors over which she has little control:

> I've cut back on sodium almost altogether. Diet, exercise . . . rather than
> taking the elevator, take the stairs. [Making] little changes in your life
> so that it becomes more of a way of living. . . . I walk whenever possible.
> And I try to take breaks every day and just give myself time just to not
> do anything. . . . Anyone, regardless of your economic level, can do those
> kind of things. . . . But I think on a larger scale, I have to find a better way
> to deal with the stress factors that are . . . external, that I really feel like I'm
> powerless to control in the big picture.

In chapter 3, Ms. Jamison spoke of the repeated insults of racism and
the subsequent behaviors (e.g., comfort eating, smoking) to which such
experiences often led. As she saw it, "things in your life that hurt you,"
"the stress factors that are . . . external"—at root, the oppressive relations
between unequal groups that create harm—ultimately militate against
the efficacy of behavioral modifications that one could engage in, regardless of economic status.

Another participant, Ms. Hernandez, who earlier in this chapter
described having to drop out of community college for lack of funds,
suffers from not only hypertension but also severe arthritis that significantly limits her ability to exercise. She recounted how her health care
providers constantly pressured her to lose weight, disregarding her physical limitations:

> Well, I've been getting [pressure] mostly from the doctors that I've spo-
> ken to . . . all pretty much tell me the same thing: they tend to take your
> condition less seriously if you're overweight. And I have a feeling that they

seem to think that your weight problem is something that you force upon yourself, you know. And so, that's almost like a recurring theme, that if you lose weight, your blood pressure will probably stabilize. . . . I don't know if that's necessarily true, but you know, it gets to be almost a mantra with them. . . . I'm still going to have the stresses in my life. . . . I mean those stresses from my job, from my personal life and everything else, those are still going to be there. . . . It bothers me that they emphasize the fact that losing weight is going to make you all better. . . . To me it's almost like a vicious circle. . . . I've gotten to the point where I just say, "Forget about it. I'll be the way I am," you know? And whatever is going to happen is going to happen.

Ms. Hernandez believed that her hypertension was caused by the chronic stresses of her marginal job as a temporary clerk and the economic insecurity that suffuses her daily survival, and the pain of her unfulfilled dreams to obtain an education and build a better life for herself. From this vantage point, then, her providers' persistent admonitions to lose weight were both insensitive given her arthritis and physical limitations and likely ineffective as a means to treat her high blood pressure.

Many lay people I interviewed grew up in fairly humble circumstances and spoke of their limited access to nutritious foods. Ms. Joe, the African American woman whose parents were sharecroppers and whom we met in chapter 3, described how sharecropping left her family with few resources to spend on food. Thus her childhood diet consisted of foods cooked in animal fat, meat preserved in salt, and calorie-dense starchy foods. Ms. Joe, as well as other African American informants, made clear that their culinary traditions emerge from generations of exposure to rampant racism and material inequalities. Thus they view dietary habits as shaped at least as much by historical and current intersectional relations of power and social hierarchy, where classed and racialized social relations are interwoven with one another, as by "culture," "preferences," and "tastes."

Similarly, Geline Laroya, the Filipina with hypertension, described how immigrants arriving in the United States find an overabundance of processed foods that promote their excessive consumption while constraining the availability of more healthful alternatives:

> One of the things I think that happens to immigrants from developing countries coming to the U.S. is that you're commodity-shocked, no matter how poor you are, [by] the availability of the junk you can buy. . . . If we were more educated about it, I would have prevented [consuming] more. . . . Eggs are, for example, so cheap here. . . . In the Philippines, you don't make certain kinds of dishes all the time because it involves the use of eggs. . . . So there's just a lot of things you could go in excess of without knowing about it and without understanding that health-wise . . . you're going beyond the level of unhealthy consumption, just because you thought back where you first grew up, the deprivation of those kinds of things is more the problem. You know, it's like the amount of calories that's possible, available. . . . Here, even though you're struggling and you're the main breadwinner, you could afford to buy those things, and it can shock you. In some ways there are so many processed ingredients here that are available to the immigrant communities.

Such dietary excesses, from an epidemiologic standpoint, would tend to be racialized as "cultural" preferences, as described in chapter 3. In contrast, people of color instead indicate how larger structural forces, such as power relations institutionalized in racial and class hierarchy, as well as the complex political economy of food production and commodification in the United States and their systematic interactions with class circumstances and life chances, are influential in shaping the diet of different groups.

However, the divide between epidemiologists' recurrent references to culturalist constructions of class and race and lay persons' mostly structural understandings of their effects on heart disease was not always neat and clean. In their interviews, people of color sporadically fused structural and more individualistic explanations for class differences in the same contradictory manner. For example, Ms. Chavez, whom we met earlier, considers herself middle class but speculated that someone who's lower class might be not as well educated or might not have the resources that I have. . . . Not to sound terrible, but there are people who have been on welfare for generations and they don't have much money and they have a tendency to eat more inexpensive and junk food, and they're hurting their bodies and they don't know it. That's all they can afford. And people aren't taught a lot of health information in school, and if they go to the average school and they don't have a doctor that really cares about them because he sees a glut of people and he doesn't have much time, they're going to suffer because of it. . . . I'm treated a little better, and I do have more information and I would see a better type of doctor because I can afford it. And I'm not just, you know, seen for five minutes and that's it. And I can afford better food. I [am subject to] less prejudice.

Here, Ms. Chavez contextualized the health-related "choices" of the poor by noting the structural constraints they face in diet, lifestyle, and health maintenance, yet she occasionally lapsed into reductionist language, alluding to generations on welfare and living in a social milieu in which people "wouldn't know any better." In this case, the lack of knowledge and awareness that leads to risky behaviors and unhealthy lifestyles is conceptualized as at least partly rooted in deviant local cultures and pathological environments, from which individuals should pull themselves out "by their own bootstraps."

Many of the lay participants I interviewed spoke at considerable length about how they had been told to monitor their blood pressure and fat and salt intake and to practice other methods of behavioral self-surveillance. Some, like Ms. Fielding, wholeheartedly take up dominant health imperatives:

When I'm eating the way I'm supposed to . . . forcing my body to walk, I feel good. . . . It's just hard work. You have to do it. . . . Exercise is a little difficult, but I'm seeing [that] walking does it. . . . But every now and then . . . I have a taste for sugar [laughs]. And I eat a little piece of candy, and I say, "Aaah! There it goes back into your blood again!" . . . I know with hypertension, it can lead to many things like blindness in the eye from the arteries exploding from too much pressure, heart attacks, stroke. . . . I know that to force myself to walk . . . eat right and take my medication will keep [the hypertension] down. It's like a thing that you have to keep doing, consistent—keep doing, keep doing. I have to remind myself, "Get up, you lazy! Do it because this is your life!" . . . See, if you care about yourself, and if you're really in tune that you want to live, then you have to be determined. . . . The pressure on the heart and taking no medicine, eating whatever you want whenever you want—it'll kill you. It will kill you.

Ms. Fielding's constant vigilance about the effects of her behaviors on her long-term health status is therefore as much dictated by her physician's rhetoric as by her own acute sense of being "at risk."

Those with heart disease often expressed guilt and frustration when recounting how they "slip," "indulge," or are otherwise undisciplined in maintaining behavioral changes that biomedical professionals recommended or that they themselves decided to take up. As Joe Irving conceded, "My health is bad because I probably don't care as much. . . . I could do better. My diet is . . . not good because I eat what I want. . . . I don't restrain . . . myself. . . . I know better, so my conscience bothers me about that." David Trimble, who in chapter 3 spoke so authoritatively and compellingly about people being the product of their oppressed environments, still believes that "people must manage themselves. The health care system can only offer treatment, and they can offer educational factors, but in the end it's the person who must manage [her- or himself] and be prudent as far as smoking, excessive drinking, and excessive ingestion of fatty foods [are concerned]."

Thus, dominant health imperatives work to normalize the constant surveillance and disciplining of our actions, behaviors, and bodies. The ways in which such discursive constructions of the poor are entangled with efforts to offer more structural explanations reflect the pervasiveness of ideologies that in effect "blame the victim" and echo "culture of poverty" arguments.[2] The ready availability of these rhetorics to serve as familiar, convenient, and safe explanations, though partial ones, for the class stratification of cardiovascular risk is, then, a measure of their success in manufacturing consent to class and health inequality.

The Intersectional Meaning versus Scientific Measurement of Class

Additional aspects of meaning-making around class reveal other underlying differences between epidemiologic and lay constructions of class. The final set of differences I observed bear on issues related to the measurement and operationalization of class and class identity. Epidemiologists widely perceived current conventions for measuring economic position and status to be inadequate because they fail to capture many of the important ways in which social class affects the distribution of heart disease. In the absence of well-developed or convincingly valid alternatives for operationalizing class dynamics, researchers found it difficult to avoid using the routinized, though inadequate, methods and measures of socioeconomic status. Many standard components of socioeconomic status were also commonly used by lay people to characterize their understandings of their economic positions, but they often augmented these with more complex descriptions of wealth and class as a social relationship. In addition, I found class identity for people with heart disease to be highly intersectional, intertwined in particular with experiences of race.

With regard to the measurement of class, the current default standard of practice in epidemiology is to use variables of income (individual, family, and/or household), occupation, and/or educational attainment, often in combinations that may vary from study to study. These measures constitute components of socioeconomic status, which is, according to all the researchers I spoke with, a key and routine ingredient in almost any epidemiologic investigation. But epidemiologists also pointed out that one fundamental weakness with using such ritualized measures of socioeconomic status is the lack of context: They argued that the expression of socioeconomic status as an absolute number or category (e.g., income in dollars, or occupational groupings) does not embody the reality of class position as a *relative* characteristic. As Dr. Mia Henderson explained,

> education and income . . . you have to look at those in terms of context. . . . If you live in Silicon Valley and make $40,000 . . . you're on the lower end, versus if you live in the middle of Illinois and you make $40,000, you'd be living like a queen. . . . You really have to look at the context of that, [and] look at how many people are in the household [and] are sharing that income.

Another researcher, Dr. Sheila Morris, likewise questioned the meaning of absolute measures of socioeconomic status: "When you use multiple socioeconomic indicators . . . are those variables . . . completely parallel to what somebody's social class and exposure and availability to certain common factors are? . . . Things like status incongruity would be more important. . . . It becomes very difficult to figure out how you get a grasp on this concept of social class, socioeconomic status." That is, many of the epidemiologists I spoke with understood that an important aspect of social class lay in its dimensions as a relational and positional characteristic, that any indicator of access to economic resources made sense only when seen contextually, in comparison with what it takes to maintain a style of life and what others are able to afford. In this sense, epidemiologists argue, the *status* aspect of socioeconomic status is central to its meaning and its consequences for health.

Another perceived methodological flaw with the routine variables of socioeconomic status is the failure of these measures to take into account the long-term systemic effects of class over the life course (and, indeed, over generations). Epidemiologists I interviewed readily invoked a longitudinal view of the effects of class on cardiovascular health. For example, Dr. Morris argued:

> I really think you have to start with the beginning of someone's life and follow them from *in utero* all the way until their death . . . to really

understand the impact of social factors and socioeconomic factors on people's survival. . . . I think we tend to look very close to the outcome, maybe too close to the outcome if the damage has probably been accumulating over a period of time and the social factors are way back that we're not even accounting for. So we're only seeing a piece of the pie.

From this perspective, which was relatively common among the epidemiologists I spoke to, prior class position is perceived to affect present and future status indelibly. It follows, therefore, that, as one scientist put it, "You don't just fix the problem at the end point," that changing a person's current income would likely do little to alter the health benefits and disadvantages which that person had accumulated throughout their life as a result of their class status.

However, epidemiologists pointed out that the conventional time frame of most health research makes it almost impossible to appropriately offset this and many of the other shortcomings in the measurement and operationalization of class.[3] In cardiovascular epidemiology, much of the most prominent and productive research has been in the form of cohort studies, despite their significant financial costs. But many epidemiologists I interviewed speculated that this may be changing as investments in such long-term research diminish and resources shift to faster and cheaper study designs. Moreover, most cohort studies include only adult participants (although this is shifting to some degree) and therefore are limited in their ability to trace the long-term effects of class on cardiovascular health in the ways that Dr. Morris and other epidemiologists advocate. Finally, even with a longitudinal cohort study design, epidemiologists recounted difficulties accounting for class factors that they know are important but that are methodologically unmanageable in some way. For example, they cited that individual measures of class or socioeconomic status are not stable (with the usual exception of educational attainment) but instead change over the lifetime of study participants and the course of a study. Thus, it remained unclear to epidemiologists how they should account for the fluid economic status of, for instance, a person who enjoys a middle-class life as part of a dual-income couple but then drops into poverty following a separation, or the man who moves from a poverty-stricken childhood to homelessness then to gainful employment in a relatively well-paying though physically strenuous job, or someone else who is working-class or poor for much of her life.

In short, epidemiologists routinely conceded that class, because of the complex and fluid ways in which its various dimensions impact material conditions and health, is problematic to measure accurately and reliably. As described earlier in this chapter, epidemiologists could easily conceptualize multiple, complex class dynamics that shape cardiovascular risk, ranging from health behaviors, access to resources, and chronic stress, but they emphasized that comprehensive measures of these effects have yet to be elaborated and widely accepted. But such measurement and analytic dilemmas, rather than raise political concerns or fundamental doubts about the value and meanings of measures of class, as they did for race, were quite often perceived as resolvable through more precise science. That is, epidemiologists I spoke to tended to articulate the problems as technical ones—in which study design and data collection procedures could be modified—and as an issue of research funding, in which sufficient resources should be committed in order to implement longitudinal studies that can study long-term and systemic effects of class on heart disease. Most researchers believed that taking better advantage of existing techniques and developing new ones would allow for the subsequent collection, availability, and analysis of more and "better" socioeconomic and class data. Thus methodological advances were seen as ultimately able to settle contentions over the causal or mediating role of social class in heart disease. Investigations into the role of social class in heart disease and health status more generally were viewed predominantly not as involving politically charged issues about the nature of the concept itself, as they are for race, so much as technical problems that can be remedied through "better" science.

People with heart disease used heterogeneous definitions and ways of describing their class background that often were somewhat congruent with the standard epidemiologic measures of socioeconomic status, such as income and education. However, lay people tended to supplement such basic measures with more complex indicators of economic status. For example, when asked to characterize their "economic situation" or "class background," most informants provided descriptions of home and property ownership, parents' as well as their own occupations, and the extent to which their parents' and their own incomes provided for food, clothing, housing, cars, and other kinds of resources for everyday life. Compared with epidemiologists, participants of color with heart disease were also much more explicit about the relationality of class—that is, the dependence of the haves upon the have-nots, and how hierarchical relations of power allow for the production of both economic advantages and status distinctions, at the expense of other classes. Bonnie Joe, for example, whose parents' work as sharecroppers was a fundamental determinant of her class status growing up, invoked class relations as she explained the exploitative labor relations that existed between landowners and sharecroppers: "the people the land belonged to—those are the ones that made the money off of it." Juanita Miller, the African American woman with diabetes, hypertension, and congestive heart failure whose story opened this book, expressed quite succinctly her understanding of how relations of power determine who draws the short straws in life and how both class and health are stratified: "I just think it's terrible that people with means can afford to live longer than people who don't have the means. . . . That's what it's all about. Money. It revolves around money. Who has the most checkers, I've found that's who has the better chance of surviving."

Finally, perspectives on the interconnections of class and race differed significantly between epidemiologists and some of the respondents who are living with heart disease. Epidemiologists almost invariably expressed concern over statistical confounding between class and race (but not with sex or gender), and I observed in interviews and at scientific meetings a continuing preoccupation with how to eliminate this technical conundrum. Epidemiologists frequently noted, for example, that adjusting for socioeconomic status "tends to wash out" much (but not all) of the disparities by race. They proposed hypotheses that African Americans and whites of equal education have more similar risk profiles than do African Americans from different socioeconomic circumstances. Many researchers thus appeared to understand the role of class in cardiovascular risk as *separable* and *independent* from that of race, such that their respective effects can be uncoupled through methodological techniques.

In contrast, the situated perspectives of people of color with heart disease significantly differed from this position. When asked how they would describe their *class* background, people of color with heart disease often interjected experiences related to *race*, or when asked about their *racial* identity, they recounted aspects of their *class* circumstances. For example, in response to my query about economic background, Rahel Clayton explained that, unlike many African Americans of that time, her family owned property, but that this economic advantage was diminished by their being African American and living in a racially segregated neighborhood. Similarly, several others described their families as "middle class" but qualified this: "In the end, however, we were black." That is, family income, occupational status, and relative wealth could never trump or overcome the disadvantages of their race. Other people of color I interviewed likewise consistently used more than one axis of difference or inequality to account for their biographical experiences and their health histories. When I asked whether being Latina made any difference at all for her health, for instance, Mabel Rodriguez stressed that she was in fact "a *poor* Mexican *woman*" (her own emphases)—that her gender and poverty mattered greatly, shaping her identity and lived reality as a Mexican in particular ways. Thus, when articulating the effects of *race* on cardiovascular health, many participants incorporated the effects of *class and gender* into their responses and repeatedly used *racial* indicators to give shape to their descriptions of their *gender and class* backgrounds. Such usage conveys the intimate linkages between the meanings of one dimension of difference to those of another and points to the lived intersections of race and class and gender.

Thus those living with heart disease argued that the conceptual and material distinctions between class, race, and gender are less meaningful—or are meaningful in different ways—than epidemiologists who aim to dissect their effects realize. Lay participants pointed out that the meanings of such socioeconomic indicators as income differ for people from different racial groups; only a few epidemiologists made this same observation.[4] Many researchers framed the "problem" in terms of how to *isolate* the distinct effects of class *from* race, but such a conception seems unable to portray accurately the biographical experiences and lived identities of those with heart disease. Instead, lay participants in their interviews underscored how race, class, and gender *intersect* and *interact with* one another.

Conclusion: The Paradox of Conceptions of Class

In contrast to their deep divisions on the subject of race, epidemiologists and lay people living with heart disease sounded quite similar in their multifaceted understandings of class and its significance for risks, resources, and health. They offered—unprompted—notions of the long-term and cumulative class-based advantages and disadvantages that systematically accrue to those positioned at different rungs on the socioeconomic ladder. They understood the class–health relationship as multiply realized—that is, class shapes and stratifies health through manifold pathways and mechanisms that can compound, interact with, and counteract one another.[5]

But despite this apparent consensus on the structural and social nature of class, some disagreements between epidemiologists and lay people emerged. First, people of color with heart disease provided more complex and nuanced understandings of class-based mechanisms and offered more sustained critiques of risk factor epidemiology and health promotion rhetoric. For example, my data indicate that "modifiable risk factors" such as smoking, obesity (and related measures such as body-mass index), physical activity, and diet are often used to "explain" some percentage of the "excess risk" of groups of color and lower socioeconomic status. Epidemiologists repeatedly noted that such groups have higher rates of high-fat and high-sodium diets, obesity, sedentary lifestyles, and smoking; lower levels of health knowledge and literacy; lower compliance with medical regimens; and inappropriate care seeking. The net effect of this epidemiologic practice is to discursively represent those risk factors as the products of *individualized* lack of knowledge, lifestyle choices, and the inappropriate use of health care.

Lay people I spoke with acknowledged that individual learning, self-education, and self-transformation are certainly possible and indeed often desirable. Yet, they continually pointed out there are multiple structural barriers to absorbing health knowledge and realizing its benefits through self-surveillance and lifestyle modification. They did not deny that differences in risk factor prevalence among groups of varying socioeconomic status are significant to cardiovascular health, or that cultural factors of various sorts play a part in shaping health behaviors that ultimately impact heart disease. Rather, their arguments focused on the deep, complicated, and layered nature of health inequalities and the strikingly disparate capacities of different individuals, groups, and communities to capitalize upon the health-related knowledges that proliferate or the potential gains to health status they offer.

Second, epidemiologists were almost uniformly consumed with the perceived conundrum of the confounding of race by class, and vice versa. That is, their own inclinations, and those of their discipline, to technically tease apart the health effects of class from those of race eclipsed lay people's argument that power relations in the contemporary United States couple these together in order to effect stratification. For their part, lay persons with heart disease clearly saw the relational nature of class, the different ways in which economic status and position can be characterized (capturing different salient aspects of class), and the inseparability and intersectionality of class with race and gender. Thus, epidemiologists' fixation on issues of measurement misses the complex, intertwined meanings that participants living with heart disease make of the class and racial gradients in health. Feminist scholars have widely argued that race and class, along with gender and multiple other dimensions of social difference, are highly intersectional.[6] Epidemiologists seemed largely unaware of such dynamics when asked to reflect on their inclusion of race and class and their interpretations of group differences.

These important rifts that underlie apparent agreement about the consequences of class for heart disease therefore yield a complex picture about epidemiologic and lay conceptions of class. On the one hand, epidemiologically and clinically inflected notions of individual responsibility and difference effect a kind of stratified biomedicalization. By understanding and studying humans as atomistic and individualized bodies, cardiovascular epidemiology attributes inequalities in cardiovascular risk to cultural, behavioral, and socioeconomic differences of individuals, rather than the product of socially constructed power relations between groups. The mobilization of race and socioeconomic status as markers of cardiovascular risk also serves to inscribe individuals' perceptions of themselves as "at risk" in racialized, classed, and gendered ways. In addition, this heightens people's sense that they must maintain particular vigilance to monitor, maintain, and intervene in their own health in accordance with contemporary biomedical imperatives. In biomedicalization, such individualized responsibilities extend to the accumulation and appropriate deployment of biomedical information and the assumption of proactive and neoliberal subjectivities in the pursuit of health. As a regime of power-knowledge, epidemiologic claims about "difference" govern relations between self and self, between self and others, within institutions and communities, and between self and state. In so doing, cardiovascular epidemiology often operates as a form of governmentality, furthers processes of stratified biomedicalization, and reproduces inequalities in cardiovascular health.

Yet on the other hand, researchers and people with heart disease largely concurred that class differences work through multiple *structural* dynamics—including access to medical care, health information, and nutritious foods; experiences of economic insecurity; constrained occupational and educational opportunities; and their lived environments—that then shape cardiovascular risk factors and behaviors. Both groups of participants viewed class inequality as a potentially modifiable aspect of social life and as processes that clearly mediate the effects of biological and genetic causes of heart disease. This perhaps is not surprising, given the significant (though often marginalized) traditions in epidemiology that focus on social determinants of health.[7] By providing explanations for disparities in heart disease rooted in the structural dynamics and consequences of class stratification, epidemiologists and lay people in my study for the most part eschewed individualistic accounts in favor of arguments that cardiovascular risk is shaped by local material contexts and societal economic policies and factors. This stands in marked contrast to their perspectives on sex and gender. As we will see in the next chapter, there were significant differences in the ways in which epidemiologic and experiential accounts frame cardiovascular risks in relation to gender.

5

The Dichotomy of Gender

As the last of the three dimensions of difference explored in this book, sex and gender pose an interesting counterpoint to race and class. The title of this chapter refers to two ways in which I found gender to be dichotomized. First, both epidemiologists and lay people alike do not question that gender and sex are binary in nature, and self-evidently so. But in a second sense, gender is viewed and constructed in fundamentally contrasting ways by epidemiologists and lay people. While epidemiologists overwhelmingly and consistently constructed gender differences in cardiovascular risk as attributable to biological, hormonal distinctions between men and women, people with heart disease viewed these differences as rooted in the structural effects of gendered relations of power and their intersections with race and class. In this chapter, therefore, I show how there are, on the one hand, significant agreements between epidemiologists and people living with heart disease on the *operationalization* of sex and gender, yet on the other, deep differences in how they believe "gender" as a dimension of difference should be *conceptualized.*

Sex and Gender as a Binary Category

The first dimension in which sex and gender are dichotomized is in their operationalization as a binary characteristic of individuals. Numerous feminist scholars have argued for the conceptual distinction between biologically determined or defined "sex" as "female" or "male," from the cultural and social processes that construct one as a "man" or "woman," or one's "gender."[1] Moreover, some also argue that this binary classification itself is a cultural construction and that given biological realities, it is more accurate to consider sex as a continuum, or at least as a categorical system of more than two groups.[2] But the epidemiologists and lay participants in my research clearly operationalized both sex and gender as dichotomous and self-evident; the categorical dilemmas encountered in the characterization of class background and in racial–ethnic identity were simply nonexistent here. My direct queries of both groups of participants revealed that "measuring" and "identifying" one's sex or gender were never at issue.

For instance, epidemiologists responded with genuine confusion when I asked them how they defined or measured "gender" or "sex," as illustrated by an exchange between me (JS) and Dr. Anita Yu (AY):

JS: Can we take a step back for a second? How do you conceive of the variable of gender or sex? How do you conceptualize it?

AY: Conceptualize what is so-called "woman" or "man"?

JS: Yes, or the variable of gender.

AY: A person who's not a man is a woman. It's just two levels of category. Are you asking—what are you asking?

Similarly, when I asked men and women with heart disease to "describe your gender identity," their responses reflected their perception of the query as bordering on the ridiculous. For example:

js: Okay. The other thing I wanted to ask you about is your gender. First of
all, how do you identify yourself in terms of gender?

sc: I'm a girl [laughs]!

These kinds of clumsy and awkward exchanges over the categorization
of sex and gender indicate the extent to which these dimensions of "difference" are seen as a matter of fact, hardly an issue for "measurement" or a
question of self-identification, as they are for race and social class. For both
groups of participants, gender categorization and identity were transparent
and obviously dichotomous. That there are but two categories of sex (female
or male) and of gender (one is "a woman or a man," or a "girl" or a guy) that
are exhaustive and mutually exclusive was clearly taken for granted.

A few epidemiologists acknowledged that the term "gender" is used
interchangeably with "sex," often as an alternative terminology thought
to be more politically correct. Its use is therefore an adaptation of the
scientific vocabulary to the sociopolitical context of the times without
altering the underlying conception itself. One such epidemiologist, Dr.
Lena Kelleher, for example, said, "I think it ['gender'] is the P.C. [politi-
cally correct] word to use, and I think that's another reason why maybe
more people in medicine will use 'gender,' too. That's sort of the correct
term to use. I don't know if there's a lot of thought put behind it. It's just
using another term." This mirrors a practice common in the biomedical and biological disciplines, as many have noted[3] and substantiated
through examinations of the literature.[4] This widespread use of "sex"
and "gender" as interchangeable terms and as reductionist attributes of
individuals largely preclude considerations of the interplay between—the
"entanglement" of—sex and gender and risk essentialist thinking about
the impact of such differences on disease.[5] In short, as the remainder
of this chapter shows, the lexical conflation of sex with gender (which
I indicate with the term "sex/gender")—and the reduction of gender to
sex that this practice effects—achieves a kind of gender-blindness, refut-
ing and rendering invisible the bodily harms of intersectional gendered
power relationships.

The Binary Conceptualization of "Gender"

The second way in which gender was dichotomized was in its conceptualization. On the one hand, epidemiologists almost uniformly understood the cardiovascular influence of gender as mediated through its biological and hormonal effects—the "estrogen connection," as one epidemiologist put it. In contrast, lay people with heart disease were inclined to attribute gender's impact on health to its significance as a dimension of social inequality with systematic and differential effects for women, particularly women of color. In so doing, lay participants pointed to the intersectional nature of sexism with racism and classism and their material effects on women's bodies and life chances. The following two subsections outline these aspects of the science–lay divide.

The "Estrogen Connection"

Binary, conflated, and essentializing constructions of both sex and gender clearly have consequences for epidemiologic practices that study the roles these differences play in heart disease risk. My interview and observational data indicate that sex/gender (again, as conflated with each other) was considered such a central axis of analysis because of its definition as a *biologically* meaningful difference. Epidemiologists regularly limited samples to just men or just women, stratified samples by sex, or collected data from both men and women but conducted statistical analyses separately for each sex. In epidemiologic conferences, presenters rarely explicitly justified engaging in such practices, but their interpretations of sex/gender–differentiated results most often relied on biological explanations. In interviews, when asked to explain the significance of sex or gender in heart disease causation, epidemiologists predominantly cited physiological differences between women and men.

In fact, prevailing themes related to sex and gender in these interviews were hormone replacement therapy and menopause—or as one epidemiologist put it, addressing "the estrogen connection." As Dr. Max Oliver saw the issue:

> Obviously of course we'll always look at [gender] and measure it, but yet I think there's very little evidence that the response to diet and lifestyle variables really differs in any important way by gender. . . . There are specific reasons to think that there are differences such as looking at hormones in men and women—obviously that, there's likely to be some differences.

Here, Dr. Oliver juxtaposed the questionable existence of gender differences in behavioral risk factors—that is, *culturally* and *socially* influenced variations in diet, smoking, physical activity, and the like—with the near-certainty that *biological*, hormonal differences do, in contrast, have a significant impact. Later in the interview, he elaborated that as a general rule, "in most situations, I don't think it's necessary to have equal power, sufficient [statistical] power in men and women separately," except in a condition like heart disease where "the disease really seemed inherent[ly] to be behaving differently in men and women. . . . Where there [is] a strong hormonal contribution, then in that situation you might want to have adequate power in the separate groups." Researchers I interviewed and observed frequently mentioned the "basic epidemiological fact" that women tend to develop heart disease at lower rates than men at any age or do so later than men by approximately ten years. Epidemiologists' motivations to explore the possible mechanisms for this fact, then, largely drive their study of the ways in which heart disease is hormonally, physiologically, and biologically sexed. Rarely did epidemiologists discuss at any length or even invoke alternative understandings of gender differences and their effects on cardiovascular risk.

It would seem that highly publicized clinical trial results[6] showing that hormone replacement therapy (HRT) is not effective in lowering women's risk for heart disease (in fact, HRT increased risk of some cardiovascular events) would potentially threaten the stability of the "estrogen connection." In fact, two epidemiologists raised this issue in my interviews with them. However, of these, one repeated "the basic epidemiological fact" that women tend to develop heart disease later than men. She then added that women often have other medical conditions concurrently, reminded me that women often misperceive that their greatest health threat is breast cancer when in fact it is heart disease, and voiced her feeling that had exclusion criteria for the trial been more strict, its results might have been different. Thus she reacted by reiterating the very statistical basis for the hypothesis that male–female differences in heart disease arise from biological differences of sex, stressing that heart disease is still a major problem for women, and providing an alternative explanation of the negative results of recent clinical trials. The second epidemiologist responded by stating that "it hasn't been discounted that the woman's natural hormone milieu is one of the things that protects [sic] her" and by arguing that perhaps HRT is not as efficacious as "natural" estrogen, thereby further reinforcing the construction of sex/gender differences as biological.

Thus, inside epidemiology, the default construction of "gender" is as sex, as a biological characteristic. This construction is an exceedingly persistent and robust one. Researchers referred to the multiple, infinitesimal, and perhaps immeasurable biological differences between the two sexes. Given this, then, epidemiologic techniques of limiting study samples to just one sex, stratifying samples, and analyzing data separately by sex represent the best ways to account for such complex and potentially unknowable differences. Therefore constructions of sex differences, again seen to be interchangeable with gender differences, shape not only ideas about cardiovascular risk but also the consideration of study designs and analytic methodologies used in the conduct of heart disease research. In these ways, representations of innate, "natural" differences of sex shape the distribution of research dollars and resources along particular lines.[7]

In marked contrast, men and women with heart disease very rarely mentioned cardiovascular risks rooted in biological differences of sex. The sole exception among the lay participants was Sharon Chavez, who spoke extensively and somewhat fearfully of her understanding of the consequences of her sex for her cardiovascular risk:

I went for a regular checkup at a clinic and the doctor told me . . . that women can have heart attacks after menopause, and because they've been shielded by estrogen, when they do have a heart attack, if they do, it can kill them—unlike a man. . . . And he said that I had hypertension and that I was at high risk for dying. . . . I would like to be healthier so that when I do become menopausal, I don't just fall over and die. I mean, after the doctor told me, I saw this ad with this beautiful older woman and she was a corpse, and [the ad] said, "You know, if you're a woman and have a heart attack [after menopause], this can happen to you." . . . It was an ad for taking care of yourself so that you don't wind up like that if you're female, because a lot of people don't know that. I didn't know that.

Ms. Chavez expressed a high level of alarm about the increased risk that menopause poses for women, and especially for those women like her who already have preexisting risk factors for heart disease such as hypertension. Her concern, originating in warnings from her physician and fueled by public service announcements on television, was that the reduction in estrogen levels accompanying menopause would produce a sudden and precipitous increase in risk. Her understanding of the role of sex and gender in cardiovascular risk, then, was clearly mediated by the biomedicalized construction of male–female difference as hormonal, or biological, in nature.

However, while Ms. Chavez's account was striking in its level of alarm and anxiety, none of the other participants living with heart disease whom I interviewed invoked biological constructions of gender as sex to account for their cardiovascular risk. Instead, their discourses regarding the causes of heart disease are peppered with notions of gendered dynamics and roles, and how these intertwine with experiences of racialization and classism. I examine such structural and intersectional constructions of gender next.

The Intersectionality of Gender, Race, and Class

Amidst epidemiologists' predominantly *biological* construction of gender differences in cardiovascular risk, a few researchers did speculate that some *social* aspects of gender relations may plausibly affect cardio-vascular health. Three epidemiologists I interviewed expressed some ambivalence about the "estrogen connection." For instance, Dr. Lena Kelleher argued, "I am just very uncomfortable using the word 'sex.' For me again, it's 'Oh, we're going to interpret these findings in biological terms.' . . . [But] why would my body be operating very differently than a [man's]?" Dr. Sheila Morris, another epidemiologist who questioned the almost exclusive biological construction of sex/gender, commented:

> There are definite things we know are biologically different between . . . [the] two sex groups. And it's easy just to [attribute] every-thing off to that biological difference without actually exploring or think-ing about some of the other possibilities that could explain for it. . . . So there can be a mechanism that acts independently of biological differ-ences. . . . Until it's explored, I think the safest bet is to give everything that you possibly think that accounts for the differences and not just restrict yourself to what you think is the easiest answer, because it may be totally wrong and I think it's misleading in medical research, and especially things that are implied in terms of policy to make sweeping generaliza-tions that haven't been explored yet. And then for every paper to echo the same sentiment, so people begin to think it's fact, and it's not . . . I think that's real frustrating in doing gender research. . . . [In] racial research . . . I think . . . people realize that there are so many things, whereas in gender, biology is the easy explanation and not many people contest it.

When pressed, Dr. Morris speculated that processes related to gender discrimination and perhaps the stress of both attempting to conform to as well as resist normative gender roles could be reasonably hypothesized to affect cardiovascular health.

Additionally, three other researchers very briefly discussed the pos-sibility that gendered behaviors—such as those related to social support, responses to stress or hostility, and health behaviors—could mediate rela-tionships between certain risk factors and heart disease risk. For example,

Dr. Carolyn Munson suggested that the possibility of these gender differences, combined with the paucity of information about heart disease risk in women, warranted separate statistical analyses for women and men, even if no variations in disease outcomes were expected or found:

> Certainly you want studies to include both men and women, or you want good studies on men and good studies on women of varying social class and race–ethnicity. It no longer makes sense to really combine them because even if . . . you haven't found gender differences in the outcome, there's still such a dearth of prevalence or incidence data on, you know, kind of the absolute values of health behavior and risk factors in women . . . that you don't want to combine them because the levels are very different. The age of onset of health behaviors are very different. So, you know, to me . . . you want things separate by gender . . . because there are differences, there are probably different mechanisms. Certainly, you know, hormonal status, menopause—things that are gender-specific—have to be considered in cardiovascular risk. And just knowledge in starting to present all the information for women is really important because that descriptive epidemiology hasn't even been done on a number of groups of women.

As she alluded to here and subsequently elaborated later in the interview, Dr. Munson considered the possibility that gendered differences in "attitudes and beliefs and knowledge"—that is, behavioral factors related to gender rather than to biological distinctions of sex—may contribute to the male–female differences in the onset and incidence of heart disease. In her view, however, such gendered differences tend to be mediated through health behaviors and are articulated only briefly amidst a much larger and extended discussion of biological differences.

Similarly, in my observations at scientific meetings, while the overwhelming majority of researchers either implicitly or explicitly attributed gender disparities to differences of sex, a very few did present research on the effects of gendered social relations. For instance, one study investigated the cardiovascular effects of multiple roles that African American women fulfilled at work, in the household, and as caregivers. But while I did encounter several examples of such alternative conceptualizations, they were isolated instances. Moreover, scientists expressed little hope that the conceptual work to develop expanded notions of gender differences will ever become a priority for the mainstream epidemiologic research agenda. Biological differences between women and men are perceived as so clear-cut and potently related to heart disease as to displace scientific inquiries into the social and cultural dimensions of gender.

In stark contrast, participants of color with heart disease widely viewed risks as rooted in the *structural* effects of gendered relations of power and their intersections with race and class. They traced multiple manifestations of such gendered, racialized, and classed dynamics to inequalities in the distribution of cardiovascular risk between women and men. The dynamics most commonly cited include sex and racial segregation in the labor market, gender discrimination in the workplace and in health care, the gendered and racialized division of social reproduction, and the experiences and consequences of domestic violence.

First, as we saw in chapter 3, almost all of the women I interviewed who had been or are currently in the workforce described interlocking dynamics of race, class, and gender that stratified their educational opportunities as working-class women of color and that structure a racially and sex-segregated labor force and market. Most of them worked in low-paying, insecure jobs, with limited or no opportunities for advancement or control over their working conditions, their hours, or the work process. For instance, Juanita Miller and Carmen Hernandez worked as low-wage, low-skilled office workers; Bonnie Joe had been a seamstress; Mercedes Portes had worked as a seamstress and cleaning offices; Yolanda Montenegro just started working part-time as a hotel desk clerk; and Mabel Rodriguez had worked as a housekeeper, home health aide, and a cannery worker and in food service. Social processes and forces of racism and racialization, classism, and sexism intersect to define and structure the terms under which people of different classes, races, and sexes are made to do different kinds of work. Particularly with the shift from a manufacturing economy with relatively better-paying jobs to a service economy with increasingly bifurcated occupational and income hierarchies, such dynamics contribute to what the political scientist Frances Fox Piven and the sociologist Richard Cloward call "the rise of a predominantly female and minority service sector proletariat."[8]

Second, once in the workplace, many of the participants had to contend with the assumptions and ideologies of gender roles in male-dominated work environments. Ms. Chavez, for example, observed that

> women are treated a little more shabbily than men are and they're expected to be perfect. . . . Men are socialized to expect help from people around them, and women . . . have to be perfect people or, you know, they're not a good person. And that's changed a lot, but it's still true. And that's pretty stressful. It's a kind of prejudice. . . . If you're assertive, then you're not a good person or you're considered aggressive, even if it's not so. If you get angry, it's not okay. That adds to stress, too—the way you're treated and how you have to deal with things because you're female. I've always thought that I could just be a person and not have to worry that I was a female, and be treated as an equal. . . . Applying for a job as a chef and being told that chefs are men . . . it's really aggravating. It makes you fume.

As Ms. Chavez understood it, heart disease was a "stress-related illness" and people can "have a much greater risk of . . . stress-related illnesses because of the way they're treated." Thus she saw women, as well as "people of different races," as especially vulnerable to conditions like heart disease because of their experiences in gender hierarchies.

Likewise, Ms. Miller encountered a great deal of resistance from her own family when she first began working outside the home as a young mother in the 1960s. Such experiences of gender discrimination exacerbated the impact on her health of managing work and household duties, contributing to her heart disease, and they exemplify the deep intersections of race and gender in relation to work and home. When I asked her if being a woman made things different for her, she responded:

> It made it harder. . . . Well, just the fact that I'm black. I was black back then and female back then which, you know, all these rights and things weren't easily acknowledged back then, you know. . . . I wanted to go to work. . . . [My ex-husband] refused. He said I could never work. . . . I didn't do nothing but watch TV and stay pregnant. . . . That's how he wanted it—barefoot and pregnant. . . . But I just got so tired of that. I said, "I'm going to work anyway." . . . He said, "I tell you what, if you go to work you gonna have to start cleaning, washing, doing everything." . . . I got lucky and got a job as a file clerk. . . . He wouldn't help me do anything after that. . . . He was determined for me not to work and made it as hard as possible.

Here, Ms. Miller highlighted the interconnections between her gender and race, pointing out that several dimensions of social power intersected and worked synergistically, rather than independently, to create particular kinds of experiences and risks for her.

Moreover, as Ms. Hernandez pointed out, these gendered ideologies about work can also have consequences for the diagnosis, treatment, and the social experience of accounting for heart disease among women:

> How doctors treat you . . . they can understand a man being overweight because . . . they might think, "Well, he's got a family to take care of. He's got a stressful job. He's got this, he's got that. Maybe that's why he's overweight. Maybe that's why he's got hypertension." For a woman, I think that they think, "Well, there's no reason in the world why she should be like that." . . . Possibly what they think—and this is only a perception on my part—is that we don't have that thing of having to be the provider, even though as a single woman I have to provide for myself. . . . And number two, why I can't do something about—I mean that I should be able to have more willpower to do something about my weight because I don't have any outside factors, you know, family or job or whatever stresses to deal with. . . . Sometimes when they make an

off-hand remark or something like that, and then you think, "Well, hey! But why it should be any different for a woman than a man?"

More dramatically, one of the most glaring forms of gender domination—and the cardiovascular risk posed by it—emerges from the alarmingly prevalent narratives of domestic violence and its reverberations for parenting and family relations. Lynn Fielding, for example, understood stress to exacerbate her hypertension, and she enumerated a litany of particularly gendered contributors to the stress in her life:

> What makes me tense is my past, in that I can't change it because I was married, divorced—it will be twenty-one years in January. My husband used to beat me. . . . Three children, divorce and then [to] have them taken away from you—I don't know if that's a thing that I'll never get over, or is that the reason why I got hypertension, or if I was going to have it if I had a normal life anyway. . . . I worry about that all the time. I worry that the kids—they know me, but blame me for it. . . . That bothers me, even today.

Third, gender's intersections with class and race become a significant structural contributor to cardiovascular distress in the unequal division of both paid and unpaid reproductive labor. Feminist scholars have termed this kind of labor social reproduction, referring to the array of activities involved in the cultural, social, and physical maintenance of people, families, and households on a daily and intergenerational basis.[9] The occupations of several of the women I interviewed exemplify the kind of service work that results from the commodification of reproductive labor: Ms. Portes' work as a seamstress and janitor, and Ms. Rodriguez's labor as a housekeeper, home health aide, and food service worker. Women of color are disproportionately employed to carry out such lower-level "public" reproductive labor.

The gendered and classed dynamics of social reproduction are also manifested in the "private" sphere: Participants with heart disease speak of the cardiovascular effects of the dual burden of fulfilling duties at work as well as family and household responsibilities at home. Three of the women, Yolanda Montenegro, Lee Tsan, and Geline Laroya, assumed primary responsibility for caregiving and sometimes financial support for their aging parents, a frequently all-encompassing and emotionally exhausting commitment motivated by the often twinned obligations of love and their family's—and their own—expectations of the role of daughters. Although they all appreciated the opportunity to have cared for their parents, they readily acknowledged the stress and physical toll of their experiences and directly attributed their cardiovascular conditions to them.

Many of the other women I interviewed are single mothers who described extensively the burdens of providing financially for their families and solo parenting of their children. For example, in chapter 3, we heard from Ms. Rodriguez that the strain of both working and raising her children on her own—"all this running around, all this worrying about money, money, money"—contributed to her high blood pressure. As she elaborated:

> My husband was never around. . . . So I had to do everything myself. . . . I think that's what developed me for having high blood pressure. . . . I had to start going to work . . . to support [my children]. . . . I started getting sick. . . . I was getting only minimum wages . . . $3 an hour. You can't live on $3. . . . I had to go through all kinds of strings because . . . [my husband] would hide [income] from me, not to pay child support. . . . I think that has a lot to do, too, with high blood pressure. You're constantly on the go. You have no time for yourself. And it's hard. And I had no one around to help me. So it made it worse. . . . I think all of that is what caused me to have the high blood pressure that I'm having right now. . . . I think it affected me all—my whole body.

Even those mothers who shared parenting and household duties with others found that the gendered division of that labor was highly unequal. In fact, Diane Jamison believed that this is a major reason why the cardiovascular risks for women and men differ in significant ways:

My husband works a full-time job. I also work a full-time job. But for some reason, he goes home and when he's home, it's like total down time. He gets to just relax and watch television and possibly help my son with his home- work. . . . And I realize that when I go home, I don't sit down. I immediately put my bag away, wash my hands, go in the kitchen and start cooking dinner. And it's just like that until about 9 o'clock. So, I'm thinking, god! . . . if I could really work all day and go home and just relax, I'd be a different person. And so I was trying to make him see the difference, and he was like, "Well, I do things, too." Yeah, but it's not the same. Mine just is constant. Because even on week- ends, I mean you may mow the lawn, okay, great, whatever. But I have to sort of oversee everything else getting done. . . . Of course there are some marital relationships that have changed the norm, but they are few. . . . Women still do much more at home. And so if you add work to that then you have much more, and I think that, to me, is a contributing factor [to the risk for heart disease].

Ms. Tsan concurred:

I think that the dynamics going on in our home [are] that I tend to take on everything. So then I tend to be the worried one [laughs], while [my husband] says, "Oh, she's going to take care of it." So he's not going to worry about it. "Oh, she's planning that," or "She's calling that person or calling—" you know. . . . It's a gender thing. . . . It's a lot of pressure. I think so. And then I'm sure that's the stress portion of the blood pressure.

Moreover, as Ms. Laroya elaborated further, some practical consider- ations in response to gender inequity in work and pay further promote the unequal division of reproductive labor:

I think that as a mother, it's not myself that I count first. It's my children and then my husband, even though on that score, you know, if you asked me intellectually, I would respond and say, "Oh, me first before him." But just roles: . . . men have more possibility to get higher-paying positions in terms of practical questions about how your family's finances are set up. You know, you would tend to give in more, you know, to subordinate yourself more to the situation that allows for more income to be brought in. You know, like I wouldn't jeopardize my husband's work standing by insisting that he do more of the doctor's visits for my kids or the sports—driving around and stuff like that. . . . I would tend to look more for a job situation set-up that would allow me to have a little bit more flexibility than that. You know, so it's like you're just set up to think of others first. . . . The self-motivation [to exercise and engage in other forms of risk reduction] is already a struggle. . . . And then I think the conditions around your role as a mother . . . that contributes to it greatly.

Thus, in addition to gendered power relations in the workplace and the commodified forms of reproductive labor, women viewed the gendered division of social reproduction in the home as a significant source of cardiovascular risk. These personal experiences are more widely shared by many women, as evidenced in recent studies of how work in the home is still unequally distributed between women and men, with women spending more time, taking on more tasks, and multitasking in ways that affect their well-being.[10]

Furthermore, the intersections of gender with race in reproductive labor create chronic stresses that are unique to women of color. Ms. Jamison pointed this out to me:

In all honesty, a lot of African American women, and possibly other women of color . . . we live and deal with a lot of stress. And I think sometimes that it's not always internal factors, but external factors. I think that we're constantly in this feeling of being tense, and I think that that sort of contributes to it. . . . Internal meaning more like what we eat—and I think that our diets play a part in it, you know, what we eat—lots of food and possibly greasy foods, and being overweight. Those kinds of things I think contribute definitely, but I think even more so, external factors.

Ms. Jamison then gave two examples of these "external" factors that she felt contributed to the differential stress-related hypertension of

African American women. First, she related that her son was labeled as being "overly aggressive" by his teachers who then maintained that he had learning disabilities and needed to be tracked into special education classes. She fought this label throughout his childhood and insisted that he remain in the mainstream classroom (he is now, she noted with satisfaction, doing well in college). Second, when Ms. Jamison's son was a teenager, he was riding a bike he received as a birthday gift when he was stopped by police who thought the bike had been stolen. Significantly, these experiences happened to her son; thus the intersections of race with gender are reflected not only in her experience as a mother of color but also in those of her son as a young African American male. As Ms. Jamison summed up:

I mean, just those kind of things—and they're like compounded daily— those, I think, contribute greatly. I think a lot of women and people of color—and men—have to deal with that. And I think that if you don't have the education to know that you have rights and that you don't have to deal with it, it's even more stressful. I really thought about the number of mothers who would have said, "God! I trust this teacher and they're saying that my kid has disabilities. Let me do what they say to do." And that really scared me and kept me up like lots of nights. And even now I have flashbacks, like, God! that was so scary. And I realized that it probably happens a lot. So those kind of factors really contribute to feeling like you're just constantly having to battle, you know? That's just a hard feeling to have to deal with all the time.

Such experiences led Ms. Jamison to view her gender and its contribution to her hypertension as secondary to that of race: "In all honesty, if I had to say which was more of a hindrance, being a woman or being African American, I would have to say being African American. . . . Race is just the bigger issue, you know. And then, being female is the second issue."[11] Other women of color, however, seemed to disagree. Ms. Hernandez, for example, pointed out that gendered assumptions made accounting for heart disease more difficult for her as a woman per se, but not because she was Latina: "I think just being a woman, you know, makes it extremely difficult—just having to deal with everyday life, you know. I don't necessarily think it's a case of being a Latina woman, but just having to deal with a very male-oriented society." Thus while most of the women most of the time spoke of the intersecting and compounding burdens of gender with race and class, they also engaged in a kind of parsing of which of their experiences and perceptions could be attributed to their race and which to gender. It is significant that epidemiologists likewise attempted to tease out the "independent" effects of, say, race and class on health status. Both of these phenomena, I argue, reflect Western scientific epistemology and its tendencies to dichotomize and disaggregate, and to reduce phenomena to elemental, presumably independent and separate parts as a means of understanding.

The women with heart disease I interviewed understood gender relations as relations of power and experienced their manifestations as embodied sources of distress, grief, regret, and anger that they explicitly constructed as significant risks to their cardiovascular health. They understood these experiences as mediated through idioms of stress, anxiety, and depression—all associated with cardiovascular disease incidence and outcomes. These experiences were, by and large, narrated by women participants and not by men. However, this does not mean that gender does not shape the lives of men in ways that impact their cardiovascular risks. Intersectionality theorists, as well as feminist and masculinity theorists, have long argued that "gender" does not equal women[12] (much as "race" does not equal people of color, and "class" the poor and working class). For example, as the sociologist Elianne Riska argues, the domain of heart disease historically has focused on the costs of masculinity to middle-class men's health.[13] With etiologic theories centered on constructs like Type A personality and hardiness, medical and public discourse clearly implicated gender as a cardiovascular risk for men.

But such constructs, notions of masculinity, or the disproportionate burden of heart disease on men did not arise in my interviews with lay people, even though I tried always to be careful to pose questions even-handedly (asking about experiences and effects for both "men and women," for instance). Perhaps my participants' focus on the impacts of gender for women, then, signals something about how being on the margins makes certain social arrangements more visible, how what one sees can depend on where one stands. The sociologist Lynn Weber suggests that "how we interpret our 'truths'—our lives, the meanings we take from our experiences—is also revealed as much in our silences and the things we take for granted as in our spoken words. Those silences are most likely to occur in areas where we experience privilege."[14] Indeed, one of the participants, Ms. Jamison, expressly reflected in chapter 3 that those categories considered to be "the norm," "the base group," and the default enjoy the privileges of invisibility and normativity. In the specific stories of gender that many of my participants told, men were privileged—at least relatively speaking. Thus the women with heart disease whom I interviewed clearly saw their bodies and their ways of knowing as implicated in structural patterns of gender oppression that had material consequences for their health. Even while gender identity seemed self-apparent, uncomplicated, and manifestly binary to them, it did not lead to biological constructions of gender as sex, nor did it displace social constructions of gender, as it seemed to do for epidemiologists. The lived and embodied experiences of gender power and inequality clearly implicate structural notions of gender inequality that act, in concert with other dimensions of "difference," as critical sources of cardiovascular risk.

Conclusion

In sum, sex and gender initially seemed the least problematic of the three dimensions of social power, at least on the issue of *operationalization*. Epidemiologists readily explained how they think about class and race as variables, why they believe them to be important or not to the study of cardiovascular risk, and in what ways. People with heart disease similarly described in detail their class backgrounds and racial–ethnic identities and often invoked the fluidity and "messiness" of those categories in lived experience. But the operationalization of sex and gender, in contrast, was unambiguously and uncontestedly seen as binary and transparent, and as categorically unproblematic.

However, analyzing the *conceptualization* of sex and gender reveals striking divergences between the constructions of epidemiologists and those of lay people. The role of sex and gender differences in heart disease causation was usually interpreted by scientists as composed largely of hormonal differences, a construction that has historically proven to be extremely robust and particularly effective in reifying fundamental dichotomies between the two biological sexes.[15] Epidemiologists' use of "gender" as a more politically correct alternative to "sex," a prevalent practice in the biomedical and biological disciplines and literature, had the effect of equating the two. Their understanding of *gender* as synonymous with the biological differences of *sex* thus contributes to naturalizing and routinizing their conflation. Their use of the term "gender" in such ways effectively rendered their science gender-blind—neglecting the toll that social, hierarchical constructions of gender, the institutional and everyday practices of inequality built upon them, and their deep intersections with racial and class stratification had on psyches, bodies, and life chances. For those with heart disease, the "risk" of gender lay not in its reference to sex differences but instead was rooted in a society structured by normative ideals of gender roles and intersectional power relations, including the gendered, racialized, and classed division of paid and reproductive labor, gender discrimination, and domestic violence.

* * *

Chapters 3 through 5 have dwelled on scientific and lay thinking about the impacts of race, class, and sex and gender on heart disease, and various angles of what emerged as a science–lay divide in their understandings of what exactly about social differences influence health. Lay people with heart disease asserted the links between their health and the manner in which their social relationships and environments were racialized, classed, and gendered in complex, layered, and—critically important—*intersectional* ways. They viewed themselves as members of *groups* and their positions in society as *relational*. Their perspectives thus largely reflect the intersectionality argument that race, class, and gender

> are historically specific, socially constructed *systems of oppression*; they are *power relationships* . . . in which one group exerts control over another, securing its position of dominance in the system, and in which substantial material resources . . . are at stake. . . . [They] are not just rankings of socially valued resources—who has *more* education, income, or prestige. They are power relationships: who exerts power and control over whom; how the privilege of some results from the exploitation of others.[16]

The lay participants in my study understood their lived experiences as marked by the ways in which representations and ideologies of "difference" shape the histories of social relations and structural dynamics *between* their own and other groups. Health inequalities emerge as the effect of these larger social relations and structural contexts on oppressed populations. Race, social class, and gender mattered in their lives and to their health because they act synergistically to shape the conditions into which they were born, the opportunities they had throughout their life course, the problems or risks they encountered at different stages of life, and their treatment by other people and institutions. Inequalities in access to resources like knowledge, money, power, prestige, and social connections—effected through social relations and structures—influenced multiple health outcomes, including cardiovascular ones, and therefore act as fundamental causes of disease.[17]

In contrast, the constructions of "difference" circulating in cardiovascular epidemiology tended to cultivate the notion that any health inequalities which happen to fall along racial, class, or gender lines must be due to individual biological or behavioral characteristics because their causes are not viewed as socially skewed or the result of relational dynamics of power.

The essentializing practices I have described in epidemiologic knowledge production accomplish three things that contribute to social hierarchy. First, they further stabilize the notion that "race," "class," and "gender" refer to features of and dynamics occurring within *individual* bodies, rather than to social relations characterized by inequality and power among differently defined groups. Second, they construct and naturalize supposed differences between those categories of bodies. Epidemiologic practices render risk an essentialized attribute of raced, classed, and sexed bodies and construct those bodies as "problems" and points of intervention. And third, the selective inclusion of social differences as intrinsic attributes of individuals achieves the strategic exclusion of structural forces and the obscuring of the social relations of power that produce health inequalities.

Through such processes and effects, epidemiologic conventions and practices can be seen as resonating with and mutually reinforcing ideological discourses about the place and effects of race, class, and gender that exist within the sciences and permeate contemporary U.S. culture. And as the philosopher and gender scholar Iris Marion Young observes, "The categories according to which people are identified as the same or different . . . carry and express relations of privilege and subordination, the power of some to determine for others how they will be named, what differences are important for what purposes."[18] In the United States, the meanings attached to race, class, and gender—and to specific racial, class, and gender groups—both underwrite epidemiologic tools for knowing and intervening in individuals and populations and structure particular histories of experiences and life conditions that in turn shape exposure to injury and disease and access to resources. In these ways, understandings of racial, class, and gender differences and disparities in cardiovascular epidemiology tend to maintain existing structures of privilege and distributions of wealth and resources.

Thus the interplay between socially constructed discourses on difference and the material relations they structure and through which they become consequential produce people's positions within hierarchical orders. Race, class, and gender privilege or disadvantage are social phenomena that mutually construct, reproduce, and synergistically oper- ate to structure forms of social organization that shape daily life, from educational and employment segregation, to encounters with the agents and agencies of the state (police, welfare, health care), to the private lives of families and households. In turn, these tightly bundled and interlock- ing forms of social organization, practices, and institutions constitute the everyday worlds that help to shape epidemiologists' and lay people's perceptions of the dynamics of race, class, and gender in general, and with respect to health and cardiovascular risk in particular.

Yet, much of what lay people feel and know in their bodies undermines their cardiovascular health becomes decontextualized, oversimplified, and erased in epidemiology. This erasure is consequential because epidemiol- ogy remains our most commonly used and socially credible optic with which to "see" and ascertain disease risks and causes. The conceptions of difference constructed from embodied and lived experiences highlight some of the incompatibilities that can arise when epidemiologists attempt to measure and study socially constructed relations and intersections of power in scientifically manageable ways. Such efforts are premised on principles and methods that work to identify and separate out the effects of different determinants on what are most often conceived of as indi- vidual health outcomes. As a result, although epidemiologists are able to articulate more structural views on social class—a dimension of differ- ence they clearly locate in the "external" and social environment—they persist in interpreting gender as a biological characteristic and race as a cultural attribute of individuals. They also either neglect or actively work to tease apart the intertwining of multiple dimensions of inequality. In short, through its treatment of the intersecting processes of racial, class, and gender marginalization, exclusion, and inequity, epidemiology enacts projects of stratified biomedicalization and stratified biopolitics. In the following chapter, I explore further why, and how, this is so.

6

Individualizing "Difference" and the Production of Scientific Credibility

Scientific practices as well as their products—scientific claims, facts, and the content of what counts as "science"—bear the imprint of social, political, historical, and economic forces. In previous chapters, I described epidemiologists' and lay people's accounts of the effects of race, class, and gender on cardiovascular risk and disease causation. In this chapter, I turn my attention to the paradigms, practices, and technologies that govern epidemiologic research on heart disease, in order to illuminate the linkages between how the science is practiced—under what conditions and constraints, and with what tools—and the content of the scientific claims being produced.

In particular, I try to make sense of two puzzles: The first is that even though epidemiologists *think* about race, class, and gender in very *different* ways, the discipline as a whole *treats* and incorporates these differences in research in largely *similar* ways. Little about race seems to be natural or settled in the world of epidemiology: neither its measurement, nor its validity, nor its meaning. In contrast, the meanings of class and its significance for health are relatively well established (although best practices for measuring it are not). And finally, the practice of equating gender difference to biological sex is uncontroversial and unremarkable. Despite such variations, however, I found that epidemiology treats and manages racial, class, and gender differences in very analogous ways, as individual-level attributes whose inclusion is viewed as necessary and routine. A second puzzle I also address is the ritualized and ubiquitous practice of individualizing social differences and including them in research, even though this practice is seen by many within (and outside) the epidemiologic community as a conceptually suspect and methodologically inadequate custom.

I argue that this process of epidemiologic individualization—the "usual suspects" approach I introduced in the opening of this book—allows researchers to satisfy a number of contingencies that must be met in order to achieve and maintain scientific credibility. That is, epidemiologists continually (if only provisionally) define the "usual suspects" approach as the "right tool for the job" and a "good enough" means to get their work done.[1] Specifically, the "usual suspects" approach helps epidemiologists comply and cope with certain requirements, mandates, and constraints. As such, not only does the use of individualized sociodemographic variables come to be routinized, but it in turn institutionalizes particular conceptions of human, bodily "differences" in cardiovascular epidemiology, ideas about what constitutes disease "risks" and "causes," and how inequalities in heart disease can be addressed.

The "Usual Suspects" Approach and Its Consequences

As described in the preceding chapters, epidemiologists overwhelmingly operationalized differences of race, class, and gender as individualized, unitary, demographic attributes of racial categories, socioeconomic status, and sex.[2] Both observational and interview data indicate that these variables were routinely and often uncritically used to limit or describe study samples, as well as to stratify and adjust results. Researchers referred to their inclusion as just something everyone has to do, to the "holy trinity" of race, sex, and age as absolutely requisite variables in statistical analyses. As Dr. Carolyn Munson catalogued,

> Well, it's hard to believe that you wouldn't ask [about these variables]—I mean you have to ask gender if you have both. . . . You have to ask race/ethnicity . . . unless you've limited it to a homogeneous race/ethnicity group. You need a measure of socioeconomic status, otherwise . . . the interrelationship between ethnicity and social class is going to be confused.

In presentations of research methods and results, multiple scientists I observed spoke of controlling for "the usual suspects," "traditional risk factors," or "traditional demographic risk factors" as shortcut references to the ritualized adjustment for race, socioeconomic status, and sex. This matter-of-fact, habitual mention of including and controlling for the usual suspects without any explicit rationale indicates a practice that is now so taken for granted as to be a standard operating procedure with which epidemiologists must comply.

As I outlined in the introductory chapter, I argue that the "usual suspects" approach has important consequences for research on the etiology of heart disease and the health effects of social differences. First, the routinized inclusion of the "usual suspects" reinforces individualistic dimensions of race, socioeconomic status, and sex as scientifically legitimate and appropriate ways to think about what I assert are group distinctions and social dynamics. As a result, the conceptual devolution of social inequalities to individual traits of race, socioeconomic status, and sex becomes increasingly taken for granted and institutionalized in epidemiologic analyses.

Second, these individualized variables very often serve as first-resort and final explanations for any differences in outcomes seen among population groups. I observed that in cases where these "usual suspects" could at least partially account for group differences in outcomes, epidemiologists perceived this not as a phenomenon to be further investigated but as an expected result, precisely because of the construction of these sociodemographic variables as the usual suspects. But as one epidemiologist pointed out, adjusting for race, socioeconomic status, and sex in fact may "adjust away" the very disparities and distinctions to which epidemiologists should attend. That is, if variations in risk and incidence may be attributable to differences in the composition of populations, the "usual suspects" approach may in fact erase evidence of this by smoothing out and statistically equalizing demographic divergences from place to place. In turn, such an erasure serves to focus causal, etiologic investigations on factors *other* than the effects of race, social class, and sex/gender. As Dr. Lena Kelleher explained, social inequalities such as minority status and social class are not considered to be "the real cause" of cardiovascular risk and disease; instead, adjusting for their effects through the inclusion of the "usual suspects" is "taken as the first step" in analyses geared toward evaluating other potential causal dynamics. Any statistically significant results obtained from research aimed at investigating sociodemographic disparities are then used as additional confirmation of the necessity to control for such differences in other epidemiologic work.

A third consequence of the "usual suspects" practice is that it eliminates the opportunity to explore *intersections* among race, social class, and gender. For example, as several epidemiologists explained, investigations of racial differences in cardiovascular disease and risk would likely control for the effects of socioeconomic status. In that case, then, interactions between race and socioeconomic status rarely enter the analytic lens given that confounding between the two variables is of much greater concern.

Finally, when epidemiologists did study sociodemographic variations, the "usual suspects" approach encouraged them to make assumptions about what mechanisms produced those variations, rather than directly and explicitly investigate a range of possible race-, class-, and gender-related dynamics. For example, I observed that epidemiologists whose results diverged by race often proposed other kinds of differences—cultural, socioeconomic, and physiological—as explanations for those racial variations, often without, or as a substitute for, actually studying those differences directly. Consequently, the very variables that are being used as controls fade from the investigational arena and become technical details and routines warranting only a general mention in describing analytic procedures, rather than the focus of study in and of themselves. Measures of categorical race, socioeconomic status, and sex are conceived as technically important for statistical adjustment but much less often as substantively interesting *in and of themselves.*

I argue that the cumulative consequence of the "usual suspects" approach in cardiovascular epidemiology is therefore that differences of race/ethnicity, social class, and gender are decontextualized from lived experience and individualized into attributes of racial categories, socioeconomic status, and sex. The approach extracts social processes, forces, and relations associated with the definition and construction of human "differences" out from under the epidemiologic lens. Rather, the phenomena considered more legitimate and appropriate objects of study are often those associations that remain *after* adjusting for the effects of social differences. In turn, such circumscription of the "job" of the epidemiology of heart disease etiology—limited to what is perceived to be the "objective" and apolitical study of determinants and causes perceived to be preventable and subject to remediation—serves to further the individualization and decontextualization of social differences in cardiovascular disease.

In the end, the lack of explicit discussion of systematic associations found between heart disease incidence and race, socioeconomic status, and sex reflects a truncated investigation, what I call a "terminal analysis," seen as sufficient unto itself. This kind of terminal analysis leaves the impression that such associations are to be expected given the populations in question and thus require no additional study. Such consequences further concretize the notion that non-intersectional and individualistic constructions of difference like measures of racial categories, socioeconomic status, and sex account for and help explain the distribution of health and illness, pushing aside uncertainty and ambiguity over what *exactly* about one's race, class, and sex/gender shapes risk for heart disease and how.

Yet, paradoxically, the "usual suspects" approach is simultaneously subject to some fairly fundamental questioning, which I explore next.

Disputing the "Unseen Hand"

As I discussed in chapter 2, a significant movement within epidemiology questions the conventional and routinized measurement and inclusion of categorical race, socioeconomic status, and sex. In my research, disputes over the "usual suspects" approach focused primarily on two sets of issues. First, some of the scientists I interviewed argued that the mere inclusion of the "usual suspects" in epidemiologic analyses by itself fails to shed light on the dynamics and origins of sociodemographic inequalities in cardiovascular risk and disease. While such questions were never raised with regard to the inclusion of sex, it happened occasionally for socioeconomic status, and more often in the context of race, where some researchers called for epidemiology to move beyond simply including it as a variable to identifying some of its mechanisms. For instance, according to Dr. Karen Verceau, ideally

> the question is always, what does one believe may be the mechanism of why there are different responses? Are they genetic? Then you need to look much more at genetic lineage. Are they more habits and socialization and cultural issues? Then measure those. . . . I think in measuring things, one needs to be mindful of what is it you are trying to get at here.

Dr. Kelleher argued that "asking *about* the proxies I think is a good way to . . . learn more about it, instead of keep sticking in our dummy variables of race, ethnicity" (emphasis added).

Published commentaries also provide points of contestation against what one account calls the "unseen hand"[3] that guides the inclusion of presumptions of racially deterministic analysis and interpretation. For example, a "Statement of Opinion on Race, Genes, and Causal Inference," issued by the Epidemiology and Prevention Council of the American Heart Association, stated:

> Serious discourse on race in our society does not usually start from bio-logical determinist premises. At least not when these premises are stated explicitly. . . . In practice, however, analytic methods are often used that channel the investigation into a deterministic path. . . . The existence of this "unseen hand" . . . can be inferred from two closely related, observ-able features of this literature. First, the field has in general embraced a transparently fallacious idea that "control" for social characteristics can be achieved by using self-reported education and income. Second, the explicit inference is routinely made that specific genes explain popula-tion differences in complex phenotypes, like hypertension, left ventricu-lar hypertrophy, and atherosclerosis, when no direct or indirect evidence exists to suggest this is the case.[4]

Nancy Krieger, a social epidemiologist, likewise notes in an extended com-mentary that controlling for the "usual suspects" smooths out the very demographic differences that should be the focus of etiologic research.[5] She also argues that instead of merely controlling for features like race and class, one should use samples of specific class and racial groups and construct case histories of communities, effectively changing the traditional approach to the unit of analysis. These scientists, like those I interviewed, therefore believe that the simple inclusion of race (and, somewhat less often, socio-economic status) as demographic variables sheds little light on exactly how such dimensions of "difference" shape cardiovascular well-being.

A second point of contestation over the "usual suspects" approach addresses their questionable validity and reliability. Epidemiology favors measures that are stable, easily quantifiable, and seemingly objective. That is, the scientists I interviewed saw epidemiologic measures as most trustworthy when they were replicable over time and represented quantifications of bodily symptoms or features measured with technologies relatively (or seemingly) less subject to human interpretation, such as a blood pressure reading or body-mass index. However, as described in earlier chapters, racial categories, socioeconomic status, and sex do not count among such measures. For example, epidemiologists I interviewed themselves pointed out that racial classifications and socioeconomic status not only vary over time but also, because the mechanisms through which they shape cardiovascular risk are unclear, their ritualized measures may in fact fail to capture or serve as good proxies for the underlying determinants of heart disease. Perceptions of *relative* wealth or poverty may be as important as or more important than absolute income or other measures of socioeconomic status. (In a similar vein, gender identification can differ from one's biological sex, and biological sex is not, strictly speaking, a binary variable[6]—though these aspects of methodological ambiguity were not noted by the epidemiologists I interviewed or observed.) Thus, operationalizing and using such variables can be fraught with uncertainty and methodological and other difficulties.

Because of the sources of methodological and conceptual imprecision that often accompanied the measurement and inclusion of categorical race and socioeconomic status (and also arguably true of sex), epidemiologists constantly faced doubts about what their data were telling them—whether their measures were actually capturing the most relevant phenomena and disease mechanisms, whether those phenomena were "real," or whether something else was actually going on. In the absence of good measurement tools that specifically operationalized those aspects of social difference that shape cardiovascular health, epidemiologists found themselves constantly making do with blunt classification systems, fairly primitive analytic methods, and proxy variables that many, if not most, acknowledged are imprecise.

Black Boxing the "Usual Suspects" Approach

Yet while there was some controversy over the "usual suspects" approach, the general categories of inputs to be included in order to produce credible outputs seem relatively settled and self-evident. Epidemiologists took for granted that they must incorporate individual-level characteristics of race, socioeconomic status, and sex; that is, this practice was increasingly "black boxed."[7] As noted in the introductory chapter, the concept of the black box originates from cybernetics, where it is used in diagrams as a quick way of alluding to some complex process or piece of machinery: In its place, one draws a box and indicates only the input and the output, thereby sidestepping the need to detail the content of the box itself.

This metaphor captures critical aspects of the character of technoscientific facts and routinized procedures: Hidden inside, as the sociologist Steven Epstein argues, "is an entire social history of actions and decisions, experiments and arguments, claims and counterclaims—often enough, a disorderly history of contingency, controversy, and uncertainty."[8] The process of constructing and closing the black box and rendering invisible this unruly social history involves the continual use of discursive techniques and actions to strengthen the case being made. To follow Epstein,[9] scientists take epidemiologic observations (for example, "the incidence of heart disease and its risk factors are associated with race, socioeconomic status, and sex"), transpose them into claims ("it is important to examine the potential roles of racial, socioeconomic status, and sex differences in heart disease") that are accepted by others ("the significance of racial, socioeconomic status, and sex differences in heart disease") and may eventually become facts ("risks for heart disease include racial, socioeconomic status, and sex differences"). The "usual suspects" approach helps to construct a seemingly intelligible and orderly story about the unequal distribution of cardiovascular health. Over time, such "facts" then themselves act as obligatory passage points[10] through which epidemiologists who follow must pass in order to further their own scientific claims and interests. When a black box has embedded itself as a taken-for-granted, standardized procedure, its history and all the elements incorporated into it cannot be easily picked apart or disputed piece by piece without potentially incurring significant costs.

A central finding here therefore is that this particular black box—of transposing social relations of race, class, and gender into standardized racial categories, socioeconomic status, and sex and then including them as demographic adjustments in epidemiologic analyses—can exist quite robustly even though its interior is frequently opened up and challenged by epidemiologists themselves. While those using the "usual suspects" approach may insist that the inner workings of this black box are uncertain, problematic, and potentially even scientifically irrational, the techniques themselves still continue to *function* as a black box.[11]

As I asked in the beginning of this book, why and how is it that the "usual suspects" approach has become so black-boxed, even if the content and validity of the black box are routinely contested? I argue that it is because the individualization of race, class, and sex/gender and their inclusion in epidemiologic research are integral to the construction of scientific credibility and the management of uncertainty in cardiovascular epidemiology. In the following section, I propose and explicate a number of reasons for how this particular practice contributes to the production of credibility in the eyes of both the public and epidemiologic and larger scientific communities.

A "Good Enough" Tool for the Job: Managing Uncertainty and Producing Credibility

The ability to make scientific claims in epidemiology—as in many other disciplines—depends upon compliance with a series of processual requirements and standards.[12] These methodological contingencies are technical procedures and criteria, characteristic of the practice and culture of epidemiology, upon whose satisfactory completion scientific and social credibility rests. I argue that through its ability to minimally comply with these contingencies, the use of the "usual suspects" approach promotes the production of credible epidemiologic claims. That is, by providing convenient ways to nominally satisfy a range of methodological contingencies, individualized variables of race, socioeconomic status, and sex persist in epidemiologic work. Researchers most consistently mentioned three contingencies: what I term the "measurement imperative," U.S. regulations requiring the inclusion of minorities and women in health research, and organizational and economic constraints on epidemiologic work. In the face of these contingencies, constraints, and conventions of practice, the "usual suspects" approach becomes constructed as a convenient and "good enough" alternative to get the job done.

The Measurement Imperative

The work of epidemiologists often involves research on indeterminate phenomena using uncertain methods. In cardiovascular epidemiology, for example, part of the objective of much research is to determine the complex etiology of one disease or a set of related diseases whose multiple determinants can be synergistic, counteracting, overlapping, or independent and may vary from person to person, place to place, and time to time. In the face of such ambiguities, grounds for the credibility of a piece of research must be carefully constructed.

One way in which a case for credibility can be built is through the comprehensive measurement and inclusion of all possible contributing, intervening, and mediating factors to the phenomenon in question. Investigators therefore experience pressures to quantify and incorporate *all* variables that *may* play a role. I call these pressures the "measurement imperative." Dr. Sheila Morris explained how epidemiologists go about complying with this mandate to measure and include, describing the scientific function that the measurement imperative fulfills:

> I mean, anything that you definitely know already has been an established risk factor for cardiovascular disease, you definitely should measure at least in the most standard method . . . things like blood pressure, age, gender, and race. So that's how I begin doing it. And then there are other things that are putative risk factors that haven't been well established but have been suggested by different sources that, if possible, you know you'd

like to measure at least to add more evidence to that literature, or help to minimize some of the residual confounding. If that factor is actually associated with your outcome, you want to eliminate its impact.

Dr. Lance Daly similarly described the inventory of variables known to potentially bear on cardiovascular risk factors and heart disease, and the need to collect data on as many of them and as comprehensively as is feasible:

> If you're trying to determine whether one particular factor is etio-logic . . . then you obviously want to get a very good history of the exposure to that particular variable. And then . . . to get some kind of assessment of the major risk factors . . . you'd at least want to know the blood pressure status, hypercholesterolemia (ideally you'd want to know about subfrac-tions), smoking, diabetes, obesity, physical activity, diet (if you can get it in a reasonable way, but diet takes a fair amount to get good information on), family history . . . body weight (like obesity, lack of obesity). And race, gender, age—basic demographic data. And also certainly measures of social class or education—those types of things have been shown in a variety of studies to be involved in risk, and those are some of the things for which the role is still being elucidated. But you want to have that information as well.

Thus, as the body of evidence accumulates that something about race, social class, and sex and gender may play a role in cardiovascular risk, the measurement imperative compels researchers to include measures of these differences in their study design and statistical analyses. Indi-vidualized variables of categorical race, socioeconomic status, and sex remain crucial to the construction of credibility in part because the mea-surement imperative mandates that *some* aspects of these differences be measured in *some* fashion. In short, any measurement, even inadequate measurement, is better than no measurement at all.

Facilitating the routinization of the "usual suspects" approach as a means to fulfill the measurement imperative is the interpretive flexibility[13] of the "usual suspects"—their ability to mean different things to different people in different times and places without undermining their basic integrity. These individualized variables are quite plastic: Their definitions, their relative weight or relevance, and even their interpretations can vary from site to site without requiring complete agreement. The nature of epidemiologic sociodemographic measures as boundary objects—comprising both objects and sets of processes that have dual properties of flexibility and integrity—allows for continued coordination without the need for substantial conceptual or interpretive agreement.[14] For example, the inclusion of the variable "race" can serve as a way to measure the cardiovascular effects of racism,[15] as a proxy for genetic[16] or physiological[17] differences, or as an indicator of possible cultural or behavioral patterns.[18] All these investigations support the inclusion of the variable of "race," but for quite different political and conceptual purposes. Similar dynamics occur for socioeconomic status and sex. The conceptual looseness of these "usual suspects" in fact contributes to their standardization in heterogeneous lines of research and to their construction as "good enough" and credible enough tools for cardiovascular epidemiology.

Thus, epidemiologists—from those who agreed that current measures are ambiguous to those who were most emphatic that they are fundamentally flawed—made do with relatively crude methods of representing race, socioeconomic status, and sex and habitually included them in their research. On the one hand, researchers saw the "usual suspects" approach as an inadequate tool for the job of meaningfully advancing knowledge on the causes of heart disease disparities. Yet on the other hand, their ritualized use of the "usual suspects" approach transforms the practice into an epidemiologic standard operating procedure and institutionalizes it as a "good enough" tool for producing credible epidemiologic research. In this fashion, more fundamental ambiguities around the meanings of sociodemographic variables and their role in the incidence of heart disease are bypassed in favor of technical, methodological deliberations. An almost singular focus on operationalizing and incorporating race, socioeconomic status, and sex displaces larger questions of when and why they ought to be included. That is, concentrating attention on refining and standardizing methods emphasizes *how* things should be done, not *why*. As the sociologist and science studies scholar Susan Leigh Star observes, "Higher-level uncertainties thus became transformed into more manageable, lower-level ones."[19] These technical downshifts therefore subsume fundamental disputes and gloss over differing visions of the objectives and limits of science. It is under these conditions imposed by the measurement imperative that there can exist significant uncertainty over the adequacy of current measures of race, social class, and gender *simultaneously with* their routinized inclusion.

Inclusion, Representation, and Regulatory Formalism

Political and regulatory conditions also govern epidemiologic research and further stabilize the "usual suspects" technique as an adequate and therefore widely embedded tool for the job.[20] Among the epidemiologists I interviewed, the most prominently mentioned issue in this regard was the 1993 mandate under the National Institutes of Health (NIH) Revitalization Act that all NIH-funded clinical research include women and minorities unless a clear and compelling rationale that such inclusion is inappropriate can be provided. Steven Epstein argues that this and similar forms of legislation were made possible because of a revolution in scientific common sense, away from protecting "vulnerable" groups from research risks, toward affirming the rights of individuals to choose to assume such risks.[21] Epstein chronicles how a growing perception that previous biomedical research had been largely focused on white men raised concerns about the generalizability of study findings to other populations. A historic convergence of women's health, AIDS, and minority health activists, and the support of key members of Congress, brought about this striking shift in the re-definition of demographically diverse and inclusive research as ethically appropriate and scientifically warranted.

The use of measures of race, socioeconomic status, and sex has become a convenient means to demonstrate an attention to diversity and representation now mandated in epidemiology. The "usual suspects" therefore enable the fulfillment of regulatory criteria and the construction of political, and not just scientific, credibility. However, the degree to which representational concerns were articulated differed for different dimensions of diversity. I heard virtually no explicit calls by epidemiologists for the inclusion of individuals from diverse class backgrounds. However, because of the widespread agreement that socioeconomic status significantly stratifies cardiovascular risk and health, it seems taken for granted that socioeconomic status must be included in epidemiologic analyses in order for the results to be statistically adjusted. In contrast, the often implicit claim that women and men differ biologically led to a moderate number of arguments for the inclusion of women in cardiovascular epidemiologic research. So the inclusion of women and the attendant compulsion to stratify by (and adjust for) sex were driven more by questions of biological etiology than by political or equity concerns.

In contrast, epidemiologists in interviews and at scientific meetings very frequently invoked the controversy surrounding the inclusion of racially diverse populations. On the surface, the need for racial diversity in epidemiologic research seems to be a settled matter, as the principle of inclusion has been codified in such documents as the American College of Epidemiology's Statement of Principles: Because "epidemiologists have a critical role in reducing the marked health disparities among United States racial and ethnic groups," those racial and ethnic groups have to be represented in study samples.[22] Some epidemiologists I interviewed echoed the pragmatic justifications for such inclusion advanced by this Statement. They claimed that multiple other practical and empirically relevant concerns—increasing diversity in the U.S. population, observed differences in behaviors and treatment responses between different racial groups, and efforts to reduce spending on health care—create an imperative to maximize research representation along racial lines.

But while epidemiologists willingly acknowledged that people of color and women have for the most part been underrepresented in cardiovascular epidemiologic research, they were almost unanimously opposed to *how* they were mandated to remedy this problem. Many epidemiologists referred to the pressures of contemporary identity politics as contributing to the token inclusion of women and people of color in order to satisfy the regulatory mandate, but without sufficient statistical power—that is, in numbers far too small to render useful and credible conclusions about group differences or about a group in and of itself. Although ensuring statistically valid comparisons between sex and racial/ethnic groups was the original intent of the NIH Revitalization Act, epidemiologists perceived and witnessed that in practice, such requirements were not enforced. Thus, researchers believed that such a mandate had now devolved to a bureaucratic yet scientifically untenable rule, diminishing the scientific credibility of research at the expense of making its results more politically palatable.

As Dr. Verceau explained:

> I think the concept is an essential and important one, [that is,] the concept that we cannot just study white men and think we have the answers to everything. You must study each of these populations separately. . . . The reason for doing what I call stratified sampling by either gender or race would be because I suspect what I want to test, that the effects may not be the same—[the effects] of the particular, if you will, black box intervention. If indeed that is my question, then it becomes totally a sample size problem. I need to be able to say, what's the least effect I expect in any one of the populations, and do I have the ability to test that effect if it's there?

Dr. Verceau argued that the implementation of the NIH inclusionary policy does not in fact resolve these methodological contingencies:

> My soap box, as an epidemiologist, is that NIH has been specifically mandating how scientists need to write proposals and need to do studies in order to get funded. Unless you have a good justification for why you do or don't include certain kinds of people, you are not even likely to get past the review step. This is particularly true with gender, and it's true with all of the different ethnic categories. . . . I personally think that's a huge mistake. I would much prefer more studies that are targeting specific ethnic groups, men separately and women separately. What's happening with the mandate

that you have to check the little boxes that you include everyone . . . [is that] people comply. So they will say that they are going to get some Hispanics, they are going to get Asians—whatever that is . . . they are going to get African Americans. And the list goes on. Ultimately, any given study, unless you make a specific effort to target it, has such small numbers of those individuals in the study that if, in fact, there is a gender difference, there is an ethnic difference, and you want to identify, describe, and detect it and advance the science, it dilutes the main effect by having people from each group, just a couple of them; none large enough, in order to fully answer the research question. . . . The [NIH] reviewers don't seem to be picking up that what you're getting is what you ask for: "Yes, I will include everyone." Have I demonstrated that I will have enough Asian people, enough African Americans, in my study, so I can draw a conclusion about such individuals? No. This is what I think is one of our biggest problems right now, in terms of the science we are doing, the proposals we write, and the studies we carry out. . . . With the mandate that has been passed down, people do the knee-jerk reaction and say, "Yeah, I'm going to get everybody. Isn't that nice?" It's a waste of money. It's a waste of research dollars.

Epidemiologists in fact discursively contrasted "political" consider-ations—which they believed guide the regulatory framework regarding representation in research—in explicit opposition to "scientific" criteria. Thus, they perceived such regulatory mandates to include people of color and women in cardiovascular research, in their current form, as the wrong tools for the job of producing *scientifically* credible knowledge about the effects of differences on heart disease. Yet, on the other hand, as bureaucratic obligatory passage points, they become methodological contingencies to be satisfied solely, epidemiologists argued, for the sake of *political* credibility.[23]

Economic Constraints and Contingencies

A third contingency that sustains the ritualized inclusion of the "usual suspects" has to do with the economic conditions under which epidemiologists do their work. Specifically, epidemiologists argued that in order to come to credible conclusions about disparities in disease, they required studies with very large sample sizes and longitudinal designs. However, such studies are extremely expensive and logistically difficult to conduct. When I asked epidemiologists how they would design their ideal study and what kinds of data they would collect, some spoke at length about the need for adequate statistical power to conduct separate analyses for carefully defined social groups in order to address questions of social factors and conditions and their role in heart disease causation. As Dr. Max Oliver pointed out, "Ideally, it would be good to have sufficient detailed individual data on all demographic groups, but this is often not practical. I think the current techniques are sufficient, but the bigger problem is adequate data, which needs to be massive for the ideal study."

The epidemiologists I interviewed also advocated longitudinal research, following individuals and communities for extended periods of time, even across generations. For example, Dr. Anita Yu suggested examining cultural adaptation and lifestyle changes across generations in order to understand the cardiovascular risks of immigrants. Dr. Morris envisioned beginning data collection during pregnancy and following those children from birth until death. However, these and other epidemiologists almost unanimously ended their descriptions with comments about the financial obstacles to doing such research, specifically the enormous costs and resources required to maintain contact with cohorts of individuals and gather such in-depth data at regular intervals. However, they perceived the alternative—studies that are cross-sectional, wherein data are collected from individuals (or the units of analysis) only at one point in time, like a snapshot, or shorter-term longitudinal studies— as inappropriate for determining causality across a wide range of both proven and untested risk factors.

Moreover, even if detailed and longitudinal data sets were available, epidemiologists pointed out that conceptual models and techniques for analyzing such complex data are still in their infancy. These represent crucial tools for the job that have not yet been fully elaborated, much less stabilized or widely accepted. Some of the epidemiologists I interviewed discussed gathering data that chart complex changes not only in the economic life chances, experiences, and health of people but also in the histories of the environments and communities in which they live.[24] Dr. Mia Henderson, for example, uses ecological models that

> bridge this gap between looking at the macro influences like . . . neighborhood socioeconomic status and neighborhood disease prevalence . . . [as well as] individual determinants and individual outcome. . . . The ecological model that says, well sure, there are these individual attributes, but you can also take into account all these neighborhood attributes, more of the context—the contextual model, as they call it, in addition to individual stuff. . . . It's a relatively new sort of way of knowing about individual health behaviors versus more conventional epidemiology.

In theory, such a model "probably will explain a lot of what's going on [at] the individual level" by "accounting for these neighborhood, these environmental, sociological kinds of influences as well as individual influences." However, in practice, Dr. Henderson acknowledged, "it's much more complicated. . . . I'm still trying to figure out how to assess those [influences], how to make them work."

Dr. Morris agreed that existing methods to determine the multiple causes of heart disease are rudimentary and ultimately inadequate to model the complex, synergistic, and intersecting dynamics that characterize the impacts of race, social class, and gender. When I asked if she felt that she had the methodological tools to do the kind of research she would like to do, she replied tepidly:

> They're okay. I mean in terms of socioeconomic status and the highly correlated data, especially if you try to do things on individual's neighborhood to . . . larger spatial units, they have some hierarchical modeling techniques you can use. But I mean it's still not perfect. You know, we still don't have a way that perfectly gives us what we want to do, so I

think there's still definitely some methodological development that we still have to do in terms of measuring things, as well as doing analysis using this information. I mean we can collect tons of information, but how do we analyze that? How do we take into account your parents' economic status and your childhood economic status, and yours now, currently, and then yours when the event happened? How do we correlate all those things together and try to measure what our lifetime socioeconomic status was? . . . I don't think conceptually we've got it all worked out yet. And I think it's mainly because we haven't figured out some of the steps along the way either. It's all kind of one big mess that we're trying to understand what it is, sort out the pieces of stuff.

Epidemiologists whom I both interviewed and observed almost uniformly perceived that such methodological problems are, as one put it, "the kiss of death for funding." Thus the conceptual models and analytic techniques for examining the effects of race, class, and gender in cardiovascular risk and disease represent crucial missing tools for the job. As a result, epidemiologists reported to me that they continue to use measures of categorical race, socioeconomic status, and sex that were often regarded as scientifically inadequate yet "good enough" stop-gap techniques to nominally account for differences that epidemiologists know to be significant, though in ways they could not conclusively state.

For all their uncertainty, then, individual-level variables of racial category, socioeconomic status, and sex have to a significant degree become systems that represent standardized ways of classifying the world,[25] bringing together scientists from diverse lines of work. They allow for comparisons between individuals and studies from different geographic, social, and historical contexts. And perhaps most significantly, because they have been embedded in multiple sites and technologies throughout the infrastructures of epidemiologic research, there are very high costs to accommodating alternatives. Such sites of institutionalization include national survey instruments, the digital design of databases and computer programs, ongoing research studies and protocols, the training and expertise of researchers, and the technical, organizational, and political cultures of government agencies and health bureaucracies. Each of these sites has both shaped and been constituted by the specific ways in which sociodemographic differences have conventionally been collected, measured, recorded, stored, analyzed, and interpreted. As a result, such conventions have been co-produced along with the practices and infrastructures of epidemiologic work and, importantly, standard definitions of what counts as legitimate and "doable"[26] research. All of these elements structure the social world and work of epidemiology and, consequently, the kinds of knowledges produced. Even though emergent methods of measuring or analyzing the effects of "difference" may be highly sophisticated or greatly improved over current modalities, they often represent the "wrong" tools for the jobs of epidemiologic investigators trying to do large-scale, generalizable, comparable, and credible research testing causal hypotheses.

Because of these economic and infrastructural constraints of conducting such long-term data collection, scientists often rely on preexisting databases compiled by other researchers or by government agencies. However, the categories and methods of measurement used to collect such data are most likely to be precisely those that are not very novel, advanced, or nuanced. Instead, they are selected because they are conservative, safe, and comparable to those used in previous rounds of data collection. Dr. Kelleher, for example, who uses secondary data sets, discussed the drawbacks of being "stuck with what I have," including the absence of some racial groups she would have liked to study, and the lumping together of ethnic groups she considered to be extremely heterogeneous. Thus, the very data sets that represent a significant resource for epidemiologists struggling to produce new knowledge are most likely those that use relatively established, standardized measures, particularly of race and class. Thus this practice of using secondary data in many ways further institutionalizes a conservative bias in research, effectively curbing the use of newer conceptual and methodological techniques that might offer a better, more nuanced understanding of the effects of race, class, and gender on cardiovascular risk. That is, they discourage innovation, as Dr. Kelleher described:

> It would be kind of nice to have people that are thinking a lot about [new methods of measurement and analysis] and theorizing a lot about it, to get with the people that are designing the surveys, you know. But that's a huge bureaucratic process. . . . It's really hard just to get like a new question on a survey. . . . The National Health Interview Survey has been going on since the '50s. . . . Just getting education on the death certificate was huge. . . . I just witness people that I've worked with that have been involved in kind of redesigning some surveys and . . . you've got people who have been there for decades, you know, who have done the same thing, the same reports are produced from the same survey, and it's just I think the inertia of getting people to change. And issues of class and race are politically charged. . . . Those issues are always very sensitive. There're ownership issues within the organization—who owns what data set and authority issues. And I just think it's just a hard thing to do for a lot of different reasons. . . . I'm not trying to put them down. I think they do a really excellent job with their stuff. It's just, to come in and say, "Oh, we need to have Marxist measures of social class on this survey," . . . talking about owning the means of production, it's just not going to happen [laughs].

Economic considerations, by shaping the kinds of data collected, deeply impact the research materials available to epidemiologists and operate to constrain the ability to develop a finer-grained understanding of the racial, class, and gender orderings of cardiovascular risk. In turn, they further routinize the use of individualized variables of demographic difference in epidemiology.

Individualizing "Difference," Problematizing "Expertise"

Epidemiologists thus perceived numerous obstacles to the conceptual and methodological advancement of the field: the intrusion of political and regulatory requirements to include certain populations that in fact counter efforts to design research based on scientific criteria; the lack of theoretical models and measurement technologies to gather appropriate data; and the lack of resources to analyze such data and evaluate more complicated causal hypotheses. These forces have shaped disciplinary responses that are largely conservative and that valorize known measurement strategies, comparable and stable forms of data, and proven conceptual and analytic models. They embed within the organization and conduct of epidemiologic work a working currency of credibility, based on standards of practice that allow for one's research to be intelligibly understood by one's peers and that is consonant with and comparable to the existing scholarship. As Dr. Verceau described, "On the one hand, I would like to be adventuresome and develop all my own categories of measurement. On the other hand, there's this real desire to want to be able to compare research with previous research. If you are not careful in developing your categorization, then you are not able to compare so well." Following these standards of practice, therefore, effectively (or at least nominally) convinces fellow scientists and other audiences of the plausibility of the methods being used and in turn, the claims being made. Here, in order to produce credible epidemiologic research, epidemiologists routinely resorted to the "usual suspects" approach, wherein individual, rather than social, attributes of racial categories, socioeconomic status, and sex were incorporated as statistical adjustments and controls.

Epidemiologists were not unaware of the potential costs of knowledge production processes that are conservative and convention-bound. At least several interviewees acknowledged that the default option of the "usual suspects" approach in fact directly counters efforts to understand the effects of racial, class, and gender differences in cardiovascular risk and disease. According to Dr. Morris, "I get frustrated because more studies are being done that do the same thing, without offering solutions, or exploring other possibilities or designing studies that could answer those questions. And this has been going on since the 1950s, so that's what I think the most annoying thing about it is."

The other costs of such disciplinary conventions are that epidemiologic standards and commonsense understandings of the effects of social differences on disease mutually shape each other and, in so doing, displace considerations of alternative bases of knowledge production and claims-making. Given our ongoing confusion about the sources of health disparities, their historical persistence despite policies aimed at their reduction, and the heterogeneous perspectives (even among epidemiologists) on how social differences produce heart disease, the notion that epidemiologists might have something to gain from the diverse knowledges constructed by lay people living with heart disease would hardly seem to be a revolutionary idea. Lay people's accounts of social conditions and the role they play in heart disease offer some compelling alternatives to epidemiologic thinking about difference. Those accounts support the notion that social inequalities of race, class, and gender function as fundamental causes of disease, stratifying life chances, resources, and the conditions within which health can be promoted, maintained, and/or undermined. Thus, lived experiences of inequality and heart disease imbue lay accounts with a kind of legitimacy and authority. This authority is not rooted in training, esoteric skills, or credentialed status, as it is with expert authority. Instead, lay people's experiences provide a kind of "data" from which they construct interpretations and understandings of the linkages among social structures and representations that maintain social inequality, their everyday lives and material conditions of life, and their cardiovascular health.

Lay knowledges should not be considered as simple, direct reflections of their lived "reality" but rather as intentional, constructed, and often political narrative efforts to make meaning out of their experiences. But in this regard, lay knowledge is no different from scientific expertise, whose production similarly filters reality and offers representations and interpretations that are no less intentional, constructed, and political. Instead, both lay and expert accounts of the causes of heart disease are attempts to explain what is experienced and observed, from which knowledge is in turn produced. Despite, or perhaps because of, the very important distinctions in the institutional, political, and cultural conditions in which epidemiologic and lay knowledges are constructed, lay accounts offer alternative ways of understanding and conceptualizing the causes of heart disease that may prove instrumental in addressing cardiovascular health inequalities.

Interactions among scientific and lay knowledges have certainly occurred in other fields of scientific and medical research. For example, as detailed in this book's opening chapter, the works of the sociologists Phil Brown and Steven Epstein demonstrate the ability for lay people in the environmental justice and AIDS social movements, respectively, to learn enough of the relevant sciences to craft their own informed stances on problem definition, study design, data collection, interpretation of findings, value neutrality, and standards of proof.[27, 28] In these cases, then, lay people gained "expertise" by virtue of their acquisition and mobilization of the concepts, frameworks, and vocabularies of the scientists themselves.

In contrast, however, I consider here a situation in which there currently is no explicit organized engagement or relationship between lay and expert forms of authority. No prominent lay movement or group has undertaken efforts to acquire biomedical and epidemiologic language and technique in order to challenge official knowledge production around cardiovascular disease and its causation. There are, of course, some national organizations aimed at education and awareness. There are also general health-advocacy organizations that are quite politicized and that more nearly mimic grassroots activist groups, especially those working to promote the health of women and communities of color. But despite its status as the most common cause of mortality, heart disease does not have associated with it a visible hybrid activist-expert community of the kind that scholars have found in other medical and scientific arenas. For these reasons, in the case of heart disease—despite its being a health concern that touches so many—the challenges of conceptualizing, much less achieving, a more democratic science are especially acute.

A distinctive feature of the expert–lay divide explored in this book has been the implicit yet omnipresent question of audience. Epidemiologists, as part of a professional community of scientists, were continually preoc-cupied with how others evaluated the credibility of their causal claims. Their analyses tended to rely upon self-authenticating styles of practice, triangulation, and explanations that are widely accepted or less contro-versial. On the other hand, because lay people's analyses centered largely on the immediacy of their own lives, they seemed to be less concerned with these issues. Scientific and lay knowledges in this study thus served different purposes: Scientific knowledge was produced explicitly for peer and public consumption, while lay knowledge provided personal inter-pretations and ways of understanding the world, based in biographical experiences and deployed to make sense of them. Theirs was knowledge produced by and for themselves.

Clearly, expert and lay knowledges are not on a level playing field. This book depicts an expert–lay hierarchy as much as a divide. Epidemi-ologists are viewed as producers of scientific, official knowledge on the causes of heart disease while lay people, in contrast, construct "subjec-tive" "anecdotal" accounts. The scientific basis of epidemiologic claims about the difference that difference makes means that such claims carry a great deal of social credibility and cultural legitimacy. In that con-text, what kind of status do we accord lay knowledge, which has vastly different criteria for validity? And what are, then, the implications for the authority of science and our conventional definitions of expertise? Against the backdrop of such questions, considering alternative bases of knowledge about the causes of heart disease, and especially of the social disparities that characterize it, is no simple matter.

The discipline of scientific conventions and routines, the importance of credibility, the implications of constructing something as a "cause"—all these both engender and reveal the high-stakes consequences of expert knowledge claims for lived experiences. Epidemiology biomedicalizes differences of race, social class, and gender in very specific and strategic ways, and it is these culturalist, behavioral, biological, and individualistic dimensions of difference that predominate in clinical medicine, pub-lic health, and public discourse. In this way, epidemiology constructs commonsense, power-laden notions about the "natural" effects of *individual* differences on *individual* health and so participates in sustaining racial, class, and gender hegemony. Epidemiology therefore enacts and endorses the belief—*even if* individual epidemiologists take issue with it—that research on the etiology of heart disease can be conducted with the individual as the basic unit of analysis, that potential factors and determinants can validly be conceptualized and measured at the individual level, and that treatment and prevention efforts can be predicated on individual change and aimed at individual actors.

What, then, would it take for the field to move forward, to produce meaningful knowledge about the *social* disparities of heart disease and the influence of *social* differences in generating them? First, it requires that we address the question of how to understand and even talk about the credibility, legitimacy, and validity of knowledges in ways that do not themselves replicate experts' take on "expertise" but that instead suggest alternative terms of debate. Why is this important? Reserving the label of "experts" for those who possess specialized training, skills, language, and credentials, and for the few lay people who acquire them, highlights that, in a knowledge-stratified society, relations of expertise are relations of power, maintained by such political practices as monopolizing knowledge and asserting privilege.[29] Defining "experts" and "expertise" in these ways has the effect of reifying scientists as producers of official knowledge, whereas lay people collect "subjective" interpretations and "anecdotes" that glean personal meaning from their experiences. The relative absence of an arena in which lay and scientific claims about the causes of heart disease come into explicit interaction and contestation means that the very basis of "expertise"—as rooted in the possession of esoteric and specialized skills, concepts, and lexicon of epidemiology—remains largely taken for granted. To counter this, we must assert, as the sociologists Jennie Popay and Gareth Williams do,[30] that lay people, through their experience of life events and the conditions of their existence, accumulate an alternative body of knowledge that is authoritative in its own way and that an analysis of its content may contribute to our understanding of the relationship between social inequalities and health inequalities.

Simultaneously changing how we define and think about experts and expertise also requires that we take into account the conditions under which expert knowledge is being produced. I do not believe that the epidemiologists in my study were simply being myopic about the social causes of disease; rather, they work within a system of rules, standardized routines, rewards, and institutional practices that all shape sanctioned causal claims in particular ways. Infrastructure matters for the production of any commodity, and here it is deeply consequential for the scientific knowledge being made. The inclusion of race, socioeconomic status, and sex as variables is a routinized practice, not because epidemiologists see it as conceptually or methodologically robust but because it helps them to satisfy a number of contingencies that must be met in order to achieve credibility. This practice, however, legitimates individualized, astructural, and (seemingly) apolitical notions of difference and sustains a focus on individual risks rather than on social causation.

Thus my work shows that devoting additional funding to the epidemiology of disease disparities—as critical as that is, and as important a political accomplishment that would be—will not be enough. Under existing conditions of production, further epidemiologic research will continue to generate results that largely replicate what we already know about individual-level risks and health-related behaviors. It will not, in contrast, tell us how complex social processes related to the representation and organization of race, class, and gender structure life chances and so limit and offer avenues for modifying and responding to disease risks. Neither will it tell us how relations of power act as fundamental causes of disease, placing people defined as different "at risk of risks."[31] We need a different set of answers to the question of what difference does difference make, and for that, we need a different way of obtaining those answers, a different way of producing knowledge.

Alternative knowledge production is a question of both definition and infrastructure, of culture and of structure; that is, problematizing the social prominence and cultural authority that we place on scientific expertise in our society means problematizing the conduct of science. These in turn are all questions about power: Expertise is a critical resource in the struggle for status and privilege, and thus the bases of expertise and its acquisition are fiercely defended domains. Even seemingly esoteric debates about epidemiologic methods are embedded with assumptions, practices, and frameworks that are thoroughly social and political. There is no science that can be separated from culture, society, or politics. To assume so is to leave untouched ideas and practices that pose fundamental obstacles to producing a new and different knowledge about difference and its consequences for the body and psyche, and for individuals and communities. Thus remaking race, class, and gender in our investigations of heart disease involves fundamentally rethinking our definitions of expertise and credibility and, consequently, of the political economic, social, and institutional conditions under which we produce knowledge about health, disease, and populations.

In short, it involves confronting the politics of knowledge. Most obviously this means initiating and contributing to conversations about the social production and causation of disease. But this also means analyzing why people imbue "difference" with such different meanings, calling attention to the ramifications of our standards for authoritative knowledge, and problematizing those criteria that hinder our efforts to improve societal well-being. In the pursuit of equity in health, we must recognize that both disease *and* difference are socially created and thus must be sociologically understood. It is to this ongoing conversation that this book seeks to contribute.

Conclusion

Despite more than a century and a half of medical and epidemiologic research into the causes of social inequalities in heart disease, vast, systematic differences persist in who develops it, who lives with it, and who dies from it. These durable disparities in heart disease incidence and outcomes have raised public concerns and prompted research explicitly aimed at uncovering the causes for such inequalities. Thus racial, socioeconomic, and sex categorizations of various forms have consistently been a part of the epidemiologic endeavor, in which population variations are identified and mined for clues to the etiology of disease. However, when considering such research, the meanings of bodily and social differences must be understood as socially constructed, capable of mobilizing a broad scope of social, political, economic, institutional forces that render such differences consequential and thus "real."[1] Grasping the array of such conceptions, who holds which conceptions, and the dynamics of power that underlie these politics of knowledge construction is therefore critical.

I did not embark on this research with the *a priori* idea that I would find wide distinctions in how scientific epidemiologists and lay individuals articulate, define, and interpret sociodemographic differences. Instead, I was motivated by some fairly exploratory questions, among them: What do racial, class, and gender differences that I take to be socially constructed "look" like in epidemiologic research? In what ways are they taken up and articulated in lived experience? I was interested in how scientific epistemologies, standards of proof, and criteria for legitimacy and validity condition what differences are considered and how they are managed in epidemiologic investigations. I also wanted to explore whether lay people's own analytic frameworks, biographies, lived experiences, and embodiment of heart disease would shape their conceptions of difference and its role in health and well-being, and how. Finally, I hoped to understand how these conceptions were constructed, as well as their interplay, overlaps, consonances, and contradictions. In doing so, I found what I have characterized as a science–lay divide.

Stratified Biomedicalization: Producing Knowledge, Producing Health

In many ways, the science–lay divide cleaves along major fault lines in our understandings of how health and illness, and knowledge about them, are produced. I argue that the production of knowledge about disease causes on the one hand, and the production of health on the other, are both social, and synergistically so. By this I mean that the ways in which we conceive of the causes of disease are part and parcel of the ways in which we go about studying them, and the ways of knowing that we bring to bear on disease (and those that we do not) are deeply consequential for how we seek to act upon and intervene on disease. These processes of knowing and acting are thoroughly embedded in our culture, political conflicts, history, and the social organization of power relations. In the arena of heart disease—its incidence and distribution, scientific and public concerns over its inequalities, and people's experiences of living with it—the social production of health and the social production of knowledge can be characterized, in a phrase, as stratified biomedicalization.

In the contemporary United States, the most authoritative body of knowledge about the causes of heart disease is epidemiology. Even from its beginnings in Framingham, Massachusetts, cardiovascular epidemiology and its study of heart disease incidence and risks have been constituted and shaped not only by scientific and technical considerations but also by social ideas, archetypical cultural narratives, and political debates about normality, pathology, difference, and hierarchy. As the epidemiologic gaze expanded to include whole communities and then entire populations, it became an instrument of Foucauldian biopower,[2] but one that places the bodies, behaviors, and traits of some groups under greater surveillance and discipline than others.[3] Epidemiology has become a veritable knowledge production industry, and policymakers and the public have increasingly turned to its science for guidance on cardiovascular risk identification, assessment, and management. But public reactions to and frustrations with the often contradictory and piecemeal claims emanating from epidemiologic research undermine the social credibility of the claims being produced. Moreover, as evidenced by the research in this book, the relevance, validity, and utility of its claims have been subject to greater scrutiny by epidemiologists themselves, who do not speak with one singular voice.

Yet at the same time, cardiovascular epidemiology remains a powerful and largely authoritative means of producing knowledge about heart disease risks and causes. As we saw, epidemiologists in my study, in practice, tend to conceptually devolve differences of race, class, and gender to individualized, demographic variables. My interview and observational data showed that researchers at times implicitly and explicitly resort to biological interpretations of racial differences. They also widely construct "race" as cultural or "ethnic" differences that affect heart disease via risk factor behaviors. Various aspects of this cultural prism—its discursive opposition to biology, its perceived observability and verifiability, its resonance with health promotion ideologies, and finally its conceptual flexibility—make it a popular, and scientifically and politically safe, construction of race. Epidemiologists almost exclusively construct sex/gender difference in biological, hormonal terms; their use of the language of "gender" is in most cases due to its perception as a more politically correct lexical choice. Little note is being taken, it seems, of an emerging literature which asserts that sex and gender are not the clear, biological binaries we have imagined them to be.[4] Finally, class appears to be somewhat of a different kind of difference. In my study, epidemiologists generally agree with lay people that class differences stem from structural forces that stratify access to resources and opportunities, and from exposure to risks of stress and environment. Both groups speak rather extensively about class-based social processes. However, *in practice* most epidemiologists almost exclusively utilize individual-level variables of income, education, and/or occupation.

The use of such decontextualized variables realizes and actualizes in epidemiologic practice the precepts of individualism, the notion that phenomena related to disease and illness—ranging from causes, progression, manifestations and symptoms, outcomes, treatment and amelioration—can be understood at the level of the individual. The researchers I interviewed and observed therefore enacted the belief—even if they took issue with it—that in research on disparities in heart disease, the individual is the conventional, institutionalized unit of analysis. Thus potential determinants under study are conceptualized and measured at the level of the individual and, concomitantly, treatment and prevention are aimed at individual actors and understood to hinge on individual change. In so doing, epidemiologists effect and enforce the biomedicalization of race, class, and gender as individual-level differences. This pattern is characteristic, I and others argue, of the rest of the discipline as well, and, as such, epidemiology constitutes a racial, class, and gender formation project.[5] That is, a narrowed scope of the "official facts" about the causes of racial, class, and sex differences in heart disease organize individualizing scientific practices, lifestyle and behavior-focused discourses, and ideas and practices around risk reduction and prevention. Such "common sense" in turn is underwritten by mutually reinforcing meanings of race, class, and gender, yet its ideological roots are obscured through its appeal to scientific neutrality and rationality. Epidemiology works to produce knowledge about and to legitimate the "naturalness" of social inequalities in health and the indisputability of their individual-level origins. While this work is often not explicitly marked as racialized, classed, and gendered, by disregarding the notion that deeper social, political, and structural forces and relations of power are consequential for health, epidemiology, as currently practiced, ultimately contributes to the reproduction of stratification.

In contrast, the embodied experiences and knowledges of people of color with heart disease that I analyzed point to the significance of intersecting systems of racial, class, and gender inequality for cardiovascular health. While their constructions of social differences and their effects on cardiovascular risk are highly variable, expansive, and even contradictory and paradoxical, lay people I interviewed tended to speak of race, class, and gender in structural terms in their accounts of disease causation. They invoked such dynamics as racialized interactions and segregation; the oppression of double consciousness; stratified access to economic, educational, and informational resources; racial and sex segregation in the labor market; and the gendered division of reproductive labor as being profoundly consequential for their health. They also tended to speak of their experiences as racialized, classed, and gendered individuals and as members of differentiated groups in deeply intersectional ways. Although I frequently queried them about the effects of race, class, and gender one by one on their health and in their lives, their responses consistently complicated and defied any notion of discrete categories. Their experiences of risk, illness, and inequality repeatedly bore witness to the overlapping and interlocking co-constitution of race, class, and gender and were conceptualized by lay people as fundamental causes[6] of the production and stratification of disease. They saw race, class, and gender structuring their life chances, exposures to stressors, access to information and resources, and myriad other pathways through which cardiovascular health can be promoted, maintained, and/or undermined. They understood health inequalities, and health and illness in general, as socially produced, the outcomes of relations of power based on social constructions of "otherness" and "difference" that exact material, real consequences. Indeed, how individuals with heart disease constructed the meanings and health consequences of being from particular racial, class, and gender groups was indistinguishable from their conceptions of the social relations and historical and ongoing experiences of interactions among those groups. Based on their lived and embodied experiences, lay people complicated the individualized, standardized constructions of difference that tended to prevail in epidemiologic science.

Yet even among epidemiologists themselves, there was acknowledgment that individualistic variables of categorical race, socioeconomic status, and sex are flawed conceptually and methodologically. So why, then, are they so ritualistically included in epidemiologic research, so much so that they were often referred to as the "usual suspects"? I found that multiple technical, political, and economic requirements posed within epidemiology and by numerous other social worlds are defined as necessary for the production of credibility and promote the routinization of this "usual suspects" approach. As I described in chapter 6, among the technical requirements are two kinds of methodological contingencies. First, the "measurement imperative" mandates that all potentially significant factors be measured and included in data collection and analysis. Also, political and regulatory requirements include the representation and analysis of racial and sex differences in health, which the inclusion of individualized variables helps to fulfill. Finally, economic constraints and the lack of organizational and funding support for interdisciplinary collaboration in epidemiology inhibit the availability of appropriate theoretical models, data, and domains of expertise that constitute other "tools for the job." As a result, the "usual suspects" approach becomes constructed as a convenient and "good enough" alternative. By providing relatively convenient ways to nominally satisfy a range of methodological, political, and economic contingencies, and thereby helping to build credibility, practices that work to individualize "difference" persist in epidemiologic work.

In the case of the epidemiology of heart disease, then, the "usual suspects" approach—transposing race, class, and gender into a set of racial categories, socioeconomic status, and sex, and then including them as demographic adjustments in epidemiologic analyses—operates as both a boundary object[7] and a black box even though its cover is frequently opened and its interior regularly challenged by epidemiologists themselves. Its status as a black box is solidified as its use is routinized in multiple lines of work. Its routinization promotes the selection of epidemiologic inputs of race, socioeconomic status, and sex, and the production of outputs of claims about heart disease and its disparities. Thus, ironically, this practice serves to manage uncertainty and potential disagreement among different social worlds, even though its inner workings *themselves* are often viewed as ambiguous, problematic, and conceptually and methodologically inadequate.

As such, the "usual suspects" approach still functions as a boundary object, facilitating collective work and contributing to the common identity of a scientific discipline like epidemiology. Integrity *in theory* and integrity *in practice* may be two very different estimations. In this case, the latter can be enhanced by the ability of the boundary object to meet the constraints of a host of technical, political, and economic forces shaping definitions of credible scientific practice. In short, this is not a Latourian story[8] about scientific entrepreneurs successfully persuading fellow epidemiologists of the validity of demographic variables. Scientists do not have to believe completely that the contents of a black box are self-evident, or that a boundary object is necessarily robust, in order to use it. Instead, when faced with multiple technical, political, and economic contingencies that must be met in order to construct credible science, epidemiologists constructed the use of individualized, demographic variables as a "good enough" tool for the job and constructed the "job" itself in terms that are solvable (at least nominally) with the tools they have at hand.[9]

To Bridge the Science–Lay Divide

If the story of the science–lay divide is not simply about scientific myopia but that, in fact, like lay people living with heart disease, a good number of epidemiologists believe that disease inequalities arise from complex causes, what then are the possibilities for bridging the divide? In the case of heart disease, the politics of causation stem not just from conflicts over the nature of racial, class, and gender differences but also from the politics that are embedded within the mundane, on-the-ground scientific conventions, practices, and disciplinary norms regulating legitimacy, credibility, and prestige. These findings raise some critical implications for reforming the practice and organization of epidemiology. Many of these recommendations have already been proposed by others.[10] However, this book offers substantive and empirical evidence for how the lack of these reforms has impoverished research on cardiovascular health inequalities and an analysis of how this has shaped our state of knowledge. My recommendations fall most notably in three areas: retooling the conceptual frameworks and methodological techniques for studying inequalities in health; diversifying participation in knowledge production processes and our understanding of what constitutes "expertise"; and rethinking research funding mechanisms, priorities, and disciplinary boundaries.

Retooling the Conceptual Models and Methods of Studying "Difference"

In my conversations with epidemiologists, I found that many could clearly identify numerous weaknesses in their models and methods, yet they continued to routinize the very individualized variables of "difference" that were a major focus of their critiques. Even though numerous "tools for the job" of studying inequalities in cardiovascular health are perceived to be inadequate and ambiguous, they are still critical to the production of credibility along technical, political, regulatory, and economic lines. Taking structural and social dynamics into account in studying sociodemographic difference and inequalities requires, therefore, retooling some of the most traditional conceptual and methodological instruments of epidemiology. Recommendations on what specific kinds of new and improved methods should be used in health research are outside the scope of this book; however, some general implications for conceptual models of disease causation and methods of data collection and analysis can be outlined.

First, my analysis of epidemiologic constructions of difference indicates that their devolution and individualization is inextricably tied to their conceptualization as having effects on cardiovascular risk and disease predominantly at the individual, behavioral, and biological levels. One rather obvious recommendation, then, is to reverse this reductionist tendency in health research and instead take up an overall conception of social conditions as fundamental causes of disease.[11] As one of my participants, Dr. Lena Kelleher, explained to me,

We always . . . want to get closer and closer to the body, finding things about biological or metabolic processes that are risk factors. . . . I'm not skeptical about those risk factors as being risk factors, because I know they're really important and they have been very predictive in disease. . . . [But] I think we're missing the broader picture. . . . When you're focusing more and more on the proximate risk factors, necessarily you're not focusing on what drives those factors at a population level. . . . When we're identifying these things that are closer to the more proximal risk factors, then we start, I think, focusing on the mechanisms of how that happens. It's great to understand the mechanisms, but mechanisms will change over time, and these . . . basic patterns of social equality and health outcomes will always remain the same. . . . [Heart disease] used to be a disease of the affluent. Then the mechanisms sort of changed and over time as we find out more and more about it, persons with more resources are more able to take advantage of the new knowledge, the new technology, you know, everything, so it almost

> increases the inequalities, I think, over time. . . . But just basically focusing
> on the more proximate causes just doesn't leave room for the big picture.

As Dr. Kelleher points out, in order to better understand the kinds of factors that determine heart disease incidence and distribution, research must consider multiple levels of causation at the same time. Many commentators have argued that epidemiologic and other health research is inclined to be rather theoretically impoverished and that the field would be better served by greater attention to explicating conceptual models of disease causation.[12] My research supports the notion that an emphasis on methodological dilemmas and debates tends to displace epistemological considerations. Both sociodemographic differences, as well as the dynamics and mechanisms of heart disease, must be understood as social, structural, historical, and institutional processes, and efforts to construct and operationalize them as such—no matter how provisional, uncertain, or tenuously credible—need to be supported.

Second, but related to the first, scientists must begin to consider seriously the notion that not everything that counts can be counted; that is, they must begin retooling the standards and definitions of what counts as "data." Lay people's conceptions of the relationships between their experiences of difference and their cardiovascular health underscore the complex intersectional dynamics of stratification and social inequality—ranging from access to educational and employment opportunities, to discrimination, the division of social reproductive labor, and the like. These must enter into health research in some fashion. Such dynamics, obviously, present enormous methodological dilemmas for researchers seeking quantifiable, stable, and reliable (in the conventional, statistical sense) data points. As the physician and medical historian Robert Aronowitz notes, "Not every association can be readily expressed in risk factor terms. . . . While pack-years of smoking could be entered easily into risk factor formulas, the role of farm subsidies to tobacco growers or marketing of high-fat foods [is] not so readily modeled."[13] One possibility is to consider how health research might take better advantage of existing qualitative traditions; indeed, a basic principle of scientific research is that the choice of qualitative or quantitative methods should be based on their appropriateness for the research questions being asked. Qualitative methods are sometimes currently used as a kind of supplementary method for pilot studies, or in advance of more quantitative investigations.

However, several caveats are in order here. First, simply adding "social" variables is not enough. As many have argued, there are fundamentally distinctive epistemological commitments between epidemiologic and intersectional models of health disparities. For example, Lynn Weber and Deborah Parra-Medina provide a useful catalog of some of the most important distinctions:

- *Individual as Unit Obscuring Social Structures* . . . Psychosocial and biobehavioral elaborations of the biomedical paradigm seek to "decompose" the effects of social inequality variables by looking for mediating factors—pathways or proximate causes—to explain the effects of social inequality on a particular health outcome. In contrast, intersectional approaches problematize the processes generating and maintaining the macro social structures of race, class, gender, and sexuality and seek to identify their relationships to individual and collective identities, behaviors, and health statuses.
- *Distributional or Relational Constructions of Social Inequality: Having More or Having Power Over?* . . . Distributional models employ rankings, linear, incremental measurements of inequalities; relational models examine categorical groupings in relations of dominance and subordination.
- *Independent, Single Inequalities or Intersecting, Multiple Inequalities?* . . . The psychosocial and biobehavioral models of health disparities typically address one or two dimensions of systemic inequality. . . . This practice derives from theoretical conceptualizations of the dimensions [of race, class, and gender] as separate and distinct, a balkanization of research traditions studying these dimensions as isolated entities, and the methodological requirements of survey research for very large (expensive) samples to enable statistical assessments of the "interactions" of these factors with one another.[14]

As a second caveat, the concept of biomedicalization[15] sensitizes us to the potential consequences of inviting epidemiologic and biomedical knowledge production processes to scientize what currently is the purview of experiential and embodied knowledge and indeed marginalized and dismissed as such.[16] Token inclusion would clearly be less transformative of the epidemiologic endeavor than integrating qualitative methods into health research in a truly synthetic and interactive way.[17] The use of qualitative research must be on terms that emphasize equality, shared power, and the partiality of all knowledges—all commitments of feminist qualitative research. Another possibility I explore below, therefore, is to implement explicit efforts to share the power inherent in the production of knowledge by involving lay people in all stages of the research process, from articulating research questions to generating policy implications.

Diversifying the Production of Knowledge on Health and Enriching Definitions of Expertise

I echo here others' calls for the greater inclusion of lay knowledge in research on public health. As usefully articulated by Jennie Popay and Gareth Williams, lay knowledge is relevant to health research and practice in three ways: the possibility that lay perceptions of health status predict future health; lay conceptions of the relationships between individual behaviors and life conditions—that is, the linkages between agency and structure; and lay theories about etiology.[18] Based on the research described throughout this book, I would argue that the last two are intimately intertwined with each other in the case of heart disease. Etiologic frameworks and epidemiology's examination of population variations shape assumptions about the linkages between personal behavior and structural circumstances—or the absence thereof—and, in turn, ideas about agency and structure within the domain of health help to organize theories of etiology. Conventional etiologic stories that place individual health behaviors and risk factors as central protagonists must be broadened with a sense of how social conditions and community resources both limit and offer avenues for exercising agency to modify such risks and to respond to them, especially in ways that traditional epidemiology might not see or recognize. Contextualizing individual behaviors—as many social epidemiologists have been arguing we must do—means a fuller understanding of how people with heart disease experience risk and illness and what factors they believe promote, harm, and otherwise produce health. My analysis of the knowledges of people who live with heart disease demonstrates the conceptual richness of their understandings of disease determinants and the potential of incorporating their constructions of "cause" and "difference" to deepen the complexity and improve the accuracy of epidemiologic models and frameworks.

To accomplish this would require the participation of lay people who can describe from their own biographical experiences some of the social conditions and processes that have shaped their cardiovascular risks and their health. This in turn would necessitate fundamental changes in the status accorded to such knowledge. In conventional epidemiology to date, what Popay and Williams call "epistemological hegemony . . . not only discounted certain forms of knowledge from taking part in scientific discussion, it also disempowered groups of people working outside the dominant paradigm from making any contribution to debate over the policies which science could inform."[19] Diversifying the production of knowledge on health would therefore involve the reconstruction of meanings of "expertise" and its modes of legitimation: Valid and applicable knowledge should be understood to emerge not only from the application of the scientific method but also from the analysis of embodied experience.[20]

However, where the participation of lay individuals would come from and how their input could most effectively be incorporated is unclear. Currently, although there are some national organizations aimed at education and awareness, I am not aware of any politically oppositional, widely visible groups clearly defined as taking on heart disease in and of itself. The American Heart Association (AHA), perhaps the most prominent advocacy group, is highly scientized. The AHA was founded in 1924 by cardiologists to facilitate the sharing of study results and promote further research. It currently counts among its membership a significant number of clinicians and researchers. In addition, it sponsors scientific conferences and issues scientific statements regarding research priorities and clinical treatment. Despite its assumed widespread pertinence as the most frequent cause of morbidity and mortality, heart disease does not have associated with it a nationally prominent activist community rooted in the experiences of those with heart disease specifically. In this context, then, the process of bringing lay people into the production of epidemiologic knowledge may, at least at the outset, have to look somewhat different than in other cases such as AIDS, breast cancer, and environmental activism. In those instances, activists fashioned collective identities and commitments around specific disease conditions or residential status, for example, and organized successfully to make their voices and perspectives heard in setting priorities for, designing, implementing, and interpreting research.[21]

What boosts the prospects for social activism in the case of heart disease, however, is that it shares so many risk factors with other chronic conditions, such as Type 2 diabetes, stroke, obesity, and cancer. Thus the efforts of groups working to reduce inequalities in those other conditions or health disparities in general may have collateral benefits for changing our notions of the causes of heart disease. But in order to maximize their collective effect on how public health priorities are selected, framed, funded, and studied, health advocacy organizations should embrace a more explicit commitment to promoting the notion that intersecting social determinants shape health and disease, in addition to their usual focus on raising disease awareness, reducing risks, changing health-related behaviors, and eliminating health disparities. Indeed, there is a long history of collective action, particularly by women of color, that insisted on the importance of intersectional analysis and an emphasis on the underlying causes of disease.[22] Furthermore, the quest for a less individualizing, more progressive epidemiology would also profit from the efforts of organizations working toward racial and gender equality and economic and other kinds of social justice. Such groups—to the extent that they aim to change structural and institutional as well as interpersonal forms of power—can help to sustain a focus on the fundamental social processes and forces that stratify myriad advantages and disadvantages, including health and illness.

At the same time, the case of sociodemographic inequalities in heart disease presents somewhat of an interpretive and strategic dilemma for social movements. Efforts to establish a legitimate scientific basis for investigation into racial and sex/gender differences often selectively mobilize assertions of potential biological differences[23] and may have the effect of hardening and reifying demographic categories. Given this set of circumstances, it is imperative that the terms and conditions under which lay actors participate in knowledge production help ensure the serious consideration of structural, relational, and intersectional inequalities and disease causation. To be clear, however, I am not arguing that the knowledges and perspectives of people of color with heart disease are more authentic, more authoritative, closer to "reality," or less partial than those of science. Rather, they are no less so. Indeed, what is clear from my research is that lay people's analyses of the structural processes that give rise to the conditions within which they become ill—that place them "at risk of risks"[24]—were viewed by many epidemiology outsiders and by a growing number of insiders as plausible, upstream mechanisms of disease. They were, however, given almost no serious consideration in conventional scientific frameworks and practices.

Moreover, there are a number of cautionary tales when considering the inclusion of lay perspectives and participation. In the case of AIDS activism, often viewed as among the most successful in changing scientific practices, Steven Epstein found that "lay actors have been far less capable of influencing debates about causation (a more insulated preserve of biomedicine) than those concerned with treatment (a more public and 'applied' domain)."[25] This finding suggests that lay participation to change how etiologic science is conducted may face particularly difficult challenges. And as many scholars have pointed out,[26] the results of lay participation in science-making are complicated. Moves often made by pharmaceutical companies, health care corporations, hospitals, and other biomedical institutions may co-opt lay participation, reinforce or promote biomedicalization processes, or have other less than desirable consequences.

Expert–lay divisions can be replicated within social movements themselves, and lay activists might themselves come to question the scientific value added of a more participatory and democratized science. Or, as the public policy scholar Olena Hankivsky and her colleagues argue, in the context of science about power relations and inequality, drawing attention to processes of domination and subordination and conceptions of difference may serve to inadvertently reinforce negative stereotypes and essentialism. They also wonder whether coalitions between scientists and lay people—social groups with unequal political and economic power—can avoid reproducing existing inequalities.[27] Finally, while contesting experts' take on expertise is a critical intellectual move, in our knowledge-stratified society it also runs the risk, as the anthropologist Rayna Rapp so cogently observes, of "romanticizing popular knowledge at the expense of recognizing both the practical rigor and hegemonic claims" that science asserts.[28]

Such complications and qualifications notwithstanding, lay knowledge and embodied experiences have the potential to (and perhaps already have—more on this below) measurably influence how health research is conducted. But in order to do so, epidemiology itself, as a discipline, must eventually change its own paradigms and practices. Enriching the definitions of "expertise" and "knowledge" would involve transforming what counts as "science" and what the boundaries of science are, which in turn necessitates some reconsideration of the disciplinary cultures and organizational infrastructure of health research. I turn to these implications below.

Rethinking Funding Priorities, Criteria, and Disciplinary Cultures

My research supports both a conservative critique of epidemiology—that it needs to pay attention to more than the conventional universe of variables—and a more radical critique that challenges both the science of epidemiology and its politics.[29] I found that a wide range of political, economic, and organizational conditions not only constrained the development of alternative theories and methods in epidemiology but in fact encouraged the ritualized inclusion of individualized variables in order to build credibility. Replacing such practices with more carefully considered, theoretically grounded, and complex factors requires, therefore, addressing the conditions that reinforce and perpetuate those practices. This project suggests that one place to begin is with policies surrounding research funding—its priorities, the criteria by which proposals are judged, and prevailing definitions of feasibility and fundability.

First, I found that the execution of bureaucratic mandates to include racial and ethnic minorities and women in biomedical research may result in the inclusion of token diversity in research samples, without sufficient statistical power to reveal new and useful knowledge about the role of race, ethnicity, and sex/gender in health. Rather than simply requiring the inclusion of racial minorities and women, as epidemiologists perceive the current practice to be, funding criteria could more frequently reward explicit considerations of statistical power, even if research is conducted among only a few groups or in one underrepresented group. Criteria could also explicitly mandate that researchers offer justifications for the particular groups that *are* chosen, as well as require rationales for why groups are *not* chosen, so that data collection and interpretation are guided by plausible, potential causes of differences rather than by convenience or *a priori* perceptions that differences might, or must, exist. That is, funding agencies could ask that investigators articulate the range of possible interpretations of any differences that might be found and propose ways to analyze and weigh their relative likelihood as explanations for study results. Such measures may at least partially preclude the widespread but ineffectual tendency of health research to attribute disparities to unknown or uncertain mechanisms and to issue instead repeated calls for more future research.

Second, my findings also suggest that under the current scale of research funding, researchers find it almost impossible to undertake the long-range longitudinal studies that they feel are necessary to obtaining definitive answers about the effects of social factors and environment on heart disease causation. Funding criteria and priorities that obligate funders to short- to middle-range commitments encourage parsimony and inadvertently favor cost efficiency over conceptual and methodological advances. I thus argue that funding agencies should rethink the time horizon of research and the scale of their funding: The epidemiologists I interviewed and observed almost unanimously argue that extensive, and expensive, cohort studies and more time- and labor-intensive data collection (including qualitative methods) have the best hope of contributing to our understanding of the intersecting roles of biology, behavior, and social context. One way to both address a frequently mentioned flaw in funding and potentially reduce costs by a significant amount so that more high-priced longitudinal studies could be supported is to move away from disease-specific funding. Although this project has focused on heart disease, many of its mechanisms are linked to those of other illnesses, such as various forms of cancer, diabetes, and cerebrovascular diseases. Thus one study could, with sufficient financial and personnel support, examine multiple disease factors, processes, and outcomes.[30]

Third, funding priorities and criteria also dissuade epidemiologists from using or developing emergent analytic techniques or new conceptualizations and models of disease processes and social factors. In addition, their discussions of collaboration and barriers to it point to how the disciplinary worldviews and commitments to which they and their colleagues have been socialized lead almost inevitably to the distrust of alternative methods, insularity, and boundary-building defenses. Experimentation with unproven techniques and models is sorely needed to advance research in social inequalities in health. Yet given that methodological robustness and credibility are central criteria for most funding agencies, it is no surprise that any such methodological uncertainties are seen as "the kiss of death for funding," as one epidemiologist put it. Grant programs, rather than reward conceptual and methodological conservatism, should explicitly encourage and support exploratory research in the use and elaboration of new conceptualizations of sociodemographic factors and disease mechanisms and new models and analytic techniques. In these respects, the extent to which funders can promote transdisciplinary collaboration will be important. Epidemiologists, at least many of those I interviewed and observed, seem open and even eager to explore how sociologically grounded concepts of stratification and inequality might be used in health research. Basic social science research in theory-building around health disparities can also lead to improved and new methods.[31] Such shifts in funding criteria and priorities, if structured appropriately, could support more meaningful forms of representation in study samples, more longitudinal research, and greater interdisciplinary collaboration. Certainly there are scientists whom I have interviewed and observed whose scientific and political worldviews would inspire them to undertake more exploratory and epistemologically unconventional research and experiment with uncertain methods, if only their profession more often rewarded such efforts.

However, placing the source of the problem solely at the feet of funders would be erroneous. Thus a fourth transformation advocated by many is for epidemiology to undertake a serious examination of the intersections of different dimensions of "difference" and the consequences of group-based identities. My research has shown that the health effects of race, class, and gender cannot readily or meaningfully be distinguished from one another, and that in lived experiences of heart disease, it makes little etiologic sense to do so. On a technical level, of course, studying intersectionality would require, again, ensuring sufficient statistical power to compare groups classified according to race, class, or sex. But conceptually and epistemologically, such efforts would also require a fundamental shift in how epidemiologic science thinks about and treats "difference" in the context of health. While there are social processes consequential for cardiovascular risk that are predominantly racialized, classed, or gendered, attending to their interlocking dynamics constitutes a basic reconceptualization of the nature of difference and inequality as mutually constituted, sometimes synergistic, group-based, and relational. Effecting such epistemological transformations in the practice of epidemiology would require fundamental changes on myriad fronts, from definitions of credibility and validity, to standards for publication, and to reward structures for careers in epidemiology. Among the epidemiologists I spoke with or observed, those earlier in their careers were particularly eager to take up novel conceptions of difference, group and population health, and methodologies in their work, yet they simultaneously expressed concerns about the deleterious impacts such decisions could have on their professional trajectories.[32] On the one hand, epistemological concerns about the disciplinary standards and conceptual universe of epidemiology, and on the other, organizational and logistical issues of funding, collaboration, and reward structures within the profession, all in the end underscore the politics embedded in conceptions of difference, disease causation, definitions of expertise, and the social production of health and knowledge.

On Health Inequalities and Epidemiologic Futures

For many reasons, this is a pivotal moment in which to observe epidemiology and how it responds to pushes from within and outside its professional boundaries. Based on my research, it appears that epidemiology as a discipline is currently experiencing a period of unstable equilibrium. Conflicts and problems with the neglect of disparities, individualizing techniques, and the like, expressed by members of the scientific community and from those outside it, have contributed to calls for conceptual and methodological reforms. In response, some modifications in epidemiologic practice are being made that have a surface affinity to the demands for reform. Examples include regulatory changes that mandate the inclusion of women and minorities in government-funded research; changing standards of practice regarding the necessity to include measures of race, socioeconomic status, and sex in data collection and analysis; and some experimentation with alternative methods. However, many epidemiologists, other scholars, and activists argue that such nominal reforms cannot hope to answer fundamental questions of why inequalities in cardiovascular risk and disease occur and how they are produced.

On other fronts, the practice and scope of epidemiology have begun to develop a science that more directly examines multilevel complexity and causality. For example, the subdiscipline of social epidemiology is transforming the ways in which disease causation is conceptualized, the very definitions of what constitute "causes" and "risks," and the procedures through which disease risks are identified and studied.[33] Social epidemiology—also referred to as ecological or ecosocial epidemiology, or multilevel or contextual analysis[34]—is significant to the science and politics of heart disease causation for its innovative concerns with social inequalities in disease and its methods of studying social factors and differences. Multiple other works,[35] both within and consonant with social epidemiology, examine the health effects of such social processes as racial/ethnic inequality, discrimination, neighborhood environment, poverty, and segregation. As Lynn Weber and M. Elizabeth Fore[36] point out, the call to address these concerns—to look further upstream in the causal chain, to use ecological approaches, to collect multilevel data, and to develop and use new measures of social inequality—is also echoed by many in the mainstream of biomedical research.[37]

But to conduct such a science also involves finding ways to collaborate meaningfully across disciplines. The epidemiologists I spoke with continually pointed to an acute lack of the right kinds and the right mix of researchers for the job of producing knowledge about differences in cardiovascular risk and disease. They almost uniformly argue that the very kinds of advances crucial to better illuminating the nature of race, social class, and gender, and their effects for heart disease, lie at least partly outside the boundaries of their own expertise and of their discipline's research agenda. For instance, "I don't think we've spent enough time trying to get better measurement of those [social factors]," said one of my participants, Dr. Sheila Morris; "we've left it to the sociology realm, we've left it to the psychology realm. And we really need to spend more time doing more collaborative work with them. . . . We've exhausted what we already know. The traditional stuff is not explaining things enough, that we need to start exploring some other novel pathways." While there was wide agreement among the epidemiologists I interviewed that not enough collaborative research is being done, they also agreed that their colleagues are often reluctant to explore alternative methodologies and frameworks from other disciplines. As Dr. Henderson observed, "I think researchers get really stuck . . . [in] our way, our epistemology, our ontology, this is *how* we do . . . this is *what* we do. . . . That's sort of how we define ourselves is by what we do." Or, concluded another, "We let someone else worry [about it]."

Whether and how epidemiology finds its way forward will have deep consequences for a number of high-stakes issues. As Aronowitz notes, changes in perspective as to what constitutes legitimate data, whose perspectives are most important, and what kind of disease heart disease is— all have consequences for the relationships among lay, scientific, and clinical worlds.[38] My research indicates that lay people living with heart disease understand, negotiate, and take up the individualizing implications of epidemiologic knowledge in pragmatic, purposeful, and/or resolute ways. That is, while they often insist that the health effects of racial, class, and gender differences operate through structural mechanisms and relations of power, given the lack of societal-level change, they are also variously practical about having to watch their diet, take their medications, exercise, and otherwise care for themselves. Moreover, they do so within a health care context that demands increasing levels of self-care, self-initiative, and self-knowledge, the very kind of situation that many argue serves to exacerbate health inequalities and the social stratification of risk.[39]

Epidemiologic constructions of the effects of sex, gender, race, ethnicity, culture, and class on cardiovascular health also shape how providers practice medicine. That is, such constructions influence health professionals' conceptions of the boundaries between and relevance of human categories and groups and what they observe, what questions they ask of patients, and what conclusions they draw regarding diagnosis and treatment. Given my data on the individualization of difference, risk, and interventions, the idea of chemoprevention (prevention in a pill) has been a growing and exceedingly attractive option for many.[40] Currently cholesterol- and blood pressure–lowering drugs are widely prescribed: In the United States, some 25 percent of adults 45 years of age and over were on cholesterol-lowering medications during the period 2005 to 2008.[41] In that same time period, close to 22 percent of adults 18 years of age and over were on blood pressure medications.[42] Moreover, recent amendments to therapeutic guidelines[43] have increased even further the population for whom pharmacological risk reduction is deemed appropriate (tripling it in the case of cholesterol-lowering drugs). Particularly interesting also are recent moves by pharmaceutical companies to explore the potential for tailored drugs for specific groups, based on epidemiologic and genetic studies of "druggable differences"[44] in metabolism and efficacy. One such drug, BiDil, manufactured by Nitromed, Inc., in 2005 received FDA approval to be marketed for the treatment of heart failure specifically among African Americans.[45] While lackluster sales eventually led to the demise of Nitromed and its acquisition by another company in 2009, its unlicensed patents were purchased by a French drug company.[46] Pharmaceutical products like BiDil have the potential to effect the commodification and biomedicalization of difference.[47] As important, their emergence in turn contributes to the ongoing contentious debates over racial difference and disease and the necessity, scientific validity, or obsolescence of race-based medicine and biomedical research.

Symbolic interactionist studies of health and illness, and social constructionist studies of science and medicine teach us that meaning-making is a fluid, unstable, socially emergent enterprise. Thus, current definitions of the nature of race, class, and sex/gender in cardiovascular epidemiology are constantly being remade and unmade and actively sustained and revised. Yet at the same time, social theories that seek to analyze racial, class, and gender inequality also alert us to the recycling of certain representations of "difference," and the persistent ways in which they are linked to institutional and organizational processes. These theoretical perspectives sensitize us to the nature of our knowledge of heart disease as a social enterprise in two overlapping senses: first, in the sense that its practices and content are shaped by processes that are often simultaneously scientific *and* thoroughly social; and second, in the sense that as a product of social interactions and relationships itself, it is an underdetermined phenomenon. The enormous changes over its historic or even recent past highlight just how fluid a science it is, the uncertain outcome of a multitude of interactions, negotiated orders,[48] and revised meanings.

Cardiovascular risk and disease are a critical site at which racial, class, and gender stratification, technical and structural conditions of scientific knowledge production, biographical experiences of inequality and intersectionality, and embodied knowledges about health converge to create a science–lay divide over the causes of disease, conceptions of "difference," and the possibilities for remedying health inequalities. This site provides a window into the consequentiality of institutional and everyday biopolitics of knowledge and its entwinement with the nature of relations and mechanisms of power in the contemporary world. As such, this book is an attempt to provide the basis for an intervention into the production of "official" science on cardiovascular health, an effort to re-merge the political and the technical, and to reject the categorization of knowledges as either "expert knowledge" or "mere opinion," a separation that Donna Haraway calls the "founding gesture of what we call modernity."[49] Understanding the possibilities for pursuing social justice in our everyday lives requires that we reexamine how science and epidemiology construct and legitimate knowledges that constrain the prospects for health equity and social change.

The methodological processes that I detail below and their epistemological cal foundations have many affinities and alliances. First, this research embodies many of the unique aspects of multi-sited ethnography, in which data collection and fieldwork are conducted at multiple related sites based on the notion that the local manifestations of some sociological cal phenomena can be found in numerous different places and studied in a relatively open-ended fashion.[1] Certainly, knowledge claims about heart disease are pervasive: They reside in the pages of newspapers and popular magazines, in the conversations people have with one another, in television programs and commercials, in the halls of policymaking bodies, as well as in the hospital and the laboratory. Thus, a multi-sited ethnography in this case aims to follow the people and the data to the places and in the actions through which constructions about racial, class, and gender differences and their effects on the incidence and distribution of heart disease are being articulated, negotiated, revised, and sustained. Such a methodology offers the opportunity to compare how human differences are conceptualized to matter for cardiovascular risk within diverse settings and contexts, how they circulate in those settings, and what their consequences for health practices and social conceptions of "difference" might be.

My methodological approach also shares important aspects of Michel Foucault's genealogical method.[2] Genealogy seeks "to entertain the claims to attention of local, discontinuous, disqualified, illegitimate knowledges against the claims of a unitary body of theory which would filter, hierarchise and order them in the name of some true knowledge and some arbitrary idea of what constitutes a science and its objects."[3] As such, the genealogical method is concerned with the intersections and mutual generation of scientific knowledges about the body, the spread of technologies of power, and the role of human sciences (particularly the biological and biomedical sciences) in the organizing practices of modern societies.[4] Such a method also has activist intentions, as Foucault argues:

> it is really against the effects of the power of a discourse that is considered to be scientific that the genealogy must wage its struggle. . . . A genealogy should be seen as a kind of attempt to emancipate historical knowledges . . . to render them . . . capable of opposition and of struggle against the coercion of a theoretical, unitary, formal and scientific discourse. It is based on a reactivation of local knowledges . . . in opposition to the scientific hierarchisation of knowledges and the effects intrinsic to their power.[5]

Sources of Data

Drawing from the methodological commitments of multi-sited ethnography and Foucauldian genealogy, I collected data from multiple sources. These sources were selected for their ability to explore the substance and content, the range of perspectives, patterns of similarities and differences, and conditions shaping the production of the constructions of race, class, and gender in cardiovascular risk. My aim was to map out the array of positions taken and the multiple constructions framed, rather than to determine their frequency, prevalence, or trends of central tendency among the participants (as might be the case if one were using quantitative methods). The premise underlying the juxtaposition of scientific and lay expert knowledges is that each of them engages in a different "calculus of credibility,"[6] in Steven Epstein's words. By examining and analyzing

these knowledges, I can unveil their similar and distinctive constructions of race, class, and sex/gender in the production of heart disease,
their criteria for credibility, the consequences of their stratification, and
points of potential mutual engagement. My sources of qualitative data
included: (1) participant observation in a range of settings where epidemiologic knowledge about such differences is presented and debated;
(2) in-depth, semi-structured interviews with researchers specializing in
cardiovascular epidemiology; (3) in-depth, semi-structured interviews
with persons of color living with heart disease; and (4) a content analysis of the literature on epidemiology, its methods, and its role in health
policy and public affairs.

Participant Observation

First, participant observation was conducted from 1999 to 2002 and 2006
to 2010 in several types of settings: scientific meetings and professional
conferences where epidemiologic research was presented and discussed;
events intended for lay audiences aimed at public education and awareness regarding cardiovascular health; and lectures or symposia largely
intended for epidemiologic/scientific audiences in which the methods
of epidemiology or findings of specific studies were presented and discussed. Scientific conferences included the annual meetings of such professional organizations as the American Heart Association, American
College of Cardiology, American College of Epidemiology, Society for
Epidemiologic Research, and American Public Health Association. These
include some of the most prominent national professional organizations
involved in cardiovascular epidemiologic research. To select which sessions at these meetings to observe, my first priority was to attend oral
presentation and poster sessions in which findings of racial, socioeconomic, and/or sex differences in cardiovascular risk, incidence, and outcomes were explicitly discussed in some fashion. I also tried to attend all
sessions in which papers were being given on results from epidemiologic
studies that I knew were exploring such differences, even if the specific

presentation itself was not necessarily focused on those differences. Additionally, I attended didactic sessions, workshops, and tutorials on epidemiologic methods offered at these scientific conferences. Participant observation in these instances included not only listening to the presenters themselves but also observing (and occasionally participating in) the question-and-answer periods and informal interviews with the presenters after the sessions and/or with other attendees. Finally, in my remaining time, I spoke with researchers presenting at poster sessions, which offered terrific opportunities to interact with researchers and delve more in-depth into the substance of their claims, their methods, and interpretations of their data. I was also often able to purchase tape recordings of sessions that I was not able to attend. All oral presentations were audiotaped, then transcribed and supplemented with field notes. For face-to-face interactions and exchanges, notes were taken as soon as possible and then converted into more complete field notes at the end of the day.

Professional conferences are attended mostly by insiders and other members of the biomedical, public health, and epidemiologic communities who tend for the most part to share collective understandings of science and the legitimacy of the scientific method. By conducting participant observation at conferences, I was able to gather data on how researchers collectively spoke about and defined the effects of what they characterize as racial, socioeconomic, and gender differences on heart disease and reshaped their research practices to better explore them. Although conference presentations are frequently scripted events, they are also relatively informal when compared with publications and offer spaces where epidemiologists are able to discuss their work more candidly and reflexively. Problems, dilemmas, and contradictions encountered in doing epidemiologic work rarely are discussed at length in print but often are in question-and-answer sessions, discussions with colleagues, and informal conversations.

I also conducted participant observation at lectures and presentations on cardiovascular health and risks that were intended for both scientific/

biomedical and lay audiences. These included such events as lectures, mini-conferences, and health education events. Through participant observation at these venues, I examined how scientific information is being translated and transmitted to other scientists, clinicians, and the public. By analyzing these data, I wanted to understand whether and how epidemiologic constructions of racial, socioeconomic, and sex differences in cardiovascular risk were being framed and communicated. All oral presentations were audiotaped, then transcribed and supplemented with field notes in which I noted such details as audience attendance and participation; descriptions of slides, other visual aids, and printed materials; and preliminary impressions and analyses of my own and others' reactions to the content and tenor of the talks.

Finally, I enrolled in an introductory course in epidemiology and conducted participant observation throughout its duration. I kept field notes of relevant experiences in the epidemiology course. Initially, my intent with this activity was to gain sufficient background and familiarity with the concepts, language, and methods of epidemiology in order to better understand what questions to ask of epidemiologists, but it also offered the unexpected opportunity to observe how researchers are socialized and trained in the epidemiologic method.

Interviews with Cardiovascular Epidemiologists

My second source of data was in-depth, semi-structured interviews I conducted with a total of twenty-one scientists conducting research in cardiovascular disease epidemiology. The interviews allowed "official" knowledge producers to speculate much more freely than in published accounts of their work about how they believe race, ethnicity, social class, socioeconomic status, sex, and gender operate in heart disease causation, how they operationalize these kinds of differences, and the problems and difficulties they run into when conducting their work. Epidemiologists were also able to express what they might *like* to do, as opposed to what they actually do, and their accounts of any discrepancies that might exist

between the two. I also asked the respondents to reflect on the contributions of their own and others' studies to the understanding of racial, class,
and sex/gender inequalities within a historical context. Interview data
enabled me to map out a range of variation of positions on the conceptualization, operationalization, and epidemiologic management of race,
social class, and sex/gender.

In-person and telephone interviews with epidemiologists were conducted in two phases: from 2000 to 2001 and 2008 to 2012. Each interview lasted from forty-five minutes to two hours. My inclusion criteria
for scientists were that they used epidemiologic methods to investigate
cardiovascular disease risks and incidence, though they did not have
to necessarily self-identify professionally as an epidemiologist exclusively. Investigators currently publishing results from ongoing studies on
heart disease that took racial, class, and/or gender differences as central
research questions were selectively contacted and asked to participate
in these interviews; convenience and snowball sampling were also used.
All of these participants worked in academic research and university
settings. Eleven of the epidemiologists interviewed were women and ten
were men; seven (five female and two male) were scientists of color, as
measured by self-identification. All interviews were audiotaped, then
fully transcribed and supplemented with field notes.

Interviews with People of Color with Heart Disease

I conducted a total of twenty-four in-depth interviews with people of
color diagnosed with hypertension and/or coronary heart disease, also
in two waves from 1999 to 2002 and 2003 to 2005. These interviews were
conducted at the participants' homes or in meeting rooms at nearby
medical institutions. They covered issues of how individuals understand
and incorporate medical knowledge about heart disease causes and risk
factors, assess their own risks, engage with biomedical institutions, and
consider their social status vis-à-vis race, class, and gender as influencing
these experiences. Additionally, basic demographic information such as

racial–ethnic identification, occupation, income, wealth, sex, and age were collected with a short standardized questionnaire.

Interviewees were recruited through the posting of flyers in a range of community-based health organizations and private, teaching, and non-profit medical institutions in different geographic communities. These communities were located within the larger San Francisco Bay Area; the respondents' proximity allowed me to interview them in person. Three racial–ethnic groups—Asian Pacific Americans, African Americans, and Latinos/Hispanics—were of particular interest because of their high rates of heart disease and concerns about their relationships to mainstream biomedical institutions. By recruiting from different kinds of health care institutions, I tried to secure the participation of people from different socioeconomic backgrounds. Interviewees were offered $20 to thank them for their participation. These interviews were audiotaped, supplemented with field notes on the interview, then fully transcribed.

Of the twenty-four interviews, eleven were with African Americans (seven with women, four with men), seven with Latina/os (five women, two men), and six with Asian Pacific Americans (four women, two men). At the time of their interviews, they ranged from 41 to 82 years of age, of whom twelve were under the age of 65, and the remaining twelve over 65. Approximately half of this sample had annual household incomes of less than $35,000 while the other half had incomes of $35,000 or greater. Their age at diagnosis with either hypertension or coronary heart disease ranged from as young as 20 up to 66 years old.

Review of Literature

The final source of data was a review of the epidemiologic literature on the significance and use of race and ethnicity, social class, and sex and gender. In particular, I paid attention to commentaries and opinion pieces, editorials and letters to the editor, articles detailing methodological issues, and papers addressing the discipline of epidemiology and its mission and practices, published from roughly 1985 to 2000. While I did

not conduct a formal content analysis, I used this review of the literature to understand ongoing discussions and debates about the inclusion,
operationalization, and interpretation of racial/ethnic, socioeconomic,
and sex/gender differences in research on heart disease etiology. Rather
than an examination of empirical findings on such differences in heart
disease incidence, this review was intended to capture how those in the
epidemiologic community themselves evaluated their own discipline; its
conventional practices with respect to race, ethnicity, social class, socioeconomic status, and sex and gender; and its potential to illuminate and
intervene in health disparities.

Analysis of Data

All materials, including participant observation and interview field notes,
materials collected at professional meetings, and transcripts of interviews
and taped scientific proceedings, were coded and analyzed using the
general principles of grounded theory in its more constructivist visions.[7]
Grounded theory focuses on uncovering the social processes and conditions that lie behind the phenomena in question and following their
consequences and effects. It is an analytic methodology that is especially
suited to an exploratory study of the kind conducted here, where the
general phenomena and its processes have not been fully articulated and
constant comparison (for example, between data from epidemiologists
and those from people of color living with heart disease) is central to the
analysis. Grounded theory offers a systematic process that moves beyond
description into analysis, and through which theories can be developed
inductively. Moreover, constructivist grounded theory "celebrates first-
hand knowledge of empirical worlds, . . . assumes the relativism of multiple social realities, recognizes the mutual creation of knowledge by the
viewer and the viewed, and aims toward interpretive understanding of
subjects' meanings."[8]

I began analyzing the data as they were being collected, starting
with the simultaneous processes of open coding and memoing, where

concepts were labeled and grouped into categories, and those categories were developed in terms of their properties and dimensions through the writing of memos. These codes and categories were developed around the phenomenon of interest, specifically the formation of definitions and conceptualizations of race, social class, and gender and how they affect or are affected by understandings of incidence, outcomes, and management of cardiovascular disease.

In coding and memoing, I paid particular attention to the specific content of the definitions and how those conceptualizations prevalent in epidemiologic research are formed and used in the study of heart disease etiology. Codes and categories were used to highlight the range of consequences that concepts of race, class, and gender have for our understanding of the nature of the "problem" of and "solutions" to heart disease inequalities. Additional codes and categories related to the knowledge constructions, social and economic resources, health beliefs and practices, access to and evaluation of medical information, and other factors that impinge on the health of lay people. By developing and using the same codes across the two types of interviews (with epidemiologists and with individuals with heart disease) and participant observation data, I was able to examine the variations in the meanings of "difference" and scientific and health practices across the different sources of data, facilitating their explication and categorization and serving as a kind of triangulation.

Once the coding process had been completed twice by hand, and the codes themselves and their relationships to one another preliminarily defined, all transcripts and field notes were entered into a qualitative research computer software program, ATLAS.ti. These materials were again coded, paragraph by paragraph, using a coding "tree" that organized individual codes within categories and groups. This software allowed for convenient access to coded elements, including retrieving all paragraphs tagged with a single particular code, intersection of two or more codes, and the union of two or more codes. Using these features of ATLAS.ti facilitated the comparison and contrasting of codes, and exploring their properties and relationships with other codes, which resulted in a deeper understanding of how and when codes, and the discourses, dynamics, and social processes they referred to, occurred together, overlapped, or remained distinct from one another. This in turn aided the shift from more descriptive to more analytic codes and categories and the inductive development and elaboration of concepts and theories.

Throughout the coding and memoing processes, under the principle of theoretical sampling, I allowed my changing understandings and directions of my research questions to influence my ongoing data collection decisions. Theoretical sampling argues that data collection should "be driven by concepts derived from the evolving theory and based on the concept of 'making comparisons,' whose purpose is to go to places, people, or events that will maximize opportunities to discover variations among concepts and to densify categories in terms of their properties and dimensions."[9] This is particularly useful for explorations of new areas as it allows researchers to choose those avenues of sampling that offer the greatest potential for theoretical return. As I reached theoretical saturation on some questions, I shifted my sampling, questionnaires, and data collection strategies to pursue newly articulated and redefined questions based on a different perspective or experience raised in an interview. Such decisions were intended to gather sufficient data on the range of positions and perspectives taken on the role and effects of race, class, and sex/gender on cardiovascular disease.

NOTES

NOTES TO THE INTRODUCTION

1. Omi and Winant (1994: 60).
2. American Heart Association Statistics Committee and Stroke Statistics Subcommittee (2007).
3. World Health Organization (2003).
4. American Heart Association Statistics Committee and Stroke Statistics Subcommittee 2013: e8, e109.
5. Note that because of overlap, it is not possible to add the estimated populations with these conditions to arrive at a total (American Heart Association Statistics Committee and Stroke Statistics Subcommittee 2012: e3, e54, e88).
6. Cohen and Krauss (2003).
7. American Heart Association Statistics Committee and Stroke Statistics Subcommittee (2007: e162).
8. Direct costs include medical expenditures (cost of physicians and other professional services, hospital services, prescribed medication, and home health care); indirect costs include lost future productivity attributed to premature death (American Heart Association Statistics Committee and Stroke Statistics Subcommittee 2012: e209–e210).
9. American Heart Association Statistics Committee and Stroke Statistics Subcommittee (2012: e211).
10. Unless otherwise noted, statistics are drawn from the American Heart Association Statistics Committee and Stroke Statistics Subcommittee (2012) and NCHS (National Center for Health Statistics) (1998). I refer here to various kinds of groups (e.g., "American Indians," "Hispanics") by the category labels used in these sources.
11. Hunt (2002).
12. Bibbins-Domingo et al. (2009).
13. Jolly et al. (2010).

14. Foraker et al. (2011).

15. See note 9, this chapter.

16. Byrd and Clayton (2001) and Myrdal (1954/1996).

17. For example, hypertension, a risk factor for coronary heart disease, is higher among blacks than whites and higher among men than women until the age of 65, when rates are higher among women (American Heart Association Statistics Committee and Stroke Statistics Subcommittee 2013). Hypertension is also higher among black and Mexican American women than white women (Winkleby et al. 1998). The prevalence of diabetes is higher among blacks and Mexican Americans than among whites, and death rates from diabetes are far higher for blacks than whites (American Heart Association Statistics Committee and Stroke Statistics Subcommittee 2013). Cigarette smoking has historically been and continues to be more common among persons of lower socioeconomic status, with the gap between the most educated and least educated increasing over the past few decades (NCHS 2011). Obesity is similarly more prevalent among women of lower educational status, although men of all races do not exhibit a clear educational gradient (NCHS 2011; Winkleby et al. 1998). Black and Hispanic women were much more likely to be overweight than white women (American Heart Association Statistics Committee and Stroke Statistics Subcommittee 2013). Physical inactivity is also more prevalent among blacks and Hispanics, and it is also strongly related to income for all age, sex, and ethnic groups (American Heart Association Statistics Committee and Stroke Statistics Subcommittee 2013; Crespo et al. 2000; NCHS 1998; Winkleby et al. 1998). One study indicated that many of these disparities in risk factors—including body-mass index, dietary fat intake, blood pressure, and smoking—appear much earlier in the life course than had previously been thought (Winkleby et al. 1999).

18. For example, Mexican Americans and Hispanics with hypertension are more likely to go untreated than blacks or whites (American Heart Association Statistics Committee and Stroke Statistics Subcommittee 2013). Research also reveals that Mexican Americans and African Americans are less likely than whites to receive cholesterol screening (Nelson et al. 2002). Among those screened and found to have high cholesterol, Mexican Americans and African Americans are less likely than whites (Nelson et al. 2002), and women less likely than men (Miller et al. 2000), to be taking cholesterol-lowering drugs. Studies have also found that people of color have lower age-adjusted utilization rates for higher-technology treatment *after* heart disease has been diagnosed. For example, blacks less frequently receive cardiac catheterization (Chen et al. 2001; Escarce et al. 1993; Popescu et al. 2007; Wenneker and Epstein 1989; Whittle et al. 1993), reperfusion therapy for acute myocardial infarction (Canto et al. 2000; Petersen et al. 2002), and coronary artery bypass surgery (Escarce et al. 1993; Popescu et al. 2007; Wenneker and Epstein 1989; Whittle et al. 1993) than do whites, even after controlling for payer source, co-morbidities, and other factors. Differences in cardiac

catheterization rates were found to persist regardless of the race of the physician (Chen et al. 2001). Women were also found to be less likely than men to undergo angiography and angioplasty (Ayanian and Epstein 1991) and bypass surgery (Ayanian and Epstein 1991; Bertoni et al. 2004).

19. See, for example, Shriver (1997). One study found that black patients with left ventricular systolic dysfunction have higher overall mortality than white patients (Dries et al. 1999), and young African Americans were found to have increased left ventricular mass when compared with their white counterparts (Dekkers et al. 2002). Also, genetic studies to pinpoint possible genes responsible for racial differences in cardiovascular health, for example, in left ventricular mass and contractility (e.g., Arnett et al. 2001a; 2001b), in hypertension (e.g., Suthanthiran et al. 2000), and in coronary heart disease (e.g., Wu et al. 2001) are common. Comparisons across racial–ethnic groups have also found significant differences in the effects of various risk and other factors on cardiovascular physiology (e.g., He et al. 1999; Pristipino et al. 2000; Treiber et al. 2000; Woo et al. 1997). Along differences of sex, innumerable studies are aimed at understanding the role of estrogen in coronary heart disease (e.g., Blumenthal et al. 2000; McCrohon et al. 1999; Steinberg et al. 2000).

20. For example, one study of black males in rural North Carolina found a positive relationship between blood pressure and perceptions that being black hindered one's chances for success among those actively seeking to improve their socioeconomic status (James et al. 1984). More recent investigations have analyzed the cardiovascular effects of experiences of discrimination and other potential predictors of discrimination such as skin color, socioeconomic status, and gender (e.g., Clark 2003; Guyll et al. 2001; Klag et al. 1991; Krieger 1990; Krieger et al. 1998). These studies are usually grounded within social epidemiology and work from the hypothesis that experiences of discrimination result in stress and internalized anger that in themselves constitute risk factors for heart disease. Other studies examine potential social, environmental, and dynamic mechanisms through which one's social position and experiences engender heart disease (e.g., Cubbin et al. 2001; Diez-Roux et al. 1997; Diez-Roux et al. 2000; Ford et al. 2000; Marmot et al. 1997b; Matthews et al. 2002).

21. As described in the appendix, the data on which this book is based were gathered from both epidemiologists and people of color diagnosed with heart disease. Throughout, I refer to the lay participants in my study using such terms as "lay people," "people of color," "those with heart disease," and so on.

22. Connerly is perhaps best known for spearheading the campaign to eliminate the consideration of race and gender in public education, public contracting, and public employment in California, a battle in which he was ultimately successful against the opposition of numerous grassroots organizations.

23. The measure also exempts the Department of Fair Employment and Housing, in order to comply with federal mandates and funding requirements.

24. Exner et al. (2001), Fullilove (1998), LaVeist (1996), Schwartz (2001), and Wood (2001).
25. Epstein (2007).
26. For example, Ayanian et al. (1993), Escarce et al. (1993), Wenneker and Epstein (1989), Whittle et al. (1993), and Yancy et al. (2001).
27. Schwartz (2001) and Satel (2000; 2002)
28. For example, Stolberg (2001).
29. See, for example, Bliss (2012), Fullwiley (2008), Hunt and Megyesi (2008), Montoya (2007; 2011), Outram and Ellison (2006a; b), and Whitmarsh (2008).
30. Wizemann and Pardue (2001).
31. For example, Hulley et al. (1998).
32. Hodis et al. (2003) and Manson et al. (2003).
33. For example, Bairey Merz et al. (2006), Jacobs (2006), Lerman and Sopko (2006), Quyyumi (2006), and Shaw et al. (2006).
34. NIH Office of Behavioral and Social Sciences Research et al. (2002).
35. See NIH Office of Behavioral and Social Sciences Research et al. (2001).
36. National Institutes of Health (2011).
37. Here I rely especially on discussion in Shim (2005).
38. Arksey (1994).
39. Brown (1987; 1992; 1997).
40. Brown (1992: 268).
41. Epstein (1995; 1996).
42. See, for example, Collins and Evans (2002; 2007), Evans and Collins (2008), Jasanoff (2003a; b), and Wynne (1995; 1996a; b; 2003).
43. Heart disease itself is a socially constructed and contested entity. While I do not interrogate its historical construction here, several other scholars have (e.g., Jones 2000; 2013; Pollock 2007; 2012). In this book I use "heart disease" as a shorthand term to include both hypertension (high blood pressure) and coronary heart disease, a condition wherein the coronary arteries that provide the heart tissue with blood become occluded and harden, resulting in insufficient blood supply to the heart, often leading to chest pain and heart attacks.
44. Collins (1991; 1998), Glenn (2002), McCall (2001; 2005), Schulz and Mullings (2006), and Weber (2010).
45. Clarke et al. (2003; 2010b).
46. Clarke et al. (2010a) and Shim (2010b).
47. On the concept of black boxes in science and technology studies, see Latour (1987) and Latour and Woolgar (1986).
48. Epstein (1996: 28).
49. Fujimura (1987; 1996).
50. Jasanoff (2004).
51. Shim (2000).
52. Lambert and Rose (1996) and Wynne (1995; 1996b).

53. For example, Brenner and Laslett (1986) and Glenn (1992/1996).

54. In March and April of 2008, PBS aired a series of documentaries under this title, exploring the work of numerous social epidemiologists and other allied scholars. See www.unnaturalcauses.org.

NOTES TO CHAPTER 1

1. Foucault (1997: 248).
2. Foucault (1978: 143).
3. Foucault (1978: 139).
4. Foucault (1978: 139).
5. Foucault (1997: 253).
6. Foucault (1997: 253).
7. Foucault (1997: 38).
8. Foucault (1997: 24).
9. Foucault (1997: 30).
10. Epstein (1996: 49).
11. Foucault (1978: 26).
12. Foucault (1997: 254–5).
13. Foucault (1997: 256).
14. Foucault (1978: 149).
15. Foucault (1997: 61–2).
16. Foucault (1997: 81).
17. Stoler (1995: 61).
18. Epstein (2007: 17).
19. Casper and Moore (2009: 6).
20. Clarke et al. (2003; 2010b).
21. Clarke et al. (2010a: 2).
22. Petryna (2002).
23. Petryna (2002: 13).
24. Petryna (2002: 6).
25. Rose (2007: 6).
26. Rose (2007: 54).
27. Rose (2007: 167).
28. Rose (2007: 70).
29. Rose (2007: 255).
30. See also Fassin (2009).
31. Crenshaw (1989).
32. Hankivsky et al. (2010).
33. Davis (2008).
34. These assumptions are drawn from Hankivsky et al. (2010), Schulz and Mullings (2006), and Weber (2010).
35. Spelman (1988).

36. Weber (2010).
37. Weber (2010: 34).
38. Omi and Winant (1994: 55).
39. Omi and Winant (1994: 56).
40. For example, Hankivsky et al. (2010) and McCall (2005).
41. Weber (2010: 90–2).
42. Collins (1998: 208).
43. McCall (2005). See also Davis (2008: 73).
44. McCall (2005: 1783).
45. McCall (2005: 1773).
46. Cassel (1976), Engels (1845/1978), Graham (1963), Syme et al. (1965), and Virchow (1848).
47. Link and Phelan (1995; 1996), Link et al. (1998), Phelan and Link (2005), and Phelan et al. (2004; 2010).
48. Link and Phelan (1995: 81).
49. Phelan et al. (2010: S30).
50. Link et al. (1998: 397).
51. Phelan and Link (2005: 29).
52. Carpiano and Kelly (2007), Chang and Lauderdale (2009), Glied and Lleras-Muney (2008), Link et al. (1998), Phelan and Link (2005), and Tehranifar et al. (2009).
53. Weber and Fore (2007: 210).
54. Collins (1991; 1998), Fonow and Cook (1991), and Weber and Parra-Medina (2003).
55. Weber and Fore (2007).

NOTES TO CHAPTER 2

1. Roth (1976: 48–9).
2. As mentioned in the Introduction, I use the terms "race," "class," and "gender" for the most part to refer to social relations of power, and the terms "racial category/ies," "socioeconomic status," and "sex" to refer to their transposition and devolution into individualized, discrete variables typically used in epidemiologic research.
3. Roth (1976).
4. See Hacking (1982; 1990), Lupton (1995), Porter (1986; 1995), Rose (1990), Schweber (2006), and Starr (1982).
5. Amsterdamska (2005: 30).
6. See Gordis (2000), Hennekens and Buring (1987), and Lilienfeld and Lilienfeld (1980).
7. Schweber (2006: 24).
8. Armstrong (1983), Jackson (2003), and Shim (2000).
9. Foucault (1978). Indeed, Schweber (2006: 25) argues that "Foucault's identification of 'population' as one of the primary objects of modern political power gave a

new currency to population statistics in particular"—that is, to epidemiology and other allied disciplines.

10. Canguilhem (1978).

11. Schweber (2006: 26).

12. Porter (1995: 45).

13. For historical analysis of how epidemiology fared during the era of microbiology and the germ theory, see, for example, Amsterdamska (2005), Jackson (2003), and Susser and Susser (1996a).

14. Susser (1985: 150). See also Aronowitz (1998).

15. Host factors include, for example, immunologic status, genetic background, socioeconomic level, hygienic practices, behavioral patterns, age, and the presence of co-existing disease (Evans 1978; Gordis 2000; Lilienfeld and Lilienfeld 1980; MacMahon et al. 1960; Susser 1985).

16. Bhopal (1999), Krieger (1994), Susser (1985), and Susser and Susser (1996a).

17. Amsterdamska (2005: 42).

18. Brandt (1997), Lilienfeld and Lilienfeld (1980).

19. I do not mean to suggest that the surveillance of individuals and communities was a new phenomenon emerging in the mid–twentieth century. In fact, governmental apparatuses to measure, survey, record, and regulate patterns of health and disease have been in existence since at least the eighteenth century (e.g., Armstrong 1983; La Berge 1992; Rose 1990). The nineteenth and early twentieth centuries saw a proliferation of government agencies, professional specializations, and philanthropic and volunteer organizations set up to deal with public health issues, including surveillance and intervention activities into practices of health, lifestyle, self- and (in the case of women) other-care, and hygiene (e.g., Fee and Porter 1992; Rogers 1992). However, in the case of studies undertaken to address etiologic questions of cardiovascular disease, the mid–twentieth century does represent a watershed in the mass surveillance and measurement of populations via epidemiologic techniques.

20. Dawber (1980: 15).

21. New organizational guidelines allocated research into methods of disease prevention and control to the National Institutes of Health, while projects concerned with practical control measures belonged elsewhere in the Public Health Service (Dawber 1980: 17).

22. Dawber (1980: 17–23).

23. Dawber (1980: 16).

24. See www.framinghamheartstudy.org.

25. See Karin Garrety's work (1997a; 1997b; 1998) for a thorough historical analysis of the contestations over the connections between dietary fat, blood cholesterol levels, and heart disease.

26. NHLBI (2001).

27. Susser (1985: 151).

28. Susser (1985).

29. Pollock (2007: 98).
30. Nieto (1999) and Aronowitz (1998: 223–4, note 2) cite the first published use of the term "risk factor" to a paper by Kannel and colleagues (1961). Aronowitz (1998: 97–8) notes, however, that the notion of "disease predisposition," prominent in the first half of the twentieth century, anticipated the conceptualization and identification of "risk factors" with respect to heart disease.
31. NHLBI (2001).
32. Nor, as important, did it force physicians to engage further in preventive practices so much as add to the list of conditions (e.g., hypertension, hypercholesterolemia) they could treat medically (Aronowitz 1998).
33. Susser (1985).
34. Aronowitz (1998).
35. Dawber (1980: 22).
36. Dawber (1980: 60).
37. Moreover, as Pollock (2007: 99–100) argues, the location for the study was legitimated in part through claims that Framingham was a "normal," typical, average, and therefore representative reflection of a pan-white, Euro-American town. Two additional findings from Pollock's work are worth noting here. First, this notion of a homogenous, "white" population is one that had to be actively constructed in the process of collecting, recording, and storing data on categories variously termed as "race," "national origin," and even nutrition for the Framingham Study (Pollock 2007: 111–8). And second, the language shifted fairly quickly from claims of representation to those of extrapolation, that the Framingham sample was not so "grossly atypical" that the results could not be generalized to other (white) Americans (Pollock 2007: 103–10).
38. Moreover, what we take to be "heart disease" has changed since the Framingham days. Pollock explains this through her comparison of Framingham to the Jackson Heart Study, begun in 2000 and often referred to as the "Black Framingham." Similar to Framingham, the Jackson Heart Study selected participants from the residents of a particular town, this time African Americans living in Jackson, Mississippi, to study atherosclerosis (the accumulation of fatty plaques along the walls of the coronary arteries) and its risk factors among this high-risk racial group. As Pollock argues: "Framingham has attended first and foremost to the coronary artery disease from combined risk factors of the white middle class. Jackson attends to the burden of morbidity and mortality on people of color who were left behind by America's post-war medical advances. Medical knowledge about the diseases of the heart comes to include an expanding notion of who counts as American: from WASP, to pan-white, to racially fractured, and in parallel from high SES to middle class and then also low SES" (Pollock 2007: 139).
39. Susser (1985).
40. However, Pollock (2007: 121–4) points out that the Omni Study does not include minorities in sufficient numbers to be able to make comparative claims across racial/ethnic populations.

41. Numerous epidemiologic studies examining the effects of preventive programs at the community level have also been initiated. However, as these studies investigate the efficacy of heart disease interventions, rather than the determinants of heart disease incidence and distribution, they are outside of the scope of this project and are not discussed here.

42. Porter (1995).

43. Amsterdamska (2005: 45).

44. Approximate total sample sizes are provided to give a sense of the large numbers of individuals being enrolled in these studies.

45. Syme et al. (1975).

46. ARIC Investigators (1989).

47. Friedman et al. (1988).

48. MESA Coordinating Center (2011).

49. Stampfer et al. (1985).

50. Lee et al. (1990).

51. NHLBI (1999).

52. Willett and Colditz (1998).

53. Blackburn and Epstein (1995).

54. See note 25, this chapter.

55. In the Framingham Study, Type A behavior pattern was measured through questionnaires that included the following questions and items: (1) "traits and qualities which describe you: being hard-driving and competitive, usually pressed for time, being bossy or dominating, having a strong need to excel in most things, eating too quickly"; (2) "feeling at the end of an average day of work: often felt very pressed for time, work stayed with you so you were thinking about it after working hours, work often stretched you to the very limits of your energy and capacity, often felt uncertain, uncomfortable, or dissatisfied with how well you were doing"; and (3) "do you get upset when you have to wait for anything?" (Haynes et al. 1978: 382).

56. Pooling Project Research Group (1978).

57. Blackburn and Epstein (1995: 1258).

58. Lipid fractions include low-density and high-density lipoproteins—the now fairly well-known LDL (or "bad") and HDL (or "good") cholesterol—as well as triglycerides.

59. See, for example, Hemingway and Marmot (1999), King (1997), Manuck et al. (1986), Schneiderman et al. (1989), Thoresen and Powell (1992), and Williams (1987).

60. See, for example, Berkman (1984; 1986), Berkman and Syme (1979), Greenwood et al. (1996), Hemingway and Marmot (1999), Lepore (1998), and Seeman (1996).

61. See, for example, Howard (1999), Kumanyika and Adams-Campbell (1991), LaRosa et al. (1990), and Schmieder and Messerli (1987).

62. Genest and Cohn (1995).

63. See, for example, Genest and Cohn (1995), Hsueh and Law (1998), Kaplan (1989), Liese et al. (1998), Modan et al. (1985), and Reavan (1988).
64. Syme (2000: xi).
65. Aronowitz (1998).
66. Porter (1995: 77).
67. Armstrong (1995).
68. For example, Anderson (1996), Ernst and Harris (1999), Jones (1993), Jordanova (1989), Krieger and Fee (1994), Lupton (1995), Oudshoorn (1994), Porter (1999), Reverby (2009), and Shah (2001).
69. See, for example, Clarke and Olesen (1999), Morgen (2002), Nelson (2011), Ruzek (1978), Smith (1995), and White (1994). It is important to note that many of the struggles chronicled in these works articulated racial, class, and gender oppressions as of a piece, woven together, and whose intersecting, cumulative effects impoverished the well-being of multiple vulnerable groups.
70. Waldby (1996:101).
71. Pollock (2007; 2012).
72. Angell and Kassirer (1994: 189). They are not alone in these sentiments; see also Mann (1995) and Taubes (1995).
73. Irwin and Wynne (1996a: 215).
74. For example, Irwin and Wynne (1996b) and Jasanoff et al. (1995).
75. For example, Irwin and Wynne (1996b). Irwin and Wynne (1996a: 218) conclude that "what scientists interpret as a naïve and impracticable public expectation of a zero-risk environment can . . . be seen instead as an expression of zero trust in institutions which claim to be able to manage large-scale risks throughout society." The analyses described in the following chapters seek in part to explore this proposition in the context of accounts of cardiovascular risk and causation.
76. See Marks (1997).
77. Observational data come from cohort and similar kinds of studies, where interventions or treatment are not being attempted.
78. Interestingly, a 1985 publication of results from the Framingham Heart Study (Wilson et al. 1985) indicated that HRT increased women's risk of stroke, but this finding was dismissed until the Women's Health Initiative publication in 2002 (Levy and Brink 2005).
79. In fact, because of the etiologic complexity of chronic disease, the term "risk factor" rather than "cause" is usually applied (Evans 1978: 167). Some (e.g., Dawber 1980) have gone so far as to state that "cause" is a word that epidemiologists prefer to avoid, as it connotes that a factor labeled as such would lead to disease in every case of exposure, when disease-related factors that still have a causal effect rarely if ever work in such a fashion. While the judgment of whether a particular risk factor operates in an associative or in a cause–effect manner is traditionally represented as a separate stage in the epidemiologic method, in everyday

epidemiologic parlance the terms "risks" and "risk factors" often refer to suspected direct or indirect "causes" or "causal mechanisms" of heart disease.

80. Aronowitz (1998).

81. Aronowitz (1998: 144).

82. Aronowitz (1998: 128).

83. See, for example, Kaufman and Cooper (1999).

84. Diez-Roux (1998b).

85. External validity also depends on the response rate and retention of participants throughout the course of a longitudinal study, in addition to the initial eligibility criteria for inclusion that are discussed here.

86. How cardiovascular epidemiologists manage the measurement and conceptualization of such social variables is the focus of later chapters.

87. However, Garrety (1997a: 188–90) shows that in the case of serum cholesterol, the perception that physiological measures are more reliable in this regard is not always true.

88. See Diez-Roux (1998a), Krieger (1994), McKinlay and Marceau (2000), McMichael (1995), Pearce (1996), Shy (1997), and Susser and Susser (1996a).

89. Diez-Roux (1998a), Krieger (1994), and McMichael (1995).

90. Krieger (1994: 890).

91. Diez-Roux (1998a).

92. NCHS (1998).

93. For example, McGinnis and Foege (1993).

94. For example, Crespo et al. (2000).

95. Pearce (1996).

96. See note 2 in this chapter.

97. For example, Diez-Roux (1998a), Duncan et al. (1996), and Von Korff et al. (1992).

98. For example, Diez-Roux (1998a), Susser (1998), and Susser and Susser (1996b).

99. Krieger (1994: 894).

100. Many commentators (e.g., McMichael 1995; Pearce 1996; Vandenbroucke 1994) have observed that the concept of an epidemiology that takes seriously, in theoretical and methodological terms, the influence of social relations and structural environments is not new. They argue that these kinds of approaches are in fact a return to the ecological, environmental, community, and social concerns of epidemiology's early pioneers, such as Edwin Chadwick, Friedrich Engels, William Farr, Rudolf Virchow, and John Snow. Susser (1985: 153) notes that more recently, during the mid-twentieth-century epidemiologic transition from infectious to chronic diseases as leading causes of death in the United States, it became increasingly clear that social and environmental factors were significant to the incidence of illness. Key innovators in this tradition include Cassel (1976), Graham (1963), Susser (1964), and Syme et al. (1965).

101. Diez-Roux (1998a).

102. An often-used example of an ecological fallacy is the assumption, based on observations that societies with high-fat diets have high rates of heart disease, that high-fat diets lead to heart disease. Such an assumption is impossible to make from this aggregate level of data as it is not possible to tell whether those individuals developing heart disease in a particular country are in fact those with the high-fat diets; exposure cannot be linked to the incidence of disease. However, this focus on the individual level to the virtual exclusion of group-level factors is changing somewhat; these moves are taken up in the Conclusion.

103. See, for example, Diez-Roux (1998a).

104. Diez-Roux (1998a: 220).

105. See also Susser (1998) and Susser and Susser (1996b).

106. Susser (1998: 610–11).

107. Susser (1998: 610).

108. Diez-Roux (1998b: 1029).

109. Rose (1985; 1992).

110. Poole and Rothman (1998). See, for example, Coughlin (1998), Diez-Roux (1998a), Kogevinas (1998), Koopman (1996), Krieger (1994), Krieger and Zierler (1996; 1997), Mackenbach (1998), McMichael (1995), McPherson (1998), Pearce (1996), Savitz (1997), Savitz et al. (1999), Shy (1997), Susser (1989; 1998), Susser and Susser (1996b), and Taubes (1995).

111. For example, Krieger (1994), Krieger and Zierler (1996), McMichael (1995), McPherson (1998), Pearce (1996), and Williams (1997).

112. For example, Diez-Roux (1998a), Poole and Rothman (1998), Susser and Susser (1996b), and Vineis (1998).

113. For example, Berkman and Kawachi (2000a) and Mackenbach (1998).

114. For example, Krieger and Zierler (1996; 1997), McMichael (1995), Savitz (1997), Susser (1998), and Susser and Susser (1996b).

115. Susser (1998: 609).

116. Susser (1998: 610).

117. Susser (1998: 609).

118. Bhopal (1997; 1999). Kuhn (1962/1996) argues that in "normal science," research is firmly based upon past scientific achievements that a particular scientific community accepts as the foundation for its practice. A reigning paradigm provides the conceptual means to guide current research and by which certain problems are taken to be scientific and the proper domain of scientists. Normal science continues until anomalies accumulate, producing a scientific crisis and engendering a paradigm shift. Kuhn's emphasis on the accumulation of anomalies as the driving force behind scientific crises and paradigm shifts has been critiqued by more recent works in science studies (Gieryn 1999; Hess 1997; Star 1986, 1989) as overly intellectualist and neglectful of the influence of broader social and cultural transformations within which the practice of science is always cradled.

119. Koopman (1996: 630).

120. Porter (1995: 230).
121. As Gieryn (1999: 23) argues, "[I]f the stakes are autonomy over scientists' ability to define problems and select procedures for investigating them, then science gets 'purified,' carefully demarcated from all political and market concerns, which are said to pollute truth; but if the stakes are material resources for scientific instruments, research materials, or personnel, science gets 'impurified,' erasing the borders or spaces between truth and policy relevance or technological panaceas. The sociological question is not whether science is really pure or impure or both, but rather how its borders and territories are flexibly and discursively mapped out in pursuit of some observed or inferred ambition—and with what consequences, and for whom?"
122. Richards (1991).

NOTES TO CHAPTER 3
1. OMB (1997).
2. The category labels used here are taken from the U.S. Office of Management and Budget, but the labels of the categories and the ways in which they are grouped and collapsed vary widely from study to study.
3. Collins (1998: 149, 204).
4. Young (1990: 46).
5. Omi and Winant (1994: 60).
6. Du Bois (1903/1989).
7. One final distinction between epidemiologists' and lay persons' perspectives on the measurement of race involved the interconnections of race with class and gender. This is discussed in chapter 4.
8. Schoenbach et al. (1995a: 506).
9. Others (for example, Jones et al. 1991; Williams 1994) have found these same practices in published literature on health research.
10. For example, in 1994 the National Institutes of Health (NIH) issued guidelines that all NIH-funded clinical research must include women and minorities unless a clear and compelling rationale that such inclusion is inappropriate can be provided (see Epstein 2007).
11. See Fujimura and Chou (1994) and Star (1985; 1986).
12. Omi and Winant (1994).
13. Frankenberg (1994).
14. Omi and Winant (1994: 21).
15. Frankenberg (1994: 14).
16. See Weber (2010), Weber and Fore (2007), and Weber and Parra-Medina (2003).
17. Hankivsky et al. (2010), Jackson (2003), Morgen (2006), Weber (2010), Weber and Fore (2007), and Weber and Parra-Medina (2003).
18. Du Bois (1903/1989).
19. Park (1950).

20. Frankenberg (1994).
21. Clarke et al. (2003; 2010a).

NOTES TO CHAPTER 4

1. In a separate paper, I conceptualized these class-mediated differences as *cultural health capital* (Shim 2010a).
2. As Katz (1989: 16–35) points out, culture-of-poverty arguments were originally developed and articulated by intellectuals more often regarded as liberal (e.g., Lewis 1959; 1966), who advocated for more generous and active intervention by the government on the part of the poor. They stressed the structural foundations and adaptive functions of a culture marked by lack of participation and integration into mainstream institutions, apathy and hostility, feelings of helplessness and dependence, present-time orientation and failure to defer gratification, and various behavioral pathologies often related to sex and familial relationships. However, the resonance of such characterizations with convenient and individualizing discourses on poverty and "the undeserving poor" (Katz 1989) rendered them readily subject to appropriation, and further elaboration, by the conservative right.
3. A more thorough discussion of this is taken up in chapter 5.
4. One of my participants, Dr. Carolyn Munson, for example, describes the process of interpreting potential racial differences: "Well, you say, this is controlled for social class, but if you look and you're comparing African Americans and whites who have a college degree, for instance, you can say, 'Ah! They're of like social class.' Well, they're not of like social class because of other poly-discriminatory kinds of things in our society. Because the wages that are earned by the African American compared to white—same educational level, four-year college degree— they're a lot lower. So, your education does not buy you the same kind of thing if you're a minority in America."
5. Lutfey and Freese (2005).
6. For example, Collins (1991; 1998), Dill et al. (2007), Glenn (1992/1996; 2002), Krieger et al. (1993), McCall (2001), Schulz and Mullings (2006), and Weber (2006).
7. See chapter 2.

NOTES TO CHAPTER 5

1. For example, Chodorow (1978), Martin and Voorhies (1975), Oakley (1972), Rosaldo and Lamphere (1974), and Unger (1979). For a discussion of the debate over the distinction between "sex" and "gender" and its consequences for biomedical research, see Fishman et al. (1999).
2. For example, see Clarke (1998) and Fausto-Sterling (1985).
3. Fishman et al. (1999) and Pearson (1996); see also Lewine (1994).
4. Haig (2000) and Torgrimson and Minson (2005).

5. Hammarstrom and Annandale (2011; 2012) and Springer et al. (2012).

6. For example, Hulley et al. (1998).

7. See Omi and Winant (1994) and Shim (2000).

8. Piven and Cloward (1993: 397).

9. For example, Brenner and Laslett (1986) and Glenn (1992/1996).

10. See, for example, Ochs and Kremer-Sadlik (2013) and Offer and Schneider (2011).

11. See Collins (1998: 209): "Although race, class, and gender may share equal billing under the paradigm of intersectionality as a heuristic device, most African American women would identify race as a fundamental, if not the most important, feature shaping the experiences of Black women as a group."

12. See Collins (2005), for example, on how hegemonic masculinity mobilizes very particular and intersectional constructions of gender that knit together systems of racism, sexism, heterosexism, and class oppression. She argues therefore that gender hierarchy must be analyzed for its distinctive yet interconnected consequences for women *and* men of different races, classes, and sexualities.

13. Riska (2000; 2004).

14. Weber (2010: 86).

15. See Oudshoorn (1994) and Oudshoorn and Wijngaard (1991).

16. Weber (2010: 109).

17. See the expanding literature on social conditions as fundamental causes of disease (e.g., Link and Phelan 1995, Link and Phelan 1996, Link et al. 1998, Lutfey and Freese 2005, Phelan and Link 2005, Phelan et al. 2004).

18. Young (1994/1996: 160). See also Collins (1998).

NOTES TO CHAPTER 6

1. Clarke and Fujimura (1992) argue that scientific work is enabled or constrained by the availability and accessibility of specific tools for scientific jobs—including the conditions of workplaces and workers; research materials, techniques, and instruments; theories and models; funding and sponsorship; regulatory groups; and audiences and consumers of the work. The meanings of "rightness," "tools," and the nature of "jobs" are situational and mutually constructed in interactions among the multiple social worlds that populate a scientific arena.

2. As I explain in the Introduction, I employ the terms "race," "class," and "gender" to refer to those dimensions when they are conceived of as social relations of power, whereas "racial categories" (and sometimes "race"), "socioeconomic status," and "sex" are used to refer to when those measures are conceptualized in their more individualized, reductive forms.

3. Anonymous (2000).

4. Anonymous (2000: 11).

5. Krieger (1992).

6. See, for example, Dreger (1998) and Fausto-Sterling (1993).

7. Shim (2002).

8. Epstein (1996: 28).
9. Epstein (1996: 28).
10. Latour (1987).
11. See also Jordan and Lynch (1992).
12. Gieryn (1999: 2) makes a similar point. He notes that in credibility struggles questions emerge that go to the heart of who is a scientist and what is scientific: "Is your training or expertise scientific? Did you follow methodologically proper scientific procedures? Would most other scientists agree with you?"
13. Pinch and Bijker (1984).
14. On the concept of boundary objects in general, see Star and Griesemer (1989). On boundary objects in epidemiology, see Shim (2002).
15. For example, see Krieger and Sidney (1996) and Krieger et al. (1998).
16. For example, see Borecki et al. (1998) and Williams et al. (2000).
17. For example, see Dries et al. (1999) and Gump et al. (1999).
18. For example, see Crespo et al. (2000).
19. Star (1985: 412).
20. Similarly, as Casper and Clarke (1998) argue with regard to the Pap smear, although the technology itself was particularly resistant to stabilization, the laboratory around it was much more amenable to standardization. Thus by achieving stability in the organizational, economic, and technological settings and conditions under which the Pap smear was used, the tool became (provisionally) constructed as good enough and hence the right one for the job.
21. Epstein (2007).
22. Schoenbach et al. (1995b: 503).
23. However, the divisions between scientific and political or social credibility are not as clear as these commentators indicate: Almost all of the epidemiologists I interviewed in fact supported on *scientific* grounds increased research among populations previously underrepresented in epidemiologic research, arguing that the historic lack of attention to groups of color, women, and the socioeconomically disadvantaged in health research has hampered its generalizability and applicability. Indeed, epidemiologic science has for much of its history attended to methodological criteria related to the representativeness of research populations. For example, researchers were often concerned about the degree to which a recruited sample "looks like" the intended study population, whether any sample biases arose during recruitment and retention, and external validity (or generalizability) of a study. Currently, the characteristics of the study sample used to determine whether significant differences exist between the sample and the population to which the study hopes to refer almost always include race (and, to a lesser extent, socioeconomic status). (Interestingly, comparability is viewed as untenable across sex lines; that is, results from a sample of women are almost never seen or even considered to be generalizable to men, and vice versa.) Related elements of accounting for external validity in both oral and written presentations

include describing sample sizes, recruitment methods, the location and character of recruitment sites, and detailed justifications for selecting these methods and sites. Figures that capture how successful recruitment efforts were (e.g., recruitment "yields" for each site, response and refusal rates) are often calculated and included. Researchers also regularly analyze the degree to which the actual sample "looks like" the intended sample by comparing the characteristics of those who refused to or did not respond to recruitment strategies with those of people who agreed to participate. For longitudinal studies, the concern for research representation also involves inspecting how well participants were retained and whether those retained "look" similar to or different from those lost to follow-up.

24. This is not to say that cohort studies are not being supported and funded; however, the extent to which they can employ more emergent methodologies is constrained by the relative scarcity of economic resources and political will.

25. See Bowker and Star (1999) on characteristics of classification systems.

26. See Fujimura (1986; 1996).

27. Brown (1987; 1992; 1997).

28. Epstein (1995; 1996).

29. I am indebted to Steven Epstein for discussions on this point.

30. Popay and Williams (1996; 1998).

31. See the work of Link, Phelan, and colleagues (Link and Phelan 1995, Link and Phelan 1996, Link et al. 1998, Phelan and Link 2005, Phelan et al. 2004).

NOTES TO THE CONCLUSION

1. See Thomas and Thomas (1970).

2. Foucault (1978).

3. See Armstrong (1983), Clarke et al. (2003; 2010b), and Shim (2000).

4. Chase (1998), Dreger (1998), Fausto-Sterling (1985; 1993), and Kessler (1990).

5. Omi and Winant (1994).

6. Link and Phelan (1995; 1996).

7. Star and Griesemer (1989).

8. Latour (1987) explains the concept of the black box as a claim or as an assemblage of conceptual and/or material parts that act as one, whose content is unquestioned, and that has become a self-evident fact used to build other claims.

9. Clarke and Fujimura (1992) and Fujimura (1987).

10. See, for example, Berkman and Kawachi (2000b), Diez-Roux (1998a; b), Kaufman and Cooper (1999), Krieger (1994; 1999a; b), Krieger and Zierler (1996), Marmot et al. (1997a), Nieto (1999), Popay and Williams (1996), Rose (1985), Susser (1998), Susser and Susser (1996a; b), and Williams (1997).

11. Link and Phelan (1995; 1996).

12. See, for example, Kaufman and Cooper (1999), Krieger (1994), Krieger and Zierler (1997), and Susser and Susser (1996b).

13. Aronowitz (1998: 133).

14. Weber and Parra-Medina (2003: 187–8); see also Hankivsky (2010), Morgen (2006), and Weber and Fore (2007).

15. Clarke et al. (2003; 2010a).

16. Many empirically grounded feminist qualitative studies examining biomedicalization make precisely this point (see, e.g., Fosket 2002, Mamo 2007).

17. Popay and Williams (1996).

18. Popay and Williams (1996).

19. Popay and Williams (1996: 765).

20. See, for example, Funtowicz and Ravetz (1992), Jasanoff (1990), Knorr-Cetina (1989), and Wynne (1996a).

21. For example, Altman (1996), Arksey (1994), Brown (1987), Brown and Mikkelsen (1990), Bullard (1992), Epstein (1995; 1996), and Kaschak and Tiefer (2001).

22. See Morgen (2006) for a review.

23. See Epstein (1995; 1996; 2007).

24. Link and Phelan (1995).

25. Epstein (1996: 337).

26. Epstein (1995; 1996), Laird (1993), and Nelkin and Pollak (1979).

27. Hankivsky et al. (2010: 11).

28. Rapp (1999: 315).

29. See Evans and Collins (2008: 611–14) for their discussion of science and technology studies as conservative and radical critique and, more broadly, of the very difficult question of the extent to which lay participation and producing science through a more inclusive process require substantive expertise or not.

30. A possible significant counter-trend to the constrained funding of longitudinal cohort studies is considerable investment by federal agencies in supporting gene-environment interaction studies. In theory, such studies have the potential to contribute to our understandings of social causation; however, the sociologist Sara Shostak (2013) has found that in the environmental health sciences, for example, a gene-environment interaction approach has led to the molecularization of environmental exposures. The extent to which gene-environment interaction studies in the etiology of complex diseases such as heart disease, Type 2 diabetes, and cancer actually, in practice, incorporate and conceptualize social determinants is the subject of current research I am conducting.

31. There are some encouraging signs in this respect. For example, the National Institutes of Health, spurred by efforts by the NIH Office of Behavioral and Social Sciences Research, launched in December 2001 a program to fund research on the social and cultural dimensions of health. See the final section of this chapter for additional detail.

32. Similarly, Aronowitz (1998: 167–8) observes that "while holistic notions are often appealing in the abstract, attempts to make such notions operational as research strategies, including the ability to develop a body of publishable research with which to advance an academic career, have generally failed."

33. See, for example, Berkman and Kawachi (2000a).

34. Because many concerns of social epidemiology involve dynamics and social relations occurring on levels beyond the individual, and because many of this subfield's critiques of conventional epidemiology and proposed solutions are quite similar to those of ecological and multilevel analysis, I treat them as overlapping endeavors here. See also Jackson (2003: 33–38) for an analysis of some of the important distinctions among works within this area of scholarship.
35. See, for example, Albert and Williams (2011), Anderson et al. (1989), Diez-Roux (1998a), Diez-Roux et al. (2000), Ford and Airhihenbuwa (2010), Krieger (1994; 2005), Krieger et al. (1993), Krieger and Zierler (1997), Landrine et al. (2006), Landrine and Corral (2009), Williams and Mohammed (2009), and Williams et al. (2008; 2010).
36. Weber and Fore (2007).
37. See, for example, the Institute of Medicine (2002; 2003) and National Institutes of Health (2001).
38. Aronowitz (1998: 179).
39. See Shim (2010a).
40. See, for example, Fosket (2002) for an analysis of chemoprevention in breast cancer research.
41. NCHS (2011).
42. CDC (2011).
43. This is established by the National Cholesterol Education Program (run by the National Heart, Lung, and Blood Institute) and the American Heart Association and American College of Cardiology (by their Joint National Committee on Prevention, Detection, Evaluation, and Treatment of High Blood Pressure).
44. This was the phrase used by an executive from a major pharmaceutical company, speaking at a 2001 scientific conference at which I conducted participant observation, to characterize genetic differences that lent themselves well to pharmacologic intervention.
45. Clinical trial data on BiDil's effects in a study population of whites and African Americans had previously failed to win FDA approval in 1997. However, subsequent re-analysis of the data revealed greater efficacy among African Americans, and on this basis the FDA granted approval to begin a clinical trial among a larger sample of African Americans. BiDil ultimately won FDA approval in 2005 and was the first drug to include race-specific labeling. See Kahn (2012).
46. Krimsky (2012).
47. Jameson (1984) and Kahn (2003; 2004; 2012).
48. Strauss (1978) and Strauss et al. (1964).
49. Haraway (1997: 24).

NOTES TO THE APPENDIX

1. Gupta & Ferguson (1997) and Marcus (1995).
2. For example, Foucault (1977; 1978; 1980).

3. Foucault (1980: 83).
4. More on how epidemiology is emblematic of Foucauldian power–knowledge relations is covered in chapter 2.
5. Foucault (1980: 84–5).
6. Epstein (1996: 355).
7. Charmaz (2000) and Strauss and Corbin (1998).
8. Charmaz (2000: 510); see also Guba and Lincoln (1994).
9. Strauss and Corbin (1998: 201).

REFERENCES

Albert, M. A., and D. R. Williams. 2011. "Discrimination—an emerging target for reducing risk of cardiovascular disease?" *American Journal of Epidemiology* 173(11): 1240–3.

Altman, Roberta. 1996. *Waking Up, Fighting Back: The Politics of Breast Cancer*. New York: Little, Brown.

American Heart Association Statistics Committee and Stroke Statistics Subcommittee. 2007. "Heart disease and stroke statistics—2007 update." *Circulation* 115: e69–e171.

American Heart Association Statistics Committee and Stroke Statistics Subcommittee. 2012. "Heart disease and stroke statistics—2012 update." *Circulation* 125: e2–e220.

American Heart Association Statistics Committee and Stroke Statistics Subcommittee. 2013. "Heart disease and stroke statistics—2013 update: A report from the American Heart Association." *Circulation* 127: e6–e245.

Amsterdamska, Olga. 2005. "Demarcating epidemiology." *Science, Technology, & Human Values* 30(1): 17–51.

Anderson, Norman B., Hector F. Myers, Thomas Pickering, and James S. Jackson. 1989. "Hypertension in blacks: Psychosocial and biological perspectives." *Journal of Hypertension* 7(3): 161–72.

Anderson, Warwick. 1996. "Immunities of empire: Race, disease, and the new tropical medicine, 1900–1920." *Bulletin of the History of Medicine* 70: 94–118.

Angell, Marcia, and Jerome P. Kassirer. 1994. "Clinical research—what should the public believe?" *New England Journal of Medicine* 331(3): 189–90.

Anonymous. 2000. "Race, genes, and causal inference: A statement of opinion." *AHA Epidemiology and Prevention Council Newsletter* Spring 2000: 11–12.

ARIC Investigators. 1989. "The Atherosclerosis Risk in Communities (ARIC) Study: Design and objectives." *American Journal of Epidemiology* 129: 687–702.

Arksey, Hilary. 1994. "Expert and lay participation in the construction of medical knowledge." *Sociology of Health and Illness* 16(4): 448–68.

Armstrong, David. 1983. *Political Anatomy of the Body: Medical Knowledge in Britain in the Twentieth Century*. Cambridge: Cambridge University Press.

Armstrong, David. 1995. "The rise of surveillance medicine." *Sociology of Health and Illness* 17(3): 393–404.

Arnett, D. K., Y. Hong, J. N. Bella, A. Oberman, D. W. Kitzman, P. N. Hopkins, D. C. Rao, and R. B. Devereux. 2001a. "Sibling correlation of left ventricular mass and geometry in hypertensive African Americans and whites: The HyperGEN study." *American Journal of Hypertension* 14(12): 1226–30.

Arnett, Donna K., Richard B. Devereux, Dalane Kitzman, Al Oberman, Paul Hopkins, Larry Atwood, Andrew Dewan, and D. C. Rao. 2001b. "Linkage of left ventricular contractility to chromosome 11 in humans: The HyperGEN Study." *Hypertension* 38(4): 767–72.

Aronowitz, Robert A. 1998. *Making Sense of Illness: Science, Society, and Disease*. New York: Cambridge University Press.

Ayanian, John Z., and Arnold M. Epstein. 1991. "Differences in the use of procedures between women and men hospitalized for coronary heart disease." *New England Journal of Medicine* 325(4): 221–25.

Ayanian, John Z., Steven Udvarhelyi, Constantine A. Gatsonis, Chris L. Pashos, and Arnold M. Epstein. 1993. "Racial differences in the use of revascularization procedures after coronary angiography." *Journal of the American Medical Association* 269(20): 2642–6.

Bairey Merz, C. N., L. J. Shaw, S. E. Reis, V. Bittner, S. F. Kelsey, M. Olson, B. D. Johnson, C. J. Pepine, S. Mankad, B. L. Sharaf et al. 2006. "Insights from the NHLBI-Sponsored Women's Ischemia Syndrome Evaluation (WISE) Study: Part II: Gender differences in presentation, diagnosis, and outcome with regard to gender-based pathophysiology of atherosclerosis and macrovascular and microvascular coronary disease." *Journal of the American College of Cardiology* 47(3 Suppl): S21–9.

Berkman, Lisa F. 1984. "Assessing the physical health effects of social networks and social support." *Annual Review of Public Health* 5: 413–32.

Berkman, Lisa F. 1986. "Social networks, support and health: Taking the next step forward." *American Journal of Epidemiology* 123: 559–62.

Berkman, Lisa F., and Ichiro Kawachi. 2000a. "A historical framework for social epidemiology." Pp. 3–12 in *Social Epidemiology*, edited by L. F. Berkman and I. Kawachi. New York: Oxford University Press.

Berkman, Lisa F., and Ichiro Kawachi, eds. 2000b. *Social Epidemiology*. New York: Oxford University Press.

Berkman, Lisa F., and S. Leonard Syme. 1979. "Social networks, host resistance and mortality: A nine-year follow-up study of Alameda County residents." *American Journal of Epidemiology* 109: 186–204.

Bertoni, Alain G., Denise E. Bonds, James Lovato, David C. Goff, and Frederick L. Brancati. 2004. "Sex disparities in procedure use for acute myocardial infarction in the United States, 1995 to 2001." *American Heart Journal* 147(6): 1054–60.

Bhopal, Raj. 1997. "Which book? A comparative review of 25 introductory epidemiology textbooks." *Journal of Epidemiology and Community Health* 51: 612–22.

Bhopal, Raj. 1999. "Paradigms in epidemiology textbooks: In the footsteps of Thomas Kuhn." *American Journal of Public Health* 89(8): 1162–5.

Bibbins-Domingo, Kirsten, Mark J. Pletcher, Feng Lin, Eric Vittinghoff, Julius M. Gardin, Alexander Arynchyn, Cora E. Lewis, O. Dale Williams, and Stephen B. Hulley. 2009. "Racial differences in incident heart failure among young adults." *New England Journal of Medicine* 360(12): 1179–90.

Blackburn, Henry, and Frederick H. Epstein. 1995. "History of the Council on Epidemiology and Prevention, American Heart Association. The pursuit of epidemiology within the American Heart Association: Prehistory and early organization." *Circulation* 91(4): 1253–62.

Bliss, Catherine. 2012. *Race Decoded: The Genomic Fight for Social Justice.* Stanford, Calif.: Stanford University Press.

Blumenthal, Roger S., Howard A. Zacur, Steven E. Reis, and Wendy S. Post. 2000. "Beyond the null hypothesis—do the HERS results disprove the estrogen/coronary heart disease hypothesis?" *American Journal of Cardiology* 85(8): 1015–17.

Borecki, I. B., M. Higgins, P. J. Schreiner, D. K. Arnett, E. Mayer-Davis, S. C. Hunt, and M. A. Province. 1998. "Evidence for multiple determinants of the body mass index: The National Heart, Lung, and Blood Institute Family Heart Study." *Obesity Research* 6(2): 107–14.

Bowker, Geoffrey C., and Susan Leigh Star. 1999. *Sorting Things Out: Classification and Its Consequences.* Cambridge, Mass.: MIT Press.

Brandt, Allan M. 1997. "Behavior, disease, and health in the twentieth-century United States: The moral valence of individual risk." Pp. 53–77 in *Morality and Health*, edited by A. M. Brandt and P. Rozin. New York: Routledge.

Brenner, Johanna, and Barbara Laslett. 1986. "Social reproduction and the family." Pp. 116–31 in *Sociology, from Crisis to Science? Vol. 2, The Social Reproduction of Organization and Culture*, edited by U. Himmelstrand. London: Sage.

Brown, Phil. 1987. "Popular epidemiology: Community response to toxic waste induced disease in Woburn, Massachusetts and other sites." *Science, Technology & Human Values* 12(3–4): 76–85.

Brown, Phil. 1992. "Toxic waste contamination and popular epidemiology: Lay and professional ways of knowing." *Journal of Health and Social Behavior* 33(3): 267–81.

Brown, Phil. 1997. "Popular epidemiology revisited." *Current Sociology* 45(3): 137–56.

Brown, Phil, and Edwin J. Mikkelsen. 1990. *No Safe Place: Toxic Waste, Leukemia, and Community Action.* Berkeley: University of California Press.

Bullard, Robert. 1992. *Confronting Environmental Racism: Voices from the Grassroots.* Boston: South End Press.

Byrd, W. Michael, and Linda A. Clayton. 2001. *An American Health Dilemma: Race, Medicine, and Health Care in the United States, 1900–2000.* New York: Routledge.

Canguilhem, Georges. 1978. *On the Normal and the Pathological*. Translated by C. R. Fawcett. Dordrecht: Reidel.

Canto, John G., Jeroan J. Allison, Catarina I. Kiefe, Contessa Fincher, Robert Farmer, Padmini Sekar, Sharina Person, and Norman W. Weissman. 2000. "Relation of race and sex to the use of reperfusion therapy in Medicare beneficiaries with acute myocardial infarction." *New England Journal of Medicine* 342(15): 1094–100.

Carpiano, Richard M., and Brian C. Kelly. 2007. "Scientific knowledge as resource and risk: What does hormone replacement tell us about health disparities?" Presented at American Sociological Association Annual Meeting, New York.

Casper, Monica J., and Adele E. Clarke. 1998. "Making the Pap smear into the 'right tool' for the job: Cervical cancer screening in the USA, circa 1940–95." *Social Studies of Science* 28(2): 255–90.

Casper, Monica J., and Lisa Jean Moore. 2009. *Missing Bodies: The Politics of Visibility*. New York: New York University Press.

Cassel, John. 1976. "The contribution of the social environment to host resistance: The Fourth Wade Hampton Frost Lecture." *American Journal of Epidemiology* 104(2): 107–23.

CDC. 2011. "Vital signs: Prevalence, treatment, and control of hypertension—United States, 1999–2002 and 2005–2008." *Morbidity and Mortality Weekly Report* 60(4): 103–8.

Chang, Virginia W., and Diane S. Lauderdale. 2009. "Fundamental cause theory, technological innovation, and health disparities: The case of cholesterol in the era of statins." *Journal of Health and Social Behavior* 50: 245–60.

Charmaz, Kathy. 2000. "Grounded theory: Objectivist and constructivist methods." Pp. 509–35 in *Handbook of Qualitative Research*, edited by N. K. Denzin and Y. S. Lincoln. Thousand Oaks, Calif.: Sage.

Chase, Cheryl. 1998. "Hermaphrodites with attitude: Mapping the emergence of intersex political activism." *GLQ-A Journal of Lesbian and Gay Studies* 4(2): 189–211.

Chen, J., S. S. Rathore, M. J. Radford, Y. Wang, and H. M. Krumholz. 2001. "Racial differences in the use of cardiac catheterization after acute myocardial infarction." *New England Journal of Medicine* 344(19): 1443–9.

Chodorow, Nancy. 1978. *The Reproduction of Mothering: Psychoanalysis and the Sociology of Gender*. Berkeley: University of California Press.

Clark, R. 2003. "Self-reported racism and social support predict blood pressure reactivity in blacks." *Annals of Behavioral Medicine* 25: 127–36.

Clarke, Adele E. 1998. *Disciplining Reproduction: Modernity, American Life Sciences, and the Problems of Sex*. Berkeley: University of California Press.

Clarke, Adele E., Janet K. Shim, Laura Mamo, Jennifer Ruth Fosket, and Jennifer R. Fishman. 2003. "Biomedicalization: Technoscientific transformations of health, illness, and U.S. biomedicine." *American Sociological Review* 68(2): 161–94.

Clarke, Adele E., Janet K. Shim, Laura Mamo, Jennifer Ruth Fosket, and Jennifer R. Fishman. 2010a. "Biomedicalization: A theoretical and substantive introduction."

Pp. 1–44 in *Biomedicalization: Technoscience, Health, and Illness in the U.S.*, edited by A. E. Clarke, L. Mamo, J. R. Fosket, J. R. Fishman, and J. K. Shim. Durham, N.C.: Duke University Press.

Clarke, Adele E., and Joan H. Fujimura. 1992. "What tools? Which jobs? Why right?" Pp. 3–44 in *The Right Tools for the Job: At Work in Twentieth-Century Life Sciences*, edited by A. E. Clarke and J. H. Fujimura. Princeton, N.J.: Princeton University Press.

Clarke, Adele E., Laura Mamo, Jennifer Ruth Fosket, Jennifer R. Fishman, and Janet K. Shim, eds. 2010b. *Biomedicalization: Technoscience, Health, and Illness in the U.S.* Durham, N.C.: Duke University Press.

Clarke, Adele E., and Virginia L. Olesen, eds. 1999. *Revisioning Women, Health, and Healing: Feminist, Cultural, and Technoscience Perspectives.* New York: Routledge.

Cohen, Joel W., and Nancy A. Krauss. 2003. "Spending and service use among people with the fifteen most costly medical conditions, 1997." *Health Affairs* 22(2): 129–38.

Collins, Harry, and Robert Evans. 2002. "The third wave of science studies: Studies of expertise and experience." *Social Studies of Science* 33(3): 435–52.

Collins, Harry, and Robert Evans. 2007. *Rethinking Expertise.* Chicago: University of Chicago Press.

Collins, Patricia Hill. 1991. *Black Feminist Thought: Knowledge, Consciousness, and the Politics of Empowerment.* New York: Routledge.

Collins, Patricia Hill. 1998. *Fighting Words: Black Women and the Search for Justice.* Minneapolis: University of Minnesota Press.

Collins, Patricia Hill. 2005. *Black Sexual Politics: African Americans, Gender, and the New Racism.* New York: Routledge.

Coughlin, Steven S. 1998. "Scientific paradigms in epidemiology and professional values." *Epidemiology* 9(5): 578–80.

Crenshaw, Kimberle. 1989. "Mapping the margins: Intersectionality, identity politics, and violence against women of color." *Stanford Law Review* 43(6): 1241–79.

Crespo, Carlos J., Ellen Smit, Ross E. Andersen, Olivia Carter-Pokras, and Barbara E. Ainsworth. 2000. "Race/ethnicity, social class and their relation to physical inactivity during leisure time: Results from the Third National Health and Nutrition Examination Survey, 1988–1994." *American Journal of Preventive Medicine* 18(1): 46–53.

Cubbin, Catherine, W. C. Hadden, and Marilyn A. Winkleby. 2001. "Neighborhood context and cardiovascular disease risk factors: The contribution of material deprivation." *Ethnicity and Disease* 11(4): 687–700.

Davis, Kathy. 2008. "Intersectionality as a buzzword: A sociology of science perspective on what makes a feminist theory successful." *Feminist Theory* 9(1): 67–85.

Dawber, Thomas Royle. 1980. *The Framingham Heart Study: The Epidemiology of Atherosclerotic Disease.* Cambridge, Mass.: Harvard University Press.

Dekkers, Caroline, Frank A. Treiber, Gaston Kapuku, Edwin J. C. G. van den Oord, and Harold Snieder. 2002. "Growth of left ventricular mass in African American and European American youth." *Hypertension* 39(5): 943–51.

Diez-Roux, Ana V. 1998a. "Bringing context back into epidemiology: Variables and fallacies in multilevel analysis." *American Journal of Public Health* 88(2): 216–22.

Diez-Roux, Ana V. 1998b. "On genes, individuals, society, and epidemiology." *American Journal of Epidemiology* 148(11): 1027–32.

Diez-Roux, Ana V., Bruce G. Link, and Mary E. Northridge. 2000. "A multilevel analysis of income inequality and cardiovascular disease risk factors." *Social Science and Medicine* 50(5): 673–87.

Diez-Roux, Ana V., F. Javier Nieto, Carles Muntaner, Herman A. Tyroler, George W. Comstock, Eyal Shahar, Lawton S. Cooper, Robert L. Watson, and Moyses Szklo. 1997. "Neighborhood environments and coronary heart disease: A multilevel analysis." *American Journal of Epidemiology* 146(1): 48–63.

Dill, Bonnie T., Amy E. McLaughlin, and Angel David Nieves. 2007. "Future directions of feminist research: Intersectionality." Pp. 629–38 in *Handbook of Feminist Research: Theory and Praxis*, edited by S. N. Hesse-Biber. Thousand Oaks, Calif.: Sage.

Dreger, Alice Domurat. 1998. *Hermaphrodites and the Medical Invention of Sex*. Cambridge, Mass.: Harvard University Press.

Dries, Daniel, Derek V. Exner, Bernard J. Gersh, Howard A. Cooper, Peter E. Carson, and Michael J. Domanski. 1999. "Racial differences in the outcome of left ventricular dysfunction." *New England Journal of Medicine* 340(8): 609–16.

Du Bois, W. E. B. 1903/1989. *The Souls of Black Folk*. New York: Bantam.

Duncan, C., K. Jones, and G. Moon. 1996. "Health-related behaviour in context: A multilevel modeling approach." *Social Science and Medicine* 42(6): 817–30.

Engels, Friedrich. 1845/1978. "Working-class Manchester." Pp. 579–85 in *The Marx-Engels Reader*, edited by R. C. Tucker. New York: Norton.

Epstein, Steven. 1995. "The construction of lay expertise: AIDS activism and the forging of credibility in the reform of clinical trials." *Science, Technology & Human Values* 20(4): 408–37.

Epstein, Steven. 1996. *Impure Science: AIDS, Activism, and the Politics of Knowledge*. Berkeley: University of California Press.

Epstein, Steven. 2007. *Inclusion: The Politics of Difference in Medical Research*. Chicago: University of Chicago Press.

Ernst, Waltraud, and Bernard Harris, eds. 1999. *Race, Science and Medicine, 1700–1960*. London: Routledge.

Escarce, Jose J., Kenneth R. Epstein, David C. Colby, and J. Sanford Schwartz. 1993. "Racial differences in the elderly's use of medical procedures and diagnostic tests." *American Journal of Public Health* 83(7): 948–54.

Evans, A. S. 1978. "Causation and disease: A chronological journey." *American Journal of Epidemiology* 108: 249–58.

Evans, Robert, and Harry Collins. 2008. "Expertise: From attribute to attribution and back again?" Pp. 609–30 in *The Handbook of Science and Technology Studies, 3rd Edition*, edited by E. J. Hackett, O. Amsterdamska, M. Lynch, and J. Wajcman. Cambridge, Mass.: MIT Press.

Exner, D. V., D. L. Dries, M. J. Domanski, and J. N. Cohn. 2001. "Lesser response to angiotensin-converting-enzyme inhibitor therapy in black as compared with white patients with left ventricular dysfunction." *New England Journal of Medicine* 344(18): 1351–7.

Fassin, Didier. 2009. "Another politics of life is possible." *Theory, Culture & Society* 26(5): 44–60.

Fausto-Sterling, Anne. 1985. *Myths of Gender: Biological Theories About Women and Men*. New York: Basic Books.

Fausto-Sterling, Anne. 1993. "The five sexes: Why men and women are not enough." *The Sciences* 33(2): 2–25.

Fee, Elizabeth, and Dorothy Porter. 1992. "Public health, preventive medicine and professionalization: England and America in the nineteenth century." Pp. 249–76 in *Medicine in Society: Historical Essays*, edited by A. Wear. Cambridge: Cambridge University Press.

Fishman, Jennifer R., Janis G. Wick, and Barbara A. Koenig. 1999. "The use of 'sex' and 'gender' to define and characterize meaningful differences between men and women." Pp. 2–20 in *Agenda for Research on Women's Health for the 21st Century: A Report of the Taskforce on the NIH Women's Health Research Agenda for the 21st Century*, vol. II, edited by NIH Office of the Director and Office of Research on Women's Health. Bethesda, Md.: National Institutes of Health.

Fonow, Mary Margaret, and Judith A. Cook, eds. 1991. *Beyond Methodology: Feminist Scholarship as Lived Research*. Bloomington: Indiana University Press.

Foraker, Randi E., Kathryn M. Rose, Anna M. Kucharska-Newton, Hanyu Ni, Chirayath M. Suchindran, and Eric A. Whitsel. 2011. "Variation in rates of fatal coronary heart disease by neighborhood socioeconomic status: The Atherosclerosis Risk in Communities surveillance (1992–2002)." *Annals of Epidemiology* 21(8): 580–8.

Ford, Chandra L., and Collins O. Airhihenbuwa. 2010. "The public health critical race methodology: Praxis for antiracism research." *Social Science and Medicine* 71(8): 1390–8.

Ford, E. S., I. B. Ahluwalia, and D. A. Galuska. 2000. "Social relationships and cardiovascular disease risk factors: Findings from the Third National Health and Nutrition Examination Survey." *Preventive Medicine* 30(2): 83–92.

Fosket, Jennifer Ruth. 2002. *Breast Cancer Risk and the Politics of Prevention: Analysis of a Clinical Trial*. Ph.D. dissertation, Department of Social and Behavioral Sciences, University of California, San Francisco, San Francisco, Calif.

Foucault, Michel. 1977. *Discipline and Punish: The Birth of the Prison*. Translated by A. Sheridan. New York: Vintage Books.

Foucault, Michel. 1978. *The History of Sexuality, Volume I: An Introduction*. Translated by R. Hurley. New York: Vintage Books.

Foucault, Michel. 1980. *Power/Knowledge: Selected Interviews and Other Writings, 1972–1977*. Edited by C. Gordon. Translated by C. Gordon, L. Marshall, J. Mepham, and K. Soper. New York: Pantheon.

Foucault, Michel. 1997. *Society Must Be Defended: Lectures at the Collège de France, 1975–1976*. Translated by D. Macey. New York: Picador.

Frankenberg, Ruth. 1994. *White Women, Race Matters: The Social Construction of Whiteness*. Minneapolis: University of Minnesota Press.

Friedman, Gary D., Gary R. Cutter, Richard P. Donahue, Glenn H. Hughes, Stephen B. Hulley, David R. Jacobs, Kiang Lu, and Peter J. Savage. 1988. "CARDIA: Study design, recruitment, and some characteristics of the examined subjects." *Journal of Clinical Epidemiology* 41(11): 1105–16.

Fujimura, Joan. 1986. "The molecular bandwagon in cancer research: Where social worlds meet." *Social Problems* 35(3): 261–83.

Fujimura, Joan H. 1987. "Constructing 'do-able' problems in cancer research: Articulating alignment." *Social Studies of Science* 17(2): 257–93.

Fujimura, Joan H. 1996. *Crafting Science: A Sociohistory of the Quest for the Genetics of Cancer*. Cambridge, Mass.: Harvard University Press.

Fujimura, Joan H., and Danny Y. Chou. 1994. "Dissent in science: Styles of scientific practice and the controversy over the cause of AIDS." *Social Science and Medicine* 38(8): 1017–36.

Fullilove, Mindy Thompson. 1998. "Abandoning 'race' as a variable in public health research—an idea whose time has come." *American Journal of Public Health* 88(9): 1297–8.

Fullwiley, Duana. 2008. "The biologistical construction of race: 'Admixture' technology and the new genetic medicine." *Social Studies of Science* 38(5): 695–735.

Funtowicz, Silvio O., and Jerome R. Ravetz. 1992. "Three types of risk assessment and the emergence of post-normal science." Pp. 251–74 in *Social Theories of Risk*, edited by S. Krimsky and D. Golding. New York: Praeger.

Garrety, Karin. 1997a. *Negotiating Dietary Knowledge Inside and Outside Laboratories: The Cholesterol Controversy*. Ph.D. dissertation, Department of Science and Technology Studies, University of New South Wales, Sydney, Australia.

Garrety, Karin. 1997b. "Social worlds, actor-networks and controversy: The case of cholesterol, dietary fat and heart disease." *Social Studies of Science* 27: 727–73.

Garrety, Karin. 1998. "Science, policy, and controversy in the cholesterol arena." *Symbolic Interaction* 21(4): 401–24.

Genest, Jacques, and Jeffrey S. Cohn. 1995. "Clustering of cardiovascular risk factors: Targeting high-risk individuals." *American Journal of Cardiology* 76: 8A–20A.

Gieryn, Thomas F. 1999. *Cultural Boundaries of Science: Credibility on the Line*. Chicago: University of Chicago Press.

Glenn, Evelyn Nakano. 1992/1996. "From servitude to service work: Historical continuities in the racial division of paid reproductive labor." Pp. 27–69 in *The Second Signs Reader: Feminist Scholarship, 1983–1996*, edited by R.-E. B. Joeres and B. Laslett. Chicago: University of Chicago Press.

Glenn, Evelyn Nakano. 2002. *Unequal Freedom: How Race and Gender Shaped American Citizenship and Labor*. Cambridge, Mass.: Harvard University Press.

Glied, Sherry, and Adriana Lleras-Muney. 2008. "Technological innovation and inequality in health." *Demography* 45: 741–61.

Gordis, Leon. 2000. *Epidemiology.* Philadelphia: W. B. Saunders.

Graham, Saxon. 1963. "Social factors in relation to chronic illness." Pp. 65–98 in *Handbook of Medical Sociology*, edited by H. E. Freeman, S. Levine, and L. G. Reeder. Englewood Cliffs, N.J.: Prentice-Hall.

Greenwood, D. C., K. R. Muir, C. J. Packman, and R. J. Madeley. 1996. "Coronary heart disease: A review of the role of psychosocial stress and social support." *Journal of Public Health Medicine* 18(2): 221–31.

Guba, Egon G., and Yvonna S. Lincoln. 1994. "Competing paradigms in qualitative research." Pp. 105–17 in *Handbook of Qualitative Research*, edited by N. K. Denzin and Y. S. Lincoln. Thousand Oaks, Calif.: Sage.

Gump, Brooks B., Karen A. Matthews, and Katri Räikkönen. 1999. "Modeling relationships among socioeconomic status, hostility, cardiovascular reactivity, and left ventricular mass in African American and White children." *Health Psychology* 18(2): 140–50.

Gupta, Akhil, and James Ferguson, eds. 1997. *Anthropological Locations: Boundaries and Grounds of a Field Science.* Berkeley: University of California Press.

Guyll, M., K. A. Matthews, and J. T. Bromberger. 2001. "Discrimination and unfair treatment: Relationship to cardiovascular reactivity among African American and European American women." *Health Psychology* 20(5): 315–25.

Hacking, Ian. 1982. "Biopower and the avalanche of printed numbers." *Humanities in Society* 8(3–4): 279–95.

Hacking, Ian. 1990. *The Taming of Chance.* Cambridge: Cambridge University Press.

Haig, David. 2000. "Of sex and gender." *Nature Genetics* 25(4): 373.

Hammarstrom, A., and E. Annandale. 2011. "Constructing the 'gender-specific body': A critical discourse analysis of publications in the field of gender-specific medicine." *health* 15(6): 571–87.

Hammarstrom, A., and E. Annandale. 2012. "A conceptual muddle: An empirical analysis of the use of 'sex' and 'gender' in 'gender-specific medicine' journals." *PLoS One* 7(4): e34193.

Hankivsky, Olena, Colleen Reid, Renee Cormier, Colleen Varcoe, Natalie Clark, Cecilia Benoit, and Shari Brotman. 2010. "Exploring the promises of intersectionality for advancing women's health research." *International Journal for Equity in Health* 9: 5.

Haraway, Donna J. 1997. *Modest_Witness@Second_Millenium.FemaleMan©_Meets_ Oncomouse™: Feminism and Technoscience.* New York: Routledge.

Haynes, Suzanne G., Sol Levine, Norman Scotch, Manning Feinleib, and William B. Kannel. 1978. "The relationship of psychosocial factors to coronary heart disease in the Framingham Study: I. Methods and risk factors." *American Journal of Epidemiology* 107(5): 362–83.

He, Jiang, Michael J. Klag, Lawrence J. Appel, Jeanne Charleston, and Paul K. Whelton. 1999. "The renin-angiotensin system and blood pressure: Differences between blacks and whites." *American Journal of Hypertension* 12(6): 555–62.

Hemingway, Harry, and Michael Marmot. 1999. "Psychosocial factors in the aetiology and prognosis of coronary heart diease: Systematic review of prospective cohort studies." *BMJ* 318(7196): 1460–7.

Hennekens, Charles H., and Julie E. Buring. 1987. *Epidemiology in Medicine*. Boston: Little, Brown.

Hess, David J. 1997. *Science Studies: An Advanced Introduction*. New York: New York University Press.

Hodis, Howard N., Wendy J. Mack, Stanley P. Azen, Roger A. Lobo, Donna Shoupe, Peter R. Mahrer, David P. Faxon, Linda Cashin-Hemphill, Miguel E. Sanmarco, William J. French et al. 2003. "Hormone therapy and the progression of coronary-artery atherosclerosis in postmenopausal women." *New England Journal of Medicine* 349(6): 535–45.

Howard, B. V. 1999. "Insulin resistance and lipid metabolism." *American Journal of Cardiology* 84(1A): 28J–32J.

Hsueh, Willa A., and Ronald E. Law. 1998. "Cardiovascular risk continuum: Implications of insulin resistance and diabetes." *American Journal of Medicine* 105(1A): 4S–14S.

Hulley, S., D. Grady, T. Bush, C. Furberg, D. Herrington, B. Riggs, and E. Vittinghoff. 1998. "Randomized trial of estrogen plus progestin for secondary prevention of coronary heart disease in postmenopausal women." *Journal of the American Medical Association* 280: 605–12.

Hunt, Kelly J. 2002. "Mexican Americans More Likely to Die of Heart Disease Than Caucasians." American Heart Association press release, from the Asia Pacific Scientific Forum. Honolulu.

Hunt, Linda M., and Mary S. Megyesi. 2008. "The ambiguous meanings of the racial/ethnic categories routinely used in human genetics research." *Social Science and Medicine* 66(2): 349–61.

Institute of Medicine. 2002. *Unequal Treatment: Confronting Racial and Ethnic Disparities in Health Care*. Washington: National Academies Press.

Institute of Medicine. 2003. *The Future of the Public's Health in the 21st Century*. Washington: National Academies Press.

Irwin, Alan, and Brian Wynne. 1996a. "Conclusions." Pp. 213–21 in *Misunderstanding Science? The Public Reconstruction of Science and Technology*, edited by A. Irwin and B. Wynne. Cambridge: Cambridge University Press.

Irwin, Alan, and Brian Wynne, eds. 1996b. *Misunderstanding Science? The Public Reconstruction of Science and Technology*. Cambridge: Cambridge University Press.

Jackson, Beth E. 2003. "Situating epidemiology." Pp. 11–58 in *Gender Perspectives on Health and Medicine (Volume 7): Key Themes*, edited by M. T. Segal, V. Demos, and J. J. Kronenfeld. New York: Elsevier.

Jacobs, A. K. 2006. "Women, ischemic heart disease, revascularization, and the gender gap: What are we missing?" *Journal of the American College of Cardiology* 47(3 Suppl): S63–S65.

James, S. J., A. Z. LaCroix, D. G. Kleinbaum, and D. S. Strogatz. 1984. "John Henry-ism and blood pressure differences among black men. II. The role of occupational stressors." *Journal of Behavioral Medicine* 7: 259–75.

Jameson, Frederic. 1984. "Postmodernism, or the cultural logic of late capitalism." *New Left Review* 146: 53–92.

Jasanoff, Sheila. 1990. *The Fifth Branch: Science Advisers as Policymakers*. Cambridge, Mass.: Harvard University Press.

Jasanoff, Sheila. 2003a. "Breaking the waves in science studies: Comment on H. M. Collins and Robert Evans, 'The third wave of science studies.'" *Social Studies of Science* 33(3): 389–400.

Jasanoff, Sheila. 2003b. "(No?) accounting for expertise." *Science and Public Policy* 30(3): 157–62.

Jasanoff, Sheila. 2004. "Ordering knowledge, ordering society." Pp. 13–45 in *States of Knowledge: The Co-Production of Science and Social Order*, edited by S. Jasanoff. New York: Routledge.

Jasanoff, Sheila, Gerald E. Markle, James C. Petersen, and Trevor Pinch, eds. 1995. *Handbook of Science and Technology Studies*. Thousand Oaks, Calif.: Sage.

Jolly, Stacey, Eric Vittinghoff, Arpita Chattopadhyay, and Kirsten Bibbins-Domingo. 2010. "Higher cardiovascular disease prevalence and mortality among younger black compared to whites." *American Journal of Medicine* 123(9): 811–18.

Jones, Camara Phyllis, Thomas A. LaVeist, and Marsha Lillie-Blanton. 1991. "'Race' in the epidemiologic literature: An examination of the *American Journal of Epidemiology*, 1921–1990." *American Journal of Epidemiology* 134(10): 1079–84.

Jones, David S. 2000. "Visions of a cure: Visualization, clinical trials, and controversies in cardiac therapeutics, 1968–1998." *Isis* 91(3): 504–41.

Jones, David S. 2013. *Broken Hearts: The Tangled History of Cardiac Care*. Baltimore: The Johns Hopkins University Press.

Jones, James H. 1993. *Bad Blood: The Tuskegee Syphilis Experiment*. New York: Free Press.

Jordan, Kathleen, and Michael Lynch. 1992. "The sociology of a genetic engineering technique: Ritual and rationality in the performance of the 'plasmid prep.'" Pp. 77–114 in *The Right Tools for the Job: At Work in Twentieth-Century Life Sciences*, edited by A. E. Clarke and J. H. Fujimura. Princeton, N.J.: Princeton University Press.

Jordanova, Ludmilla. 1989. *Sexual Visions: Images of Gender in Science and Medicine Between the Eighteenth and Twentieth Centuries*. Madison: University of Wisconsin Press.

Kahn, Jonathan. 2003. "Getting the numbers right: Statistical mischief and racial profiling in health failure research." *Perspectives in Biology and Medicine* 46: 473–83.

Kahn, Jonathan. 2004. "How a drug becomes 'ethnic': Law, commerce, and the production of racial categories in medicine." *Yale Journal of Health Policy, Law, and Ethics* 4: 1–46.

Kahn, Jonathan. 2012. *Race in a Bottle: The Story of BiDil and Racialized Medicine in a Post-Genomic Age*. New York: Columbia University Press.

Kannel, William B., Thomas R. Dawber, Abraham Kagan, Nicholas Revotskiw, and Joseph Stokes III. 1961. "Factors of risk in the development of coronary heart disease: Six-year follow-up experience—The Framingham Study." *Annals of Internal Medicine* 55: 33–50.

Kaplan, N. M. 1989. "The deadly quartet: Upper body obesity, glucose intolerance, hypertriglyceridemia, and hypertension." *Archives of Internal Medicine* 149: 1514–20.

Kaschak, Ellyn, and Leonore Tiefer, eds. 2001. *A New View of Women's Sexual Problems*. New York: Haworth Press.

Katz, Michael B. 1989. *The Undeserving Poor: From the War on Poverty to the War on Welfare*. New York: Pantheon.

Kaufman, Jay S., and Richard S. Cooper. 1999. "Seeking causal explanations in social epidemiology." *American Journal of Epidemiology* 150(2): 113–20.

Kessler, Suzanne J. 1990. "The medical construction of gender: Case management of intersexed infants." *Signs* 16(1): 3–26.

King, K. B. 1997. "Psychologic and social aspects of cardiovascular disease." *Annals of Behavioral Medicine* 19(3): 264–70.

Klag, M. J., P. K. Whelton, J. Coresh, C. E. Grim, and L. H. Kuller. 1991. "The association of skin color with blood pressure in U.S. blacks with low socioeconomic status." *Journal of the American Medical Association* 265(5): 599–602.

Knorr-Cetina, Karin. 1989. "Epistemic cultures: Forms of reason in science." *History of Political Economy* 23: 105–22.

Kogevinas, Manolis. 1998. "The loss of the population approach puts epidemiology at risk." *Journal of Epidemiology and Community Health* 52(10): 615–16.

Koopman, James S. 1996. "Emerging objectives and methods in epidemiology." *American Journal of Public Health* 86(5): 630–2.

Krieger, Nancy. 1990. "Racial and gender discrimination: Risk factors for high blood pressure?" *Social Science and Medicine* 30(12): 1273–81.

Krieger, Nancy. 1992. "The making of public health data: Paradigms, politics, and policy." *Journal of Public Health Policy* 13: 412–27.

Krieger, Nancy. 1994. "Epidemiology and the web of causation: Has anyone seen the spider?" *Social Science and Medicine* 39(7): 887–903.

Krieger, Nancy. 1999a. "Embodying inequality: A review of concepts, measures, and methods for studying health consequences of discrimination." *International Journal of Health Services* 29(2): 295–352.

Krieger, Nancy. 1999b. "Questioning epidemiology: Objectivity, advocacy, and socially responsible science." *American Journal of Public Health* 89(8): 1151–3.

Krieger, Nancy, ed. 2005. *Embodying Inequality: Epidemiologic Perspectives*. Amityville, N.Y.: Baywood.

Krieger, Nancy, Diane L. Rowley, Allen A. Herman, Byllye Avery, and Mona T. Phillips. 1993. "Racism, sexism, and social class: Implications for studies of health, disease, and well-being." *American Journal of Preventive Medicine* 9(6): 82–122.

Krieger, Nancy, and Elizabeth Fee. 1994. "Man-made medicine and women's health: The biopolitics of sex/gender and race/ethnicity." *International Journal of Health Services* 24(2): 265–83.

Krieger, Nancy, and Sally Zierler. 1996. "What explains the public's health? A call for epidemiologic theory." *Epidemiology* 7(1): 107–9.

Krieger, Nancy, and Sally Zierler. 1997. "The need for epidemiologic theory." *Epidemiology* 8(2): 212–14.

Krieger, Nancy, and Stephen Sidney. 1996. "Racial discrimination and blood pressure: The CARDIA study of young black and white adults." *American Journal of Public Health* 86(10): 1370–8.

Krieger, Nancy, Stephen Sidney, and Eugenie Coakley. 1998. "Racial discrimination and skin color in the CARDIA study: Implications for public health research." *American Journal of Public Health* 88(9): 1308–13.

Krimsky, Sheldon. 2012. "The short life of a race drug." *The Lancet* 349(9811): 114–15.

Kuhn, Thomas S. 1962/1996. *The Structure of Scientific Revolutions*. Chicago: University of Chicago Press.

Kumanyika, S., and L. L. Adams-Campbell. 1991. "Obesity, diet, and psychosocial factors contributing to cardiovascular disease in blacks." *Cardiovascular Clinics* 21(3): 47–73.

La Berge, Ann Elizabeth Fowler. 1992. *Mission and Method: The Early Nineteenth-Century French Public Health Movement*. New York: Cambridge University Press.

Laird, Frank N. 1993. "Participatory analysis, democracy, and technological decision making." *Science, Technology, & Human Values* 18(4): 341–61.

Lambert, Helen, and Hilary Rose. 1996. "Disembodied knowledge? Making sense of medical science." Pp. 65–83 in *Misunderstanding Science? The Public Reconstruction of Science and Technology*, edited by A. Irwin and B. Wynne. Cambridge: Cambridge University Press.

Landrine, H., and I. Corral. 2009. "Separate and unequal: Residential segregation and black health disparities." *Ethnicity and Disease* 19(2): 179–84.

Landrine, H., E. A. Klonoff, I. Corral, S. Fernandez, and S. Roesch. 2006. "Conceptualizing and measuring ethnic discrimination in health research." *Journal of Behavioral Medicine* 29(1): 79–94.

LaRosa, J. C., D. Hunninghake, D. Bush, M. H. Criqui, G. S. Getz, A. M. Gotto Jr., S. M. Grundy, L. Rakita, R. M. Robertson, and M. L. Weisfeldt. 1990. "The cholesterol facts. A summary of the evidence relating dietary fats, serum cholesterol, and coronary heart disease. A joint statement by the American Heart Association and the National Heart, Lung, and Blood Institute." *Circulation* 81(5): 1721–33.

Latour, Bruno. 1987. *Science in Action: How to Follow Scientists and Engineers Through Society*. Cambridge, Mass.: Harvard University Press.

Latour, Bruno, and Steve Woolgar. 1986. *Laboratory Life: The Social Construction of Scientific Facts*. Princeton, N.J.: Princeton University Press.

LaVeist, Thomas A. 1996. "Why we should continue to study race . . . but do a better job: An essay on race, racism, and health." *Ethnicity and Disease* 6(1–2): 21–9.

Lee, Elisa T., Thomas K. Welty, Richard Fabsitz, Linda D. Cowan, Ngoc-Anh Le, Arvo J. Oopik, Andrew J. Cucchiara, Peter J. Savage, and Barbara V. Howard. 1990. "The Strong Heart Study, a study of cardiovascular disease in American Indians: Design and methods." *American Journal of Epidemiology* 132(6): 1141–55.

Lepore, S. J. 1998. "Problems and prospects for the social support–reactivity hypothesis." *Annals of Behavioral Medicine* 20(4): 257–69.

Lerman, A., and G. Sopko. 2006. "Women and cardiovascular heart disease: Clinical implications from the Women's Ischemia Syndrome Evaluation (WISE) Study. Are we smarter?" *Journal of the American College of Cardiology* 47(3 Suppl): S59–S62.

Levy, Daniel, and Susan Brink. 2005. *A Change of Heart: How the Framingham Heart Study Helped Unravel the Mysteries of Cardiovascular Disease.* New York: Knopf.

Lewine, R. R. J. 1994. "Sex: An imperfect marker of gender." *Schizophrenia Bulletin* 20(4): 777–8.

Lewis, Oscar. 1959. *Five Families: Mexican Case Studies in the Culture of Poverty.* New York: Basic Books.

Lewis, Oscar. 1966. *La Vida: A Puerto Rican Family in the Culture of Poverty—San Juan and New York.* New York: Random House.

Liese, Angela D., Elizabeth J. Mayer-Davis, and Steven M. Haffner. 1998. "Development of the multiple metabolic syndrome: An epidemiologic perspective." *Epidemiologic Reviews* 20(2): 157–72.

Lilienfeld, Abraham M., and David E. Lilienfeld. 1980. *Foundations of Epidemiology.* New York: Oxford University Press.

Link, Bruce G., and Jo Phelan. 1995. "Social conditions as fundamental causes of disease." *Journal of Health and Social Behavior* 36(extra issue): 80–94.

Link, Bruce G., and Jo C. Phelan. 1996. "Understanding sociodemographic differences in health—the role of fundamental social causes." *American Journal of Public Health* 86(4): 471–3.

Link, Bruce G., Mary E. Northridge, Jo C. Phelan, and Michael L. Ganz. 1998. "Social epidemiology and the fundamental cause concept: On the structuring of effective cancer screens by socioeconomic status." *Milbank Quarterly* 76(3): 375–402.

Lupton, Deborah. 1995. *The Imperative of Health: Public Health and the Regulated Body.* Thousand Oaks, Calif.: Sage.

Lutfey, Karen, and Jeremy Freese. 2005. "Toward some fundamentals of fundamental causality: Socioeconomic status and health in the routine clinic visit for diabetes." *American Journal of Sociology* 110(5): 1326–72.

Mackenbach, Johan P. 1998. "Multilevel ecoepidemiology and parsimony." *Journal of Epidemiology and Community Health* 52(10): 614–15.

MacMahon, B., T. F. Pugh, and J. Ipsen. 1960. *Epidemiologic Methods.* Boston: Little, Brown.

Mamo, Laura. 2007. *Queering Reproduction: Achieving Pregnancy in the Age of Technoscience.* Durham, N.C.: Duke University Press.

Mann, Charles C. 1995. "Press coverage: Leaving out the big picture." *Science* 269(5221): 166.

Manson, JoAnn E., Judith Hsia, Karen C. Johnson, Jacques E. Rossouw, Annlouise R. Assaf, Norman L. Lasser, Maurizio Trevisan, Henry R. Black, Susan R. Heckbert, Robert Detrano et al. 2003. "Estrogen plus progestin and the risk of coronary heart disease." *New England Journal of Medicine* 349(6): 523–34.

Manuck, S. B., J. R. Kaplan, and K. A. Matthews. 1986. "Behavioral antecedents of coronary heart disease and atherosclerosis." *Arteriosclerosis* 6(1): 2–14.

Marcus, George. 1995. "Ethnography in/of the world system: The emergence of multi-sited ethnography." *Annual Review of Anthropology* 24: 95–117.

Marks, Harry M. 1997. *The Progress of Experiment: Science and Therapeutic Reform in the United States, 1900–1990.* New York: Cambridge University Press.

Marmot, Michael, Carol D. Ryff, Larry L. Bumpass, Martin Shipley, and Nadine F. Marks. 1997a. "Social inequalities in health: Next questions and converging evidence." *Social Science and Medicine* 44(6): 901–10.

Marmot, M. G., H. Bosma, H. Hemingway, E. Brunner, and S. Stansfeld. 1997b. "Contribution of job control and other risk factors to social variations in coronary heart disease incidence." *Lancet* 350(9073): 235–39.

Martin, M. Kay, and Barbara Voorhies. 1975. *Female of the Species.* New York: Columbia University Press.

Matthews, Karen A., Catarina I. Kiefe, Cora E. Lewis, Kiang Liu, Stephen Sidney, and Carla Yunis. 2002. "Socioeconomic trajectories and incident hypertension in a biracial cohort of young adults." *Hypertension* 39(3): 772–6.

McCall, Leslie. 2001. *Complex Inequality: Gender, Class and Race in the New Economy.* New York: Routledge.

McCall, Leslie. 2005. "The complexity of intersectionality." *Signs* 30(3): 1771–1800.

McCrohon, Jane A., Shirley Nakhla, Wendy Jessup, Keith K. Stanley, and David S. Celermajer. 1999. "Estrogen and progesterone reduce lipid accumulation in human monocyte–derived macrophages: A sex-specific effect." *Circulation* 100(23): 2319–25.

McGinnis, M. J., and W. H. Foege. 1993. "Actual causes of death in the United States." *Journal of the American Medical Association* 270(18): 2207–12.

McKinlay, John B., and Lisa D. Marceau. 2000. "To boldly go . . . " *American Journal of Public Health* 90(1): 25–33.

McMichael, Anthony J. 1995. "The health of persons, populations, and planets: Epidemiology comes full circle." *Epidemiology* 6(6): 633–6.

McPherson, Klim. 1998. "Wider 'causal thinking in the health sciences.'" *Journal of Epidemiology and Community Health* 52(10): 612–13.

MESA Coordinating Center. 2011. "MESA Study Population." Accessed on April 29, 2011. Available at http://mesa-nhlbi.org/population.aspx.

Miller, M., R. Byington, D. Hunninghake, B. Pitt, and C. D. Furberg. 2000. "Sex bias and underutilization of lipid-lowering therapy in patients with coronary artery disease at academic medical centers in the United States and Canada. Prospective

Randomized Evaluation of the Vascular Effects of Norvasc Trial (PREVENT) Investigators." *Archives of Internal Medicine* 160(3): 343–7.

Modan, M., H. Halkin, S. Almog, A. Lusky, A. Eshkol, M. Shefi, A. Shitrit, and Z. Fuchs. 1985. "Hyperinsulinemia: A link between hypertension, obesity and glucose intolerance." *Journal of Clinical Investigation* 75: 809–17.

Montoya, Michael J. 2007. "Bioethnic conscription: Genes, race, and Mexicana/o ethnicity in diabetes research." *Cultural Anthropology* 22(1): 94–128.

Montoya, Michael J. 2011. *Making the Mexican Diabetic: Race, Science, and the Genetics of Inequality.* Berkeley: University of California Press.

Morgen, Sandi. 2006. "Movement-grounded theory: Intersectional analysis of health inequities in the United States." Pp. 394–423 in *Gender, Race, Class, and Health: Intersectional Approaches,* edited by A. J. Schulz and L. Mullings. San Francisco: Jossey-Bass.

Morgen, Sandra. 2002. *Into Our Own Hands: The Women's Health Movement in the United States, 1969–1990.* New Brunswick, N.J.: Rutgers University Press.

Myrdal, Gunnar. 1954/1996. *An American Dilemma: The Negro Problem and Modern Democracy.* New Brunswick, N.J.: Transaction Publishers.

National Institutes of Health. 2001. *Towards Higher Levels of Analysis: Progress and Promise in Research on Social and Cultural Dimensions of Health: Executive Summary.* Washington: NIH Publication No. 21-5020.

National Institutes of Health. 2011. "PAR-10-136: Behavioral and Social Science Research on Understanding and Reducing Health Disparities (R01)." Accessed on May 24, 2011. Available at http://grants.nih.gov/grants/guide/pa-files/PAR-10-136.html.

NCHS. 1998. *Health, United States, 1998 with Socioeconomic Status and Health Chartbook.* Hyattsville, Md.: National Center for Health Statistics.

NCHS. 2011. *Health, United States, 2010: With Special Feature on Death and Dying.* Hyattsville, Md.: National Center for Health Statistics.

Nelkin, Dorothy, and Michael Pollak. 1979. "Public participation in technological decisions: Reality or grand illusion?" *Technology Review* 81(8): 55–64.

Nelson, Alondra. 2011. *Body and Soul: The Black Panther Party and the Fight Against Medical Discrimination.* Minneapolis: University of Minnesota Press.

Nelson, K., K. Norris, and C. M. Mangione. 2002. "Disparities in the diagnosis and pharmacologic treatment of high serum cholesterol by race and ethnicity: Data from the Third National Health and Nutrition Examination Survey." *Archives of Internal Medicine* 162(8): 929–35.

NHLBI. 1999. "Women's Health Initiative website." Accessed on February 18, 1999. Available at http://www.nhlbi.nih.gov/nhlbi/whi1.

NHLBI. 2001. "Framingham Heart Study website." Accessed on May 18, 2001. Available at http://www.nhlbi.nih.gov/about/framingham/index.html.

Nieto, F. Javier. 1999. "Cardiovascular disease and risk factor epidemiology: A look back at the epidemic of the 20th century." *American Journal of Public Health* 89(3): 292–4.

NIH Office of Behavioral and Social Sciences Research et al. 2001. "Social and Cultural Dimensions of Health (PA-02-043)." Accessed on December 30, 2001. Available at http://grants1.nih.gov/grants/guide/pa-files/PA-02-043.html.

NIH Office of Behavioral and Social Sciences Research et al. 2002. "Methodology and Measurement in the Behavioral and Social Sciences (PA-02-072)." Accessed on March 21, 2002. Available at http://grants1.nih.gov/grants/guide/pa-files/PA-02-072.html.

Oakley, Ann. 1972. *Sex, Gender, and Society*. London: Maurice Temple Smith Ltd.

Ochs, Elinor, and Tamar Kremer-Sadlik, eds. 2013. *Fast-Forward Family: Home, Work, and Relationships in Middle-Class America*. Berkeley: University of California Press.

Offer, Shira, and Barbara Schneider. 2011. "Revisiting the gender gap in time-use patterns: Multitasking and well-being among mothers and fathers in dual-earner families." *American Sociological Review* 76(6): 809–33.

OMB. 1997. "Revisions to the Standards for the Classification of Federal Data on Race and Ethnicity." Accessed on April 2, 2002. Available at http://www.whitehouse.gov/omb/fedreg/ombdir15.html.

Omi, Michael, and Howard Winant. 1994. *Racial Formation in the United States: From the 1960s to the 1990s*. New York: Routledge.

Oudshoorn, Nelly. 1994. *Beyond the Natural Body: An Archaeology of Sex Hormones*. New York: Routledge.

Oudshoorn, Nelly, and Marianne van den Wijngaard. 1991. "Dualism in biology: The case of sex hormones." *Women's Studies International Forum* 14(5): 459–71.

Outram, Simon M., and George T.H. Ellison. 2006a. "Anthropological insights into the use of race/ethnicity to explore genetic contributions to disparities in health." *Journal of Biosocial Science* 38: 83–102.

Outram, Simon M., and George T.H. Ellison. 2006b. "The truth will out: Scientific pragmatism and the geneticization of race and ethnicity." Pp. 157–79 in *The Nature of Difference: Science, Society and Human Biology*, edited by G. T. H. Ellison and A. H. Goodman. Boca Raton, Fla.: Taylor and Francis.

Park, Robert Ezra. 1950. *Race and Culture*. Glencoe, Ill.: Free Press.

Pearce, Neil. 1996. "Traditional epidemiology, modern epidemiology, and public health." *American Journal of Public Health* 86(5): 678–83.

Pearson, G. A. 1996. "Of sex and gender." *Science* 274(5286): 328–9.

Petryna, Adriana. 2002. *Life Exposed: Biological Citizens After Chernobyl*. Princeton, N.J.: Princeton University Press.

Phelan, Jo C., and Bruce G. Link. 2005. "Controlling disease and creating disparities: A fundamental cause perspective." *Journal of Gerontology, Social Sciences* 60B(Special Issue II): 27–33.

Phelan, Jo C., Bruce G. Link, Ana Diez-Roux, Ichiro Kawachi, and Bruce Levin. 2004. "'Fundamental causes' of social inequalities in mortality: A test of the theory." *Journal of Health and Social Behavior* 45(3): 265–85.

Phelan, Jo C., Bruce G. Link, and Parisa Tehranifar. 2010. "Social conditions as fundamental causes of health inequalities: Theory, evidence, and policy implications." *Journal of Health and Social Behavior* 51(suppl): S28–S40.

Pinch, Trevor, and Wiebe Bijker. 1984. "The social construction of facts and artefacts: Or how the sociology of science and the sociology of technology might benefit each other." *Social Studies of Science* 14: 399–441.

Piven, Frances Fox, and Richard A. Cloward. 1993. *Regulating the Poor: The Functions of Public Welfare*. New York: Vintage.

Pollock, Anne. 2007. *Medicating Race: Heart Disease and Durable Preoccupations with Difference*. Ph.D. dissertation, Program in Science, Technology and Society, Massachusetts Institute of Technology, Cambridge, Mass.

Pollock, Anne. 2012. *Medicating Race: Heart Disease and Durable Preoccupations with Difference*. Durham, N.C.: Duke University Press.

Poole, Charles, and Kenneth J. Rothman. 1998. "Our conscientious objection to the epidemiology wars." *Journal of Epidemiology and Community Health* 52(10): 613–14.

Pooling Project Research Group. 1978. "Relationship of blood pressure, serum cholesterol, smoking habits, relative weight and ECG abnormalities to the incidence of major coronary events: Final report of the Pooling Project." *Journal of Chronic Diseases* 31: 201–306.

Popay, Jennie, and Gareth Williams. 1996. "Public health research and lay knowledge." *Social Science and Medicine* 42(5): 759–68.

Popay, Jennie, Gareth Williams, Carol Thomas, and Tony Gatrell. 1998. "Theorising inequalities in health: The place of lay knowledge." *Sociology of Health and Illness* 20(5): 619–44.

Popescu, Ioana, Mary S. Vaughan-Sarrazin, and Gary E. Rosenthal. 2007. "Differences in mortality and use of revascularization in black and white patients with acute MI admitted to hospitals with and without revascularization services." *Journal of the American Medical Association* 297(22): 2489–95.

Porter, Dorothy. 1999. *Health, Civilization and the State: A History of Public Health from Ancient to Modern Times*. London: Routledge.

Porter, Theodore M. 1986. *The Rise of Statistical Thinking: 1820–1900*. Princeton, N.J.: Princeton University Press.

Porter, Theodore M. 1995. *Trust in Numbers: The Pursuit of Objectivity in Science and Public Life*. Princeton, N.J.: Princeton University Press.

Pristipino, Chrsitian, John F. Beltrame, Maria L. Finocchiaro, Ryuichi Hattori, Masatoshi Fujita, Rocco Mongiardo, Domenico Cianflone, Tommaso Sanna, Shigetake Sasayama, and Attilio Maseri. 2000. "Major racial differences in coronary constrictor response between Japanese and Caucasians with recent myocardial infarction." *Circulation* 101(10): 1102–8.

Quyyumi, A. A. 2006. "Women and ischemic heart disease: Pathophysiologic implications from the Women's Ischemia Syndrome Evaluation (WISE) Study and future research steps." *Journal of the American College of Cardiology* 47(3 Suppl): S66–S71.

Rapp, Rayna. 1999. *Testing Women, Testing the Fetus: The Social Impact of Amniocentesis in America*. New York: Routledge.

Reaven, G. M. 1988. "The role of insulin resistance in human disease." *Diabetes* 37: 1595–607.

Reverby, Susan M. 2009. *Examining Tuskegee: The Infamous Syphilis Study and Its Legacy*. Chapel Hill: University of North Carolina Press.

Richards, Evelleen. 1991. *Vitamin C and Cancer: Medicine or Politics?* London: Macmillan.

Riska, Elianne. 2000. "The rise and fall of Type A man." *Social Science and Medicine* 51(11): 1665–74.

Riska, Elianne. 2004. *Masculinity and Men's Health: Coronary Heart Disease in Medical and Public Discourse*. Lanham, Md.: Rowman and Littlefield.

Rogers, Naomi. 1992. *Dirt and Disease: Polio Before FDR*. New Brunswick, N.J.: Rutgers University Press.

Rosaldo, Michelle Zimbalist, and Louise Lamphere, eds. 1974. *Woman, Culture, and Society*. Stanford, Calif.: Stanford University Press.

Rose, Geoffrey. 1985. "Sick individuals and sick populations." *International Journal of Epidemiology* 14(1): 32–8.

Rose, Geoffrey. 1992. *The Strategy of Preventive Medicine*. Oxford: Oxford University Press.

Rose, Nikolas. 1990. *Governing the Soul: The Shaping of the Private Self*. London: Routledge.

Rose, Nikolas. 2007. *The Politics of Life Itself: Biomedicine, Power, and Subjectivity in the Twenty-First Century*. Princeton, N.J.: Princeton University Press.

Roth, Dora. 1976. *The Scientific Basis of Epidemiology: An Historical and Philosophical Enquiry*. Ph.D. dissertation, Department of Epidemiology, University of California, Berkeley, Berkeley, Calif.

Ruzek, Sheryl B. 1978. *The Women's Health Movement*. New York: Praeger.

Satel, Sally. 2000. *PC, M.D.: How Political Correctness Is Corrupting Medicine*. New York: Basic Books.

Satel, Sally. 2002. "I am a racially profiling doctor." *New York Times Magazine*, May 5.

Savitz, David A. 1997. "The alternative to epidemiologic theory: Whatever works." *Epidemiology* 8(2): 210–12.

Savitz, David A., Charles Poole, and William C. Miller. 1999. "Reassessing the role of epidemiology in public health." *American Journal of Public Health* 89(8): 1158–61.

Schmieder, R. E., and F. H. Messerli. 1987. "Obesity hypertension." *Medical Clinics of North America* 71(5): 991–1001.

Schneiderman, N., M. A. Chesney, and D. S. Krantz. 1989. "Biobehavioral aspects of cardiovascular disease: progress and prospects." *Health Psychology* 8(6): 649–76.

Schoenbach, Victor J., C. Perry Brown, James A. Ferguson, Sherman A. James, Bill Jenkins, Vickie M. Mays, John T. Nwangwu, Gladys H. Reynolds, Shiriki K. Kumanyika, and Lucina Suarez. 1995a. "Statement of principles: Epidemiology and minority populations." *Annals of Epidemiology* 5(6): 505–8.

Schoenbach, Victor J., Raymond S. Greenberg, Patricia A. Buffer, Alan R. Hinman, G. Marie Swanson, Genevieve M. Matanoski, Philip C. Nasca, and Michael B. Bracken. 1995b. "American College of Epidemiology statement of principles." *Annals of Epidemiology* 5(6): 503–4.

Schulz, Amy J., and Leith Mullings, eds. 2006. *Gender, Race, Class, and Health: Intersectional Approaches.* San Francisco: Jossey-Bass.

Schwartz, R. S. 2001. "Racial profiling in medical research." *New England Journal of Medicine* 344(18): 1392–3.

Schweber, Libby. 2006. *Disciplining Statistics: Demography and Vital Statistics in France and England, 1830–1885.* Durham, N.C.: Duke University Press.

Seeman, T. E. 1996. "Social ties and health: The benefits of social integration." *Annals of Epidemiology* 6(5): 442–51.

Shah, Nayan. 2001. *Contagious Divides: Epidemics and Race in San Francisco's Chinatown.* Berkeley: University of California Press.

Shaw, L. J., C. N. Bairey Merz, C. J. Pepine, S. E. Reis, V. Bittner, S. F. Kelsey, M. Olson, B. D. Johnson, S. Mankad, B. L. Sharaf et al. 2006. "Insights from the NHLBI-Sponsored Women's Ischemia Syndrome Evaluation (WISE) Study: Part I: Gender differences in traditional and novel risk factors, symptom evaluation, and gender-optimized diagnostic strategies." *Journal of the American College of Cardiology* 47(3 Suppl): S4–20.

Shim, Janet K. 2000. "Bio-power and racial, class, and gender formation in biomedical knowledge production." *Research in the Sociology of Health Care* 17: 173–95.

Shim, Janet K. 2002. "Understanding the routinised inclusion of race, socioeconomic status and sex in epidemiology: The utility of concepts from technoscience studies." *Sociology of Health and Illness* 24(2): 129–50.

Shim, Janet K. 2005. "Constructing 'race' across the science–lay divide: Racial formation in the epidemiology and experience of cardiovascular disease." *Social Studies of Science* 35(3): 405–36.

Shim, Janet K. 2010a. "Cultural health capital: A theoretical approach to understanding health care interactions and the dynamics of unequal treatment." *Journal of Health and Social Behavior* 51(1): 1–15.

Shim, Janet K. 2010b. "The stratified biomedicalization of heart disease: Expert and lay perspectives on racial and class inequality." Pp. 218–41 in *Biomedicalization: Technoscience, Health, and Illness in the U.S.*, edited by A. E. Clarke, L. Mamo, J. R. Fosket, J. R. Fishman, and J. K. Shim. Durham, N.C.: Duke University Press.

Shostak, Sara. 2013. *Exposed Science: Genes, the Environment, and the Politics of Population Health.* Berkeley: University of California Press.

Shriver, Mark D. 1997. "Ethnic variation as a key to the biology of human disease." *Annals of Internal Medicine* 127(5): 401–3.

Shy, Carl M. 1997. "The failure of academic epidemiology: Witness for the prosecution." *American Journal of Epidemiology* 145(6): 479–84.

Smith, Susan L. 1995. *Sick and Tired of Being Sick and Tired: Black Women's Health Activism in America, 1890–1950.* Philadelphia: University of Pennsylvania Press.

Spelman, Elizabeth. 1988. *Inessential Woman: Problems of Exclusion in Feminist Thought*. Boston: Beacon Press.

Springer, Kristen, Jeanne Mager Stellman, and Rebecca Jordan-Young. 2012. "Beyond a catalogue of differences: A theoretical frame and good practice guidelines for researching sex-gender in human health." *Social Science and Medicine* 74(11): 1817–24.

Stampfer, Meir J., Walter C. Willett, Graham A. Colditz, Bernard Rosner, Frank E. Speizer, and Charles H. Hennekens. 1985. "A prospective study of postmenopausal estrogen therapy and coronary heart disease." *New England Journal of Medicine* 313(17): 1044–9.

Star, Susan Leigh. 1985. "Scientific work and uncertainty." *Social Studies of Science* 15(3): 391–427.

Star, Susan Leigh. 1986. "Triangulating clinical and basic research: British localizationists, 1870–1906." *History of Science* 24: 29–48.

Star, Susan Leigh. 1989. *Regions of the Mind: Brain Research and the Quest for Scientific Certainty*. Stanford, Calif.: Stanford University Press.

Star, Susan Leigh, and James R. Griesemer. 1989. "Institutional ecology, 'translations' and boundary objects: Amateurs and professionals in Berkeley's Museum of Vertebrate Zoology, 1907–39." *Social Studies of Science* 19(3): 387–420.

Starr, Paul. 1982. *The Social Transformation of American Medicine*. New York: Basic Books.

Steinberg, Helmut O., Giancarlo Paradisi, Jessica Cronin, Kristin Crowde, Annette Hempfling, Ginger Hook, and Alain D. Baron. 2000. "Type II diabetes abrogates sex differences in endothelial function in premenopausal women." *Circulation* 101(17): 2040–6.

Stolberg, Sheryl Gay. 2001. "Shouldn't a pill be colorblind? Medicine wrestles with race and the science of healing." Pp. 1, 3 (Week in Review). *New York Times*, May 13.

Stoler, Ann Laura. 1995. *Race and the Education of Desire: Foucault's History of Sexuality and the Colonial Order of Things*. Durham, N.C.: Duke University Press.

Strauss, Anselm. 1978. "A social world perspective." *Studies in Symbolic Interaction* 1: 119–28.

Strauss, Anselm, and Juliet Corbin. 1998. *Basics of Qualitative Research: Techniques and Procedures for Developing Grounded Theory*. Thousand Oaks, Calif.: Sage.

Strauss, Anselm, Rue Bucher, Danuta Erlich, Melvin Sabshin, and Leonard Schatzman. 1964. *Psychiatric Ideologies and Institutions*. Glencoe, Ill.: Free Press.

Susser, Mervyn. 1964. "The uses of social science in medicine." *Lancet* 2: 425–9.

Susser, Mervyn. 1985. "Epidemiology in the United States after World War II: The evolution of technique." *Epidemiology Review* 7: 147–77.

Susser, Mervyn. 1989. "Epidemiology today: 'A thought-tormented world.'" *International Journal of Epidemiology* 18(3): 481–8.

Susser, Mervyn. 1998. "Does risk factor epidemiology put epidemiology at risk? Peering into the future." *Journal of Epidemiology and Community Health* 52(10): 608–11.

Susser, Mervyn, and Ezra Susser. 1996a. "Choosing a future for epidemiology: I. Eras and paradigms." *American Journal of Public Health* 86(5): 668–73.

Susser, Mervyn, and Ezra Susser. 1996b. "Choosing a future for epidemiology: II. From black box to Chinese boxes and eco-epidemiology." *American Journal of Public Health* 86(5): 674–7.

Suthanthiran, Manikkam, Baougui Li, J. O. Song, Ruching Ding, Vijay K. Sharma, J. E. Schwartz, and Phyllis August. 2000. "Transforming growth factor–beta 1 hyperexpression in African-American hypertensives: A novel mediator of hypertension and/or target organ damage." *Proceedings of the National Academy of Science* 97(7): 3479–84.

Syme, S. Leonard. 2000. "Foreword." Pp. ix–xii in *Social Epidemiology*, edited by L. F. Berkman and I. Kawachi. New York: Oxford University Press.

Syme, S. Leonard, Merton M. Hyman, and Philip E. Enterline. 1965. "Cultural mobility and the occurrence of coronary heart disease." *Journal of Health and Human Behavior* 6(4): 178–89.

Syme, S. L., M. G. Marmot, A. Kagan, H. Kato, and G. Rhoads. 1975. "Epidemiologic studies of coronary heart disease and stroke in Japanese men living in Japan, Hawaii and California: Introduction." *American Journal of Epidemiology* 102(6): 477–80.

Taubes, Gary. 1995. "Epidemiology faces its limits." *Science* 269(5221): 164–9.

Tehranifar, Parisa, A. I. Neugut, Jo C. Phelan, Bruce G. Link, Y. Liao, M. Desai, and M. B. Terry. 2009. "Medical advances and racial/ethnic disparities in cancer survival." *Cancer Epidemiology, Biomarkers & Prevention* 18: 2701–8.

Thomas, William I., and Dorothy Swain Thomas. 1970. "Situations defined as real are real in their consequences." Pp. 154–5 in *Social Psychology Through Symbolic Interaction*, edited by G. Stone and H. Farberman. Waltham, Mass.: Xeros.

Thoresen, C. E., and L. H. Powell. 1992. "Type A behavior pattern: New perspectives on theory, assessment, and intervention." *Journal of Consulting and Clinical Psychology* 60(4): 595–604.

Torgrimson, Britta N., and Christopher T. Minson. 2005. "Sex and gender: What is the difference?" *Journal of Applied Physiology* 99: 785–7.

Treiber, Frank A., Robert W. Jackson, Harry Davis, Jennifer S. Pollock, Gaston Kapuku, George A. Mensah, and David M. Pollock. 2000. "Racial differences in endothelin-1 at rest and in response to acute stress in adolescent males." *Hypertension* 35(3): 722–5.

Unger, R. K. 1979. "Toward a redefinition of sex and gender." *American Psychologist* 34(11): 1085–94.

Vandenbroucke, J. P. 1994. "New public health and old rhetoric." *BMJ* 308(6935): 994–5.

Vineis, Paolo. 1998. "Epidemiology between social and natural sciences." *Journal of Epidemiology and Community Health* 52(10): 616–17.

Virchow, Rudolf. 1848. "The public health service." *Medizinische Reform* 5: 21–22.

Von Korff, M., T. Koepsell, S. Curry, and P. Diehr. 1992. "Multi-level analysis in epidemiologic research on health behaviors and outcomes." *American Journal of Epidemiology* 135(10): 1077–82.

Waldby, Catherine. 1996. *AIDS and the Body Politic: Biomedicine and Sexual Difference.* New York: Routledge.

Weber, Lynn. 2006. "Reconstructing the landscape of health disparities research: Promoting dialogue and collaboration between feminist intersectional and biomedical paradigms." Pp. 21–59 in *Gender, Race, Class, and Health: Intersectional Approaches,* edited by A. J. Schulz and L. Mullings. San Francisco: Jossey-Bass.

Weber, Lynn. 2010. *Understanding Race, Class, Gender, and Sexuality: A Conceptual Framework.* New York: Oxford University Press.

Weber, Lynn, and Deborah Parra-Medina. 2003. "Intersectionality and women's health: Charting a path to eliminating health disparities." Pp. 181–230 in *Gender Perspectives on Health and Medicine (Volume 7): Key Themes,* edited by M. T. Segal, V. Demos, and J. J. Kronenfeld. New York: Elsevier.

Weber, Lynn, and M. Elizabeth Fore. 2007. "Race, ethnicity, and health: An intersectional approach." Pp. 191–218 in *Handbook of the Sociology of Racial and Ethnic Relations,* edited by H. Vera and J. Feagin. New York: Springer.

Wenneker, Mark B., and Arnold M. Epstein. 1989. "Racial inequalities in the use of procedures for patients with ischemic heart disease in Massachusetts." *Journal of the American Medical Association* 261(2): 253–7.

White, Evelyn C., ed. 1994. *The Black Women's Health Book: Speaking for Ourselves.* Seattle: Seal Press.

Whitmarsh, Ian. 2008. *Biomedical Ambiguity: Race, Asthma, and the Contested Meaning of Genetic Research in the Caribbean.* Ithaca, N.Y.: Cornell University Press.

Whittle, Jeff, Joseph Conigliaro, C. B. Good, and Richard P. Lofgren. 1993. "Racial differences in the use of invasive cardiovascular procedures in the Department of Veterans Affairs medical system." *Journal of the American Medical Association* 329(9): 621–7.

Willett, Walter C., and Graham A. Colditz. 1998. "Approaches for conducting large cohort studies." *Epidemiologic Reviews* 20(1): 91–9.

Williams, David R. 1994. "The concept of race in *Health Services Research*: 1966 to 1990." *Health Services Research* 29(3): 261–74.

Williams, David R. 1997. "Race and health: Basic questions, emerging directions." *Annals of Epidemiology* 7(5): 322–33.

Williams, David R., Harold W. Neighbors, and James S. Jackson. 2008. "Racial/ethnic discrimination and health: Findings from community studies." *American Journal of Public Health* 98(Suppl 1): S29–S37.

Williams, David R., and Selina A. Mohammed. 2009. "Discrimination and racial disparities in health: Evidence and needed research." *Journal of Behavioral Medicine* 32(1): 20–47.

Williams, David R., Selina A. Mohammed, Jacinta Leavell, and Chiquita Collins. 2010. "Race, socioeconomic status, and health: Complexities, ongoing challenges, and research opportunities." *Annals of the New York Academy of Sciences* 1186: 69–101.

Williams, R. B., Jr. 1987. "Refining the type A hypothesis: Emergence of the hostility complex." *American Journal of Cardiology* 60(18): 27J–32J.

Williams, Roger R., D. C. Rao, R. Curtis Ellison, Donna K. Arnett, Gerardo Heiss, Albert Oberman, John H. Eckfeldt, Mark F. Leppert, Michael A. Province, Stephen C. Mockrin et al. 2000. "NHLBI Family Blood Pressure Program: Methodology and recruitment in the HyperGEN network." *Annals of Epidemiology* 10(6): 389–400.

Wilson, Peter W. F., Robert J. Garrison, and William P. Castelli. 1985. "Postmenopausal estrogen use, cigarette smoking, and cardiovascular morbidity in women over 50— The Framingham Study." *New England Journal of Medicine* 313(17): 1038–43.

Winkleby, Marilyn A., Helena C. Kraemer, David K. Ahn, and Ann N. Varady. 1998. "Ethnic and socioeconomic differences in cardiovascular disease risk factors: Findings for women from the Third National Health and Nutrition Examination Survey, 1988–1994." *Journal of the American Medical Association* 280(4): 356–62.

Winkleby, Marilyn A., Thomas N. Robinson, Jan Sundquist, and Helena C. Kraemer. 1999. "Ethnic variation in cardiovascular disease risk factors among children and young adults: Findings from the Third National Health and Nutrition Examination Survey, 1988–1994." *Journal of the American Medical Association* 281(11): 1006–13.

Wizemann, Theresa M., and Mary-Lou Pardue. 2001. *Exploring the Biological Contributions to Human Health: Does Sex Matter?* Washington: National Academies Press.

Woo, Kam S., Jacqui T.C. Robinson, Ping Chook, Mark R. Adams, Gabriel Yip, Z. J. Mai, Chris W.K. Lam, Keld E. Sorensen, John E. Deanfield, and David S. Celermajer. 1997. "Differences in the effect of cigarette smoking on endothelial function in Chinese and white adults." *Annals of Internal Medicine* 127(5): 372–5.

Wood, A. J. 2001. "Racial differences in the response to drugs—pointers to genetic differences." *New England Journal of Medicine* 344(18): 1394–6.

World Health Organization. 2003. *SuRF Report I: Surveillance of Risk Factors.* World Health Organization, Geneva, Switzerland.

Wu, K. K., N. Aleksic, C. Ahn, E. Boerwinkle, A. R. Folsom, and H. Juneja. 2001. "Thrombomodulin Ala455Val polymorphism and risk of coronary heart disease." *Circulation* 103(10): 1386–9.

Wynne, Brian. 1995. "Public understanding of science." Pp. 361–88 in *Handbook of Science and Technology Studies,* edited by S. Jasanoff, G. E. Markle, J. C. Petersen, and T. Pinch. Thousand Oaks, Calif.: Sage.

Wynne, Brian. 1996a. "May the sheep safely graze? A reflexive view of the expert–lay knowledge divide." Pp. 44–83 in *Risk, Environment and Modernity: Towards a New Ecology,* edited by S. Lash, B. Szerszynski, and B. Wynne. London: Sage.

Wynne, Brian. 1996b. "Misunderstood misunderstandings: Social identities and public uptake of science." Pp. 19–46 in *Misunderstanding Science? The Public*

Reconstruction of Science and Technology, edited by A. Irwin and B. Wynne. Cambridge: Cambridge University Press.

Wynne, Brian. 2003. "Seasick on the third wave: Subverting the hegemony of propositionalism." *Social Studies of Science* 33(3): 401–17.

Yancy, C. W., M. B. Fowler, W. S. Colucci et al. 2001. "Race and the response to adrenergic blockade with carvedilol in patients with chronic heart failure." *New England Journal of Medicine* 344(18): 1358–65.

Young, Iris Marion. 1990. *Justice and the Politics of Difference*. Princeton, N.J.: Princeton University Press.

Young, Iris Marion. 1994/1996. "Gender as seriality: Thinking about women as a social collective." Pp. 158–83 in *The Second Signs Reader: Feminist Scholarship, 1983–1996*, edited by R.-E. B. Joeres and B. Laslett. Chicago: University of Chicago Press.

INDEX

American College of Cardiology, 11, 21, 176, 217, 243n43
American Heart Association, 21, 59, 203–204, 217, 243n43
American Public Health Association, 217
Amsterdamska, Olga, 50
Arksey, Hilary, 12
Aronowitz, Robert, 55, 66, 200, 212, 232n30
Assimilation, 89–90, 93

Bhopal, Raj, 75
BiDil, 213, 243n45
Biomedicalization: concept, 35, 202; and drugs, 213; epidemiology as, 16, 17, 21, 111, 145, 187; stratified, 16–17, 36, 78, 108–110, 137, 161, 193–195
Biopolitics and biopower, 21–22, 29–37, 39, 51, 214; and epidemiology, 23–24, 43, 49–51, 110–111, 137, 161, 193; inclusion-and-difference paradigm, 10, 34
Black box, 18–20, 75, 170–171, 177, 197–198, 241n8
Boundary object, 174, 197–198
Brown, Phil, 13, 186
Byrd, W. Michael, 7

Cardiovascular epidemiology: costs, 5; history, 50–62, 193 (*see also* Framingham Heart Study); incidence, prevalence, and mortality, 5–7, 227n19, 227n20; standard

risk factors, 2, 6–7, 54, 59–60, 66. *See also* Biomedicalization; Biopolitics and biopower; Epidemiology; Risk factor epidemiology; Social epidemiology
Casper, Monica, 34, 36, 240n20
Causal inference, 64–67, 69, 72, 168
Chemoprevention, 212
Cholesterol, 73, 212–213, 226n18, 233n58; in epidemiologic accounts, 116, 123, 173; epidemiologic research on, 53, 59, 66, 231n25, 235n87; in lay accounts, 94; as risk factor for heart disease, 54, 59, 60, 232n32
Citizenship, 38, 39; biological, 35, 37
Clarke, Adele, 35, 239n1, 240n20
Class, 14–15, 18, 25–26; access to health care, 113–114; access to health information, 114–115, 121, 122–123, 127, 136, 137; classification and measurement, 4, 16, 18, 20, 129–133, 159–160, 174, 180–181, 183 (*see also* Socioeconomic status); confounding with race, 26, 133–135, 136, 156; and cultural attributes, 70, 121–123, 125–129, 135–136; as cumulative, 130–132, 181; economic insecurity, 115–117, 125–126, 137–138, 195; educational stratification, 16, 118–119, 121, 137–138, 195, 200; exposure to and mitigation of risks, 112, 115–117, 123–125, 126; inclusion in epidemiology, 147, 176, 187–188, 194; intersections with gender, 26, 102–104, 117–118, 122–123,

Class (*Continued*)
134, 136–137, 148–149, 151–154, 158–161, 195–196; intersections with race, 26, 78, 102–104, 107, 117, 122–123, 133–135, 148–149; occupational stratification, 16, 26, 102–104, 117–119, 148–149; physical and social environment, 119–120, 137–138; as relational, 16, 46, 120–121, 123–124, 130, 133–135, 136–137, 159, 196; and risk for heart disease, 6–7. *See also* Biomedicalization, stratified; Intersectionality; Socioeconomic status; Usual suspects approach

Classification, 4, 23–24, 50, 60–62, 160, 169, 181, 209; of race, 9, 25, 77–84, 96, 169; of sex, 140–141

Clayton, Linda, 7

Cloward, Richard, 149

Cohort study. *See* Prospective (or longitudinal) cohort study

Collins, Harry, 242n29

Collins, Patricia Hill, 41–42, 81, 239n11, 239n12

Colorblindness, 9, 106

Conceptual flexibility. *See* Interpretive (or conceptual) flexibility

Congestive heart failure, 1, 2, 6

Connerly, Ward, 9, 227n22

Co-production, 20, 76, 182

Coronary heart disease, 5–7, 220, 221, 228n43; epidemiologic research on, 53, 57, 59, 227n19, 232n38; standard risk factors for, 60

Credibility, 240n12, 240n23; critiques of epidemiologic credibility, 63–64, 74–75; of epidemiology as discipline, 49, 161; and expertise, 187–190, 216–217; norms of, 184, 198, 208, 210; of usual suspects approach (*see* Usual suspects approach). *See also* Economic constraints on epidemiology; Inclusion as trend in health research; Measurement imperative

Crenshaw, Kimberle, 37

Cultural health capital, 238n1

Cultural prism or culturalist understandings, 14, 25, 88–97, 122–123, 125–129, 193–194; effects of, 108–110, 187

Culture of poverty, 128–129

Dawber, Thomas, 56, 234n79

Depression, 101–102, 120, 156

Diabetes: in participants, 2, 99, 133; as risk factor for heart disease, 7, 53, 54, 60, 173, 204, 208, 226n17

Diet: in epidemiologic accounts, 2, 73, 90, 117, 122, 126, 135–136, 173; epidemiologic research on, 54, 58, 143, 236n102; in lay accounts, 87–88, 91, 93–95, 105–106, 124–128, 154, 212; as risk factor for heart disease, 7, 59, 70, 226n17. *See also* Cholesterol

Diez-Roux, Ana, 73

Ecological models, 180, 211, 235n100. *See also* Social epidemiology

Economic constraints on epidemiology, 19–20, 76, 178–183, 189, 196–197. *See also* Funding

Epidemiology: alignments with lay accounts of class, 14, 112, 113–117, 121; alignments with lay accounts of gender, 15, 139, 140–141, 145–148; alignments with lay accounts of race, 82, 92, 93–94, 205, 209; authority of, 5, 12, 19, 22–23, 49, 186–190, 193–195; current changes in, 210–211, 231n19; disciplinary standards, 184, 189–190, 198, 207–210; heterogeneity within, 92, 141, 145–148, 193, 198; retooling models and methods, 198–202; theoretical and methodological conservatism, 184, 199–200, 208–209, 212. *See also* Cardiovascular epidemiology; Economic constraints on epidemiology; Social epidemiology

Epstein, Steven, 10, 13, 34, 36, 170, 175, 186, 205, 216

Ethnicity, 9, 14, 23, 25, 164, 167, 182; epidemiologic research on, 59; ethnicity paradigm of race, 93; and health disparities, 9; and patterns in heart disease, 7, 8, 226n17.

227n19. *See also* Cultural prism; Inclusion as trend in health research; Race

Evans, Robert, 242n29

Expertise, 17, 196; and biopower, 31, 35; epidemiology as a form of, 17, 22, 202, 211; expert-lay relations, 12–13, 24, 30, 63, 185–187, 203–206; lay forms of, 105, 108, 185–187, 188–189, 202–204; reforming definitions of, 27, 182, 188–190, 203–206. *See also* Lay knowledge

Federal Drug Administration, 213, 243n45

Fishman, Jennifer, 35, 238n1

Fore, M. Elizabeth, 211

Fosket, Jennifer, 35, 243n40

Foucault, Michel, 30–35, 36, 51, 193, 215–216, 230n9

Framingham Heart Study, 53–57, 193, 232n38, 233n55, 234n78; critiques of, 55–57, 232n37; and related studies, 54, 57

Frankenberg, Ruth, 93

Fujimura, Joan, 239n1

Fundamental causes, 22, 27, 29, 185, 189, 204–205; in epidemiologic accounts, 97, 199–200, 211–212; in lay accounts, 46, 133, 159, 185, 195; theorizations of, 43–46, 239n17

Funding, 57, 131–132, 178–183, 189, 207–209. *See also* Economic constraints on epidemiology

Garrety, Karin, 231n25, 235n87

Gender, 14–15, 44, 46; access to health care, 150–151, 226n18; as biological, 142–145, 148, 157–158, 163, 194, 205; classification and measurement, 4, 15, 16, 18, 26, 139–140, 157, 169, 194; and cultural attributes, 122–123; educational stratification, 16; gendered division of reproductive labor, 16, 123, 148–150, 151–154, 195, 200; inclusion in epidemiology, 34, 36, 49, 61–62, 66–67, 69, 71, 142, 164, 177–178, 187–188; intersections with class, 26, 102–104, 117–118, 122–123, 134, 136–137, 148–149, 151–154, 158–161, 195–196; intersections with race, 102–104,

107, 117–118, 122–123, 134, 148–150, 151–156, 158–161, 195, 239n11, 239n12; occupational stratification, 16, 102–104, 117–118, 148–149, 151; as relational, 46, 159, 196; and risk for heart disease, 7, 227n20; versus sex, 10, 14–15, 26, 141, 147–148, 158, 194, 238n1. *See also* Biomedicalization: stratified; Hormone replacement therapy; Inclusion as trend in health research; Intersectionality; Usual suspects approach; Violence: domestic violence

Generalizability, 56, 68, 175, 182, 232n37, 240n23

Gieryn, Thomas, 237n121, 240n12

Hankivsky, Olena, 206

Haraway, Donna, 214

Health care disparities, 7–8, 113–114, 127, 226n18

High blood pressure. *See* Hypertension

Hormone replacement therapy, 10–11, 46, 65, 142–144, 234n78

Hypertension (or high blood pressure), 2, 168, 212–213; in epidemiologic accounts, 116, 169, 172, 173; epidemiologic patterns of, 5–7; epidemiologic research on, 53, 59, 226n18, 227n19, 227n20; in lay accounts, 93–94, 99, 100–103, 108, 117, 119–120, 124–125, 127–128, 145, 150–155; as risk factor, 54, 60, 226n17; standard risk factors for, 7, 226n17

Inclusion as trend in health research, 36, 167–169, 175–178, 196, 207, 210; inclusion-and-difference biopolitical paradigm, 10, 34, 175, 210, 237n10. *See also* Usual suspects approach

Institute of Medicine, 10

Interdisciplinary research, 12, 49, 196, 208–212

Interpretive (or conceptual) flexibility, 90, 97, 110, 173–174

Intersectionality: analysis of, 40–42, 204–205, 209–210; in epidemiologic accounts, 16, 71, 78, 110–111, 136, 161, 165–166, 180, 200; in lay accounts, 15–16, 77–78, 97–98, 102–104, 117–119, 134–135, 148–156,

Intersectionality (*Continued*)
158–159, 195–196; patterns in heart disease, 6–7; theorizations of, 37–43, 46–47, 137, 156, 201, 234n69, 239n11. *See also* Class; Gender; Race

Irwin, Alan, 63

Jackson, Beth, 243n34
Jones, David, 228n43

Kahn, Jonathan, 243n45
Katz, Michael, 238n2
Krieger, Nancy, 69–70, 71, 168
Kuhn, Thomas, 75, 236n118

Latour, Bruno, 18, 197, 241n8
Lay knowledge, 12–13, 24, 110–111; as expertise, 105, 108, 185–187, 188–189, 202–204; expert-lay relations, 12–13, 24, 30, 63, 185–187, 203–206; inclusion in scientific research, 200, 202–206; and understanding of risk, 63, 127–128, 212
Link, Bruce, 43–45

Mamo, Laura, 35
McCall, Leslie, 42
Measurement imperative, 172–175, 196
Menopause, 11, 54, 65, 142, 145, 147
Methodological contingencies, 19–20, 27, 163, 171–172, 189, 196–197. *See also* Economic constraints on epidemiology; Inclusion as trend in health research; Measurement imperative; Usual suspects approach
Moore, Felix, 54
Moore, Lisa Jean, 34, 36
Multifactorial model of disease causation, 61–62, 63, 66, 67, 70, 72, 75; emergence of, 22, 49, 51–53, 54
Myrdal, Gunnar, 7

National Institutes of Health (NIH), 8–9, 11–12, 178, 231n21, 242n31
National Institutes of Health Revitalization Act (1993), 57, 175, 177, 237n10

Neighborhood effects on health, 6–7, 44; in epidemiologic accounts, 121, 180, 211; in lay accounts, 78, 104, 134. *See also* Class; Ecological models

Obesity (and body weight): in epidemiologic accounts, 135–136, 173; in lay accounts, 100, 120, 124–125, 150, 154; and risk for heart disease, 7, 53–54, 59–60, 66, 204, 226n17
Obligatory passage point, 170, 178
Observational studies. *See* Prospective (or longitudinal) cohort study
Office of Management and Budget, 25, 79
Omi, Michael, 38–39, 81, 93

Parra-Medina, Deborah, 201
Petryna, Adriana, 35, 37
Phelan, Jo, 43–45
Physical activity (and exercise): in epidemiologic accounts, 70, 89, 135–136, 143, 173; in lay accounts, 104, 117, 122–123, 124, 127, 154, 212; and risk for heart disease, 7, 53–54, 60, 226n17
Piven, Frances Fox, 149
Pollock, Anne, 55, 62, 232n37, 232n38, 232n40
Popay, Jennie, 188, 202, 203
Popular epidemiology, 13
Population, 4, 22, 55, 56, 84, 160, 177; and biopower, 30–36, 50–51, 52, 108, 193, 230n9; and risk, 17, 60, 61, 62, 71–72, 74, 199. *See also* Generalizability; Inclusion as trend in health research
Porter, Theodore, 51, 76
Power-knowledge. *See* Biopolitics and biopower
Prospective (or longitudinal) cohort study, 54–55, 60, 65, 67, 131, 179, 207–208, 235n85, 241n23; examples of, 58–59
Public understanding of science, 63

Qualitative health research, 200–201

Race, 14–15, 24–26, 77–78; access to health care, 7–8, 10, 100; ascription, 98–102; as biological, 8, 10, 86–88, 174, 205; classification and measurement, 4, 18, 69, 78–84, 95–96, 169, 174; and culture (*see* Cultural prism); educational stratification, 16, 118–120, 195; exposure to and mitigation of risks, 94–95, 105–108, 112, 120, 124–125, 137; inclusion in epidemiology, 57–59, 62, 66–68, 79, 84–85, 108–111, 159–160, 176–177 (*see also* Usual suspects approach); intersections with class, 26, 78, 102–104, 107, 117, 122–123, 133–135, 148–149; intersections with gender, 102–104, 107, 117–118, 122–123, 134, 148–150, 151–156, 158–161, 195, 239n11, 239n12; multiraciality, 18, 79–80, 84, 90; occupational stratification, 16, 26, 102–104, 117–119, 148–149, 195; physical and social environment, 99, 104–105, 137; policies on racial health disparities, 8–9; as relational, 16, 46, 124, 133, 159, 196; and risk for heart disease, 5–7, 70–71. *See also* Biomedicalization: stratified; Fundamental causes; Health care disparities; Inclusion as trend in health research; Intersectionality; Racial formation; Racism: in scientific studies; Usual suspects approach

Racial formation, 38–39, 81, 108, 113, 194

Racial Privacy Initiative, 9

Racism: Foucault's theorizations of, 32–34; in scientific studies, 10, 91, 122–123. *See also* Race

Randomized controlled clinical trial, 11, 13, 65–67, 143–144

Rapp, Rayna, 206

Reproductive labor. *See* Gender: gendered division of reproductive labor

Risk (and risk factor) as concept or approach, 66, 69–71, 170, 189, 200, 232n30, 234n79; emergence in epidemiology, 32, 48–49, 52–54, 55, 57, 59, 60, 74, 193; and fundamental cause theory, 27, 44–45, 46, 189, 202–203, 205; scientific and social credibility, 61, 62–64, 65, 72, 92, 193; standard risk factors for heart

disease, 7, 11, 54, 59–60, 172–173, 179, 226n17, 227n20

Riska, Elianne, 156

Risk factor epidemiology, 66, 70, 74, 75, 135, 199

Risk reduction, 189, 204, 212–213; in epidemiologic accounts, 17, 64, 91–92, 117, 122–124, 195; in lay accounts, 104–106, 117, 154

Roth, Dora, 49

Rose, Geoffrey, 74

Rose, Nikolas, 35–36, 37

Schweber, Libby, 230n9

Sex. *See* Gender

Shostak, Sara, 242n30

Smoking: in epidemiologic accounts, 114–115, 116, 122, 135–136, 143, 173; epidemiologic research on, 53, 59, 70, 200; in lay accounts, 94–95, 105–106, 124, 128; as risk factor for heart disease, 7, 54, 60, 226n17

Social epidemiology, 69, 71–74, 168, 203, 211, 227n20, 229n54

Social movements, 13, 61, 175, 186, 203–206. *See also* Lay knowledge

Society for Epidemiologic Research, 217

Socioeconomic status, 44–46; confounding with race, 26, 133–135, 136, 156; as control variable, 70–71; and cultural attributes, 25 (*see also* Cultural prism); inclusion in epidemiology, 2, 62, 67, 68, 137, 191, 210, 240n23 (*see also* Usual suspects approach); measurement, 14, 117, 129–133, 169, 180–181; and patterns of heart disease, 6–7, 226n17, 227n20. *See also* Class

Spelman, Elizabeth, 37

Star, Susan Leigh, 175

Stoler, Ann Laura, 34

Stratified biomedicalization. *See* Biomedicalization

Stress, 44, 227n20; in epidemiologic accounts, 116, 121, 132, 146; in lay accounts, 98–102, 103–104, 116, 118–120, 123–125, 149–156, 196

Susser, Ezra, 72

Susser, Mervyn, 54, 57, 72, 75, 235n100

Technical downshift, 174–175

Terminal analysis, 166

Tool for the job, 178, 179, 181, 182, 196–198

Usual suspects approach, 18–20, 26–27, 85; as
black box, 170–171; consequences, 164–
167, 184–185; construction of credibility,
163, 171–178, 181–183 (see also Credibility);
questioning of, 166–169, 171, 174, 177–178,
184–185, 194, 196–198; routinization of,
163–164, 196–197; unseen hand, 167–168.
See also Economic constraints on epidemiology; Inclusion as trend in health
research; Measurement imperative

Validity (statistical), 64, 67–69, 83, 163,
235n85, 240n23

Violence, 44; domestic violence, 2, 151

Waldby, Catherine, 62

Web of causation, 52–53, 69

Weber, Lynn, 38, 40–41, 157, 201, 211

Williams, Gareth, 188, 202, 203

Winant, Howard, 38–39, 81, 93

World Health Organization, 46

Wynne, Brian, 63, 234n75

Young, Iris Marion, 81, 160

ABOUT THE AUTHOR

Janet K. Shim is Associate Professor of Sociology at the University of California, San Francisco.